HEART ETHICS:

PURSUING CHRISTIAN LOVE ACCORDING TO THE THEOLOGY OF JOHN WESLEY

The Asbury Theological Seminary Series in World Christian Revitalization Movements in Pietist/Wesleyan Studies

Michael H. Browder, Jr

EMETH PRESS
www.emethpress.com

Heart Ethics: Pursuing Christian Love According to the Theology of John Wesley

Copyright © 2020 by Michael Browder
Printed in the United States of America on acid-free paper

All rights reserved. No part of this book may be reproduced or transmitted in any form or by any means, electronic or mechanical, including photocopying, recording, or by any information storage and retrieval system, without the written permission of the publisher, except where permitted by law. For permission to reproduce any part or form of the text, contact the publisher. www.emethpress.com.

Library of Congress Cataloging-in-Publication Data

Names: Browder, Michael Heath, 1981- author.
Title: Heart ethics : pursuing Christian love according to the theology of John Wesley / Michael Heath Browder, Jr.
Description: Nicholas, KY : Emeth Press, 2020. | Series: The Asbury Theological Seminary in world Christian revitalization movements in pietist/wesleyan studies | Includes bibliographical references. | Summary: "This book shows that John Wesley believed a person's pursuit of the greatest end of ethics is an expression of God's gift and that the giftedness of this blessing is illuminated by a critical examination of the work of the Spirit with respect to the active and passive dimensions of a human being"-- Provided by publisher.
Identifiers: LCCN 2020018710 (print) | LCCN 2020018711 (ebook) | ISBN 9781609471569 (paperback) | ISBN 9781609471576 (kindle edition)
Subjects: LCSH: Wesley, John, 1703-1791. | Love--Religious aspects--Christianity. | Methodist Church--Doctrines.
Classification: LCC BX8495.W5 B745 2020 (print) | LCC BX8495.W5 (ebook) | DDC 241/.4--dc23
LC record available at https://lccn.loc.gov/2020018710
LC ebook record available at https://lccn.loc.gov/2020018711

Contents

List of Diagrams / 7

Abbreviations / 9

Dedication / 11

Acknowledgments / 13

Chapter 1: Introducing Wesley's Ethics / 15
   Background to Wesley's Ethics: A Search for True Religion / 17
   "Virtue Ethics" in Western Tradition / 22
   Introducing Wesley's Ethics / 27
   Recent Scholarship Concerning Wesley's Ethics / 33
   Summary of this Project / 35

Chapter 2: Active and Passive / 37
   A Mighty Typology / 37
   Highlights from Eighteenth Century Libertarians / 44
   Approach for Clarifying Active and Passive / 47
   Preliminary Illustrations / 48
      Illustrations of the Active Dimension / 48
      Illustrations of the Passive Dimension / 50
   Illustrations of Focus / 51
   Two Kinds of Spiritual Growth in John Wesley's Ethics / 55
   For Wesley, Liberty is Action / 58

Chapter 3: The Will and Liberty / 63
   Other Views of the Will / 63
   The Will "Properly Speaking" / 69
   Free Will / 71
   Responding to Edwards? / 74

Chapter 4: The Heart / 79
   Desires of the Heart / 80
   Happiness / 83
   The Language of Tempers, Dispositions, and Affections / 86
   The "Fire" and "Flames" of the Heart / 93
   Practical Reason and the Heart / 95
   Responding to Secondary Literature: Clapper, Maddox, and Collins on the Affections / 99
   Summarizing the First Task of this Project / 101

Chapter 5: Fruitful Action and the Holy Spirit / 103
   The Shape of John Wesley's Theology / 104
   Active and Passive Work of the Spirit / 109
   Key Features of Fruitful Action / 113
   Fruitful Action and Free will / 117
   Wesley versus Luther / 118
   Further Analysis / 122

Chapter 6: From Sin to New Birth / 125
   The Impenitent Sinner / 125
      The Image of God / 126
      Prevenient Grace / 127
      The Ethics of an Impenitent Sinner / 131
   The Servant of God / 132
      Characteristics of the Servant of God / 132
      The Ethics of the Servant of God / 138
   The Child of the New Birth / 139
      The Beginning of Sanctification / 139
      Faith of the Newborn Child, Witness of the Spirit, and Justification / 140
      The Love of God Shed Abroad in the Heart / 143
      Instantaneous, Perceived, and Unpredictable Birth / 143

Chapter 7: From New Birth to Perfect Love & the Rewards of Heaven / 147
   The Child of the New Birth (continued) / 147
      The Repentance of Believers / 147
      Virtuous Action / 149
      The Ethics of the Newborn Child / 151

The Child of Perfect Love / 155
    Faith of the Perfected Child, Pure Heart, and the Witness of the
        Perfected Child / 157
    Instantaneous, Perceived, and Unpredictable Beginning of
        Perfection / 159
    Not Absolute Perfection / 161
    The Ethics of the Perfected Child / 163
The Inhabitant of Heaven / 166
    From Death to the Great Judgment / 166
    Final Justification and the Rewards of Heaven / 167
    The Ethics of the Inhabitant of Heaven / 171
Responding to Secondary Literature: Maddox, Collins, and
    Colón-Emeric / 172

Chapter 8: A Method for Fruitful Action / 177
An Encounter with John Wesley / 179
The Means of Grace / 181
Choosing Christian Fellowship / 183
    Joining the Methodist Society / 184
    Early-Morning, Evening, and Outdoor Preaching Services / 187
    The Covenant Service, The Love-Feast, the Watch-Night,
        and the Letter-Day / 188
Following the *General Rules* / 190
    Do no Harm / 192
        Rules for Avoiding Harm / 192
        Managing Money / 193
    Do Good / 193
        Serving the Needy / 194
        Other Rules for Doing Good / 196
        Self-Denial and Taking up the Cross / 197
    Attend the Ordinances of God / 198
        Public Worship and Liturgy, the Ministry of the Word, and the
            Lord's Supper / 198
        Prayer, Searching the Scriptures, and Fasting / 201
Following the Moral Commandments of Scripture / 203
Recommended Action Concerning Slavery and Government / 205
Summarizing this Chapter / 206

Chapter 9: Heart Ethics for Today / 209
    Is Hauerwas the John Wesley of Today? / 210
        The Authority of Scripture / 212
        Regard for Religious Experience / 213
        Truth and Ethics / 215
        Choice as Gift / 221
    Volf and Wesley / 224
    John Wesley's Theology for Today / 224
    John Wesley's Heart Ethics for Today / 228
        Approach 1: Academics / 228
        Approach 2: Determining the Relevance to One's
            Church Tradition / 229
        Approach 3: Planning and Acting / 231

Appendices
    Appendix A: Responding to Interpretations of John
        Wesley's View of Liberty / 243
    Appendix B: Consistency in Wesley's Thought / 257

Bibliography / 263

List of Diagrams

Diagram 2.1 / 235

Diagram 3.1 / 236

Diagram 4.1 / 237

Diagram 5.1 / 238

Diagram 6.1 / 239

Diagram 7.1 / 240

Diagram 8.1 / 241

ABBREVIATIONS

AM John Wesley, editor. *The Arminian Magazine.* vols. 1- 14. (London: Printed for the Editor, January 1778 – February 1791).

(BE) Frank Baker, editor in chief, *The Bicentennial Edition of the Works of John Wesley* (Nashville, Tennessee: Abingdon Press, 1975-).

ENNT John Wesley, *Explanatory Notes Upon the New Testament* (London: The Epworth Press, reprinted 1954).

(Jackson) Thomas Jackson, editor. *The Works of John Wesley.* 14 vols. (Grand Rapids: Baker Books, reprinted 2007).

Letters *The Letters of the Rev. John Wesley,* A.M., Edited by John Telford. Standard edition. 8 vols. (London: Epworth Press, 1931)

Dedication

For my parents Michael and Susan Browder
who brought me up in the life of the church.

Acknowledgments

I would like to thank Laurence Wood, Steven O'Malley, Thomas Noble, Kenneth Collins, and Randy Maddox for helpful guidance.

Chapter 1

Introducing Wesley's Ethics

Thou shalt love the Lord thy God with all thy heart, and with all thy soul, and with all thy mind, and with all thy strength. This is the first commandment. And the second is like unto it: Thou shalt love thy neighbor as thyself. There is no other commandment greater than these.[1]
—Jesus, Mark 12:30 - 31

In these words, Jesus, the One believed to be God in the flesh, sums up the greatest commandment for human living. As we will explore, it is this love that serves as the ultimate target for John Wesley's ministry and theology. For Wesley, it is a love that is not reachable by secular means or by a lazy kind of discipleship. It is a love that, as it is rooted in Christian faith, shows power and rigor. This love is the image of God and the mark of holiness. Greater levels of such love are pursued only by and with the empowering presence of the Spirit, made possible by Christ's life, death, and resurrection.

And yet, Wesley's thought has been the subject of criticism by some who fear that it implies that there is human merit in spiritual matters. Such critics tend to describe Wesley's account of pursuing Christian love as semi-Pelagian or as diminishing the glory of God.[2] Nevertheless, ev-

---

[1] This is quoted from Wesley's *Explanatory Notes Upon the New Testament*. Throughout his writings, Wesley makes many references to these verses. As we will show in chapter 7, he claims that the fulfillment of this commandment is what he means by Christian perfection.

[2] Such criticism was common among people with Calvinist sympathies. An example of such criticism may be found in the work of the Calvinist Methodist Richard Hill (Richard Hill, 'A Review of all the Doctrines Taught by the Rev. Mr. John Wesley' (Second Edition, London: E. and C. Dilly, 1772), 103). "Pelagianism" here means the view that right action may be done without God's grace. "Pelagianism" here does not necessarily refer to the view of the historical figure Pelagius who was the object of Augustine's critique.

idence in Wesley's writings shows that criticism of this kind is misguided. Over the course of this project, it will be argued that according to the view of John Wesley, a person's pursuit of Christian love is an expression of God's gift and that the giftedness of this blessing is illuminated by a critical examination of the work of the Spirit with respect to the active and passive dimensions of a human being. While this thesis offers a perspective that may strengthen Wesley's position against the critics, the purpose of this project is not to address Wesley's critics or to explore their arguments in great depth. Rather, the purpose of this project is to argue for an interpretation of Wesley's thought that until this point, has not been given adequate attention.

Parts of this book may seem a bit academic for some who are not researchers. Although this book is academic in nature, we are not arguing that Wesley believes that normal Christian living must depend on academic achievement. Wesley believes that a person does not have to have specialized education to have spiritual power and wisdom. It is possible that a person can be poor and uneducated and have more spiritual power and a much better theology than a church leader with many academic degrees. Wesley often cautions against people who are prideful because of their academic achievements. Yet, Wesley believes that, in general, the most rigorous academic and scientific achievements are good and are compatible with the truth of Christianity. Faith and reason are friends, not enemies. While the approach of the chapters ahead is academic, the nature of the content will lead us to highlight connections to a person's spiritual journey. Throughout this work, we will also be highlighting as much as possible how Wesley uses the Bible as his supreme guide for his views on Christian living.

Two important features of the Christian life that we will examine in this book are human actions and emotions, which as we will show, underly much of the active and passive dimensions of a person. Wesley always stressed that the Christian life calls people to act and to do good by putting forth as much effort as possible. This is part of what it means to follow the greatest commandment of scripture: to love God with all of one's heart, soul, mind, and strength. From his reading of the Bible, Wesley also emphasized the importance of emotions and religious experience in the Christian life. In its ideal form, the Christian life is not an ordinary or dull existence. Rather, it is a life filled with love, a love that has an amazing joy and happiness far beyond what anyone can put into words. For Wesley, this is a love that many people choose not to pursue. But this is a love that anyone can find, if one simply chooses to pursue it patiently over time. Anyone who pursues a relationship with God will find the feelings of joy and happiness, but it is not possible to fully predict or control when a person will first be aware of these states of being. Many occasions of spiritual emotions come according to God's mysterious schedule.

For those people who are coming to this work without much recent background in college or graduate school, you may find it useful to focus more attention on chapters 4, 6, 7, 8, the end of chapter 9, and maybe also the section of chapter 5 entitled, "The Shape of John Wesley's Theology." Some of the diagrams give a helpful summary of what is presented. The table of contents, of course, is also available to help you find sections that you think might most suit you.

Action and emotions are key elements of what this project describes as ethics. In this work, we describe "ethics" as a consideration of the features of the soul and how they relate as a person performs right action and pursues the highest goal of human living. As ethics is of central importance to the thesis mentioned above, we will begin this chapter by considering a background to Wesley's ethics. Next, we will illuminate what is meant by "ethics" in this project and introduce Wesley's version of it. After this, we will show how the approach of this work is different from approaches taken by other scholars who have published on Wesley's ethics. Last, in this chapter, we will summarize the steps that will be taken in the upcoming chapters in order to defend the thesis.

Background to Wesley's Ethics: A Search for True Religion

Wesley's church tradition is Anglican, which refers to the Church of England. Throughout his entire ministry, he remains a committed Anglican priest.[3] In some respects, this church tradition represents a "via media," a middle road between the Reformed tradition of the Protestant Reformation on the one side and Roman Catholicism on the other. From the birth of the Anglican church in the sixteenth century to the life of Wesley in the eighteenth century, political pressures from both sides—Reformed and Catholic—arose in Britain in various ways. To name a few examples: there was the Puritan Revolution in Britain during the middle of the

---

[3] Frank Baker, *John Wesley and the Church of England* (London : Epworth Press 2nd ed. 2000), 318-320.

Seventeenth Century that established the Reformed tradition as the reigning political power. Not long after, James II, a King with Roman Catholic inclinations, ruled Britain.[4] Finally, there was the Glorious Revolution of 1688 in which Anglican monarchs regained the throne once again and reaffirmed many previously existing Anglican doctrines and polity. From this point on, during Wesley's entire life and after, England would remain Anglican.

In England in the seventeenth century, there were a number of people who sought to express their devotion to God by means of creating or participating in religious societies. This occurred inside and outside of the Anglican church. According to one account that precedes the rise of Wesley's Methodism, the purpose of the societies was to promote "real holiness of heart and life."[5] The emphasis of holiness of heart found in these religious societies was similar to the concern for "heart theology" in the colleges of piety in Germany that arose in the seventeenth century even earlier than the English religious societies of the same century.[6] These colleges of piety were a mark of German pietism and were similar to the English religious societies in that they included time for small group Bible study and prayer.[7]

John Wesley's father Samuel Wesley shared the vision of religious societies and started his own religious society in Epworth, England in 1700, about three years before John's birth.[8] Samuel used a set of rules and practices as a guide for his religious society in their quest for promoting holiness of heart and life.[9] These rules and practices were similar to those used by the London societies. The orders of one society included a long list of practices, which included daily prayer, partaking of the Lord's Supper, censuring others, being holy in conduct, daily self-reflection concerning spiritual matters, fasting, and the reading of pious books.[10] The impact of Samuel's religious society is difficult to assess given the records available.[11] However, it is clear that many other so-

---

[4] Richard Heitzenrater. *Wesley and the People Called Methodists* (Nashville, TN: Abingdon, c1995), 15.

[5] *Orders Belonging to a Religious Society*: London: [n.p.] 1724.

[6] Heitzenrater, *Wesley and the People Called Methodists*, 19.

[7] Ibid., 20.

[8] Ibid., 27.

[9] Ibid., 27.

[10] Richard Heitzenrater. *Mirror and Memory* (Nashville TN: Kingswood Books, 1989), 38.

cieties succeeded in matters of social justice, as charitable schools were built and efforts were made to try to increase education and standards of living for the poor.[12] The purposes of the religious societies and the role of Samuel Wesley in promoting them foreshadowed similar efforts of John Wesley in the eighteenth century. The ministry of John Wesley would later become one of the highlights of a period of history known as the "First Great Awakening" and lead the rise of a Methodist movement that would involve over 120,000 people in religious societies before his death.[13]

During his life, Wesley had numerous other influences that helped to shape how he viewed religion. From his upbringing at Epworth; to his time at Oxford as an undergraduate, graduate student, and fellow of divinity; to his many travels, including his mission to Georgia during his 30s; Wesley read many books and corresponded with a wide variety of people. Wesley's development as a minister and theologian continued at a remarkable pace throughout his adult life, as he took control of the Methodist movement in the 1740s and in the decades that followed as he defended and clarified many aspects of the Methodist identity in the form of his prolific publications and letters. Such writing included dialogues and debates with figures from many kinds of theological perspectives and church traditions.

In the early stages of his ministry, Wesley faced what he considered to be an urgent problem. This was what he saw as the lack of true Christianity in culture. In his assessment of English culture, Wesley says, "We see (and who does not?) the numberless follies and miseries of our fellow-creatures. We see, on every side, either men of no religion at all, or men of a lifeless, formal religion. We are grieved at the sight; and should greatly rejoice, if by any means we might convince some that there is a better religion to be attained."[14] This concern is part of what inspired the mission of Wesley's ethics. In this same passage, Wesley goes on to define what he means as the goal of true religion. The goal of true religion is "the loving of God with all our heart, and soul, and strength, as having first loved us, as the fountain of all the good we have received, and of all we ever hope to enjoy; and the loving every soul which God hath made, every man on earth, as our own soul."[15]

[11] Heitzenrater, *Wesley and the People Called Methodists*, 30.
[12] Heitzenrater, *Mirror and Memory*, 39.
[13] Wesley, 'Annual Minutes of Some Late Conversations,' 1790, *Works* (BE), 10:733.
[14] Wesley, 'An Earnest Appeal to Men of Reason and Religion,' *Works* (Jackson), 8:3.

There is no surprise that Wesley makes loving God and one's neighbor the greatest goal of religion. These are the greatest commandments of scripture, as shown in the Old Testament, New Testament, and from the mouth of Jesus himself! A few lines later, Wesley says in reference to reaching this love: "Wherever this is, there are virtue and happiness going hand in hand."[16] These statements—concerning virtue and the greatest end of Christian living— are placed at the very beginning of his *An Earnest Appeal to Men of Reason and Religion* in 1743, which is an early defense of the Methodist movement. Wesley will repeatedly maintain this mission throughout the rest of his ministry.[17] This is the search for true religion, a pursuit different from the concerns of a troubled culture—a culture that often lacked sincerity concerning the teachings of the Bible.

For Wesley, the highest goal of the Christian life is outward directed: it is to love God and neighbor to one's fullest potential. However, there must be a way to hold Christians accountable for seeking and reaching what is truly the highest end as opposed to this highest end in disguise.[18] With scripture as his supreme guide and following the example of many religious societies before him, Wesley holds that the barometer for gauging one's progress in fulfilling the true Christian mission involves ex-

---

[15] Wesley, 'An Earnest Appeal to Men of Reason and Religion,' *Works* (Jackson), 8:3.

[16] Wesley, 'An Earnest Appeal to Men of Reason and Religion,' *Works* (Jackson), 8:3.

[17] See for example his comments in 1777 when he says, "Methodism, so called, is the old religion, the religion of the Bible, the religion of the primitive church, the religion of the Church of England. This 'old religion' (as I observed in the *Earnest Appeal to Men of Reason and Religion*) is 'no other than love: the love of God and of all mankind; the loving of God with all our heart, and soul, and strength, as having first loved us, as the fountain of all the good we have received, and of all we ever hope to enjoy; and the loving every soul which God hath made, every man on earth, as our own soul," from Wesley, 'On Laying the Foundation of the New Chapel,' *Works* (BE), 3:585. To name only several of the many other cases: he restates this mission in his Principles of a Methodist Farther Explained (Wesley, 'The Principles of a Methodist Farther Explained,' *Works* (Jackson), 8:474), in his definition of Christian perfection (Wesley, 'A Plain Account of Christian Perfection,' *Works* (Jackson), 11:394), and in the concluding remarks of a sermon he preaches in 1789 (Wesley, 'On Knowing Christ After the Flesh,' *Works* (BE), 4:106). He also says, "Christian faith"... "still is only the handmaid of love. As glorious and honourable as it is, it is not the end of the commandment. God hath given this honour to love alone. Love is the end of all the commandments of God. Love is the end, the sole end, of every dispensation of God, from the beginning of the world to the consummation of all things" (Wesley, 'The Law Established Through Faith, II,' *Works* (BE), 2:38).

[18] Wesley's theology is not self-interested for the sake of being self-interested. It is self-reflective in reaction to a widespread mindset of complicity for a practice of religion that lacks the power of religion and the example of "true religion."

perimental consideration of the heart and works that flow from the heart. As we will explore in the chapters ahead, the heart and the works that flow from it are intimately related. As the love of God is concerned much with the human heart, Wesley was known to use the phrase "heart religion."[19] Inspired by this language, we will use the phrase "heart ethics" to describe Wesley's ethics.

As argued by scholars such as T. A. Noble, Richard Heitzenrater, Randy Maddox, Henry Knight, Kenneth Collins, and others, a Wesleyan pursuit of the highest end of Christian love is a matter of relationship building.[20] According to Wesley, due to the fall of humankind and the condition of total depravity, God sent his Son Jesus to the world in order to redeem humankind from sin and death. Because of Jesus' life, death, and resurrection, God offers to each person salvation from sin and death, a restoring of the image of God, the capability of performing good actions, and the opportunity to love God for all eternity. By God's free grace, the process of relationship building begins. One example of free grace is when God touches the heart in a manner that is perceivable to the human recipient. After this, a person is able to respond to this first move by seeking Christian love and by performing fruitful action.

Concerning his understanding of Christian thought, Wesley has read a vast range of sources, consulted with an immense range of people, and had an enormous number of experiences in ministry settings. For centuries, Wesleyan scholars have attempted to determine how Wesley's sources have influenced him. Often, this task has been quite complex and difficult, if not impossible in some cases. For this project, the approach will be to focus more on the actual content of Wesley's thought and less on how his sources influenced him. In this project, when we compare Wesley's thought to his sources, predecessors, and contemporaries, it will be for the sake of bringing clarity to Wesley's thought rather than to offer a link for how his sources may have caused the shaping of his thought. We will make exceptions to this approach for certain cases

---

[19] See, for example, his comments in a 1789 sermon. Wesley, 'Prophets and Priests,' *Works* (BE), 4:82.

[20] T.A. Noble, *Holy Trinity: Holy People* (Eugene, Oregon: Cascade Books, 2013), 108; Henry Knight III, *The Presence of God in the Christian Life* (Oxford: Scarecrow Press Inc., 1987), 2; Randy Maddox, *Responsible Grace* (Nashville, TN: Kingswood Books, 1994), 68. See footnote 20 (p. 287) of Maddox for more examples of other commentators who see Wesley's view of salvation as involving relationships.

in which Wesley explicitly gives his sources and explains how he uses them. One such exception is Wesley's use of the Bible. Unlike for his other sources, Wesley openly claims that the Bible is what he considers to be the source with the highest authority.[21] For this reason, Wesley's reliance on the Bible will often be highlighted. In chapter 5, we will take a more in depth look at how Wesley says he uses his sources.

Now that we have offered some background to Wesley's ethics, we will now clarify what is meant by "ethics" in this project before we introduce Wesley's own version of it. In preparation for illuminating what is meant by ethics in this work, we will first consider a brief overview of "virtue ethics" in the western tradition.

"Virtue Ethics" in Western Tradition

Academic discussions of ethics today include but are not limited to three major branches: deontology, utilitarianism, and virtue ethics.[22] Rosalind Hursthouse claims that in the second part of the twentieth century, virtue ethics "acquired full status, recognized as a rival to deontological and utilitarian approaches, as interestingly and challengingly different from either as they are from each other."[23] Deontology is inspired by Immanuel Kant and stresses duties and rules. Utilitarianism (also known as consequentialism) is inspired by Jeremy Bentham and John Stuart Mill and emphasizes the consequences of actions.[24] According to *The Cambridge Companion to Virtue Ethics* published in 2013, virtues ethics concerns "what to do with one's life and how to make it a happy one. Answering these questions involves, among other things, reflecting on what sort of person to be and what sort of character to develop."[25] Some schol-

---

[21] Wesley says, "We believe the written word of God to be the only and sufficient rule both of Christian faith and practice" (Wesley, 'The Character of a Methodist,' *Works* (Jackson), 8:340).

[22] See, for example, Roger Crisp and Michael Slote, *Virtue Ethics* (Oxford: Oxford University Press, 1997), 1; Rosalind Hursthouse, *On Virtue Ethics* (Oxford: Oxford University Press, 2001), 1; Michael Slote, "Virtue Ethics" in *The Routledge Companion to Ethics*, ed. John Skorupski (New York: Routledge, 2010), 478; Stan van Hooft, *The Handbook of Virtue Ethics* (Bristol, CT: Acumen, 2014), 1.

[23] Hursthouse, *On Virtue Ethics*, 2.

[24] Hursthouse, *On Virtue Ethics*, 1.

[25] Daniel C. Russell. *The Cambridge Companion to Virtue Ethics* (Cambridge: Cambridge University Press, 2013), 7. Russell is speaking here in reference to

arship has attempted to show that there is overlap in these three approaches or at least potential for sharing conceptual tools.[26] However, these three areas have been distinguished due to each having points of emphasis that are different from the others.

Although virtue ethics does not have one standard definition, there are several traits that are commonly associated with it. One common mark of virtue ethics is an emphasis and concern with character or "who the person is" in relation to moral action.[27] In this way, virtue ethics is more concerned with moral psychology and anthropology than the other two approaches to ethics. Stan van Hooft says that virtue ethics "leads to an understanding of our moral psychology and is sensitive to the complexities and obscurities of our motivational lives."[28] Like deontology, virtue ethics is often concerned with right action. However, unlike deontology, virtue ethics is concerned with how right action flows from excellences of character.[29] As Michael Slote says,

> But rules/principles and consequences are not the basis for the moral evaluations virtue ethics makes. The ethical focus, rather, is on character and motive, which are naturally regarded as the key elements in determining whether someone is virtuous or has a particular virtue.[30]

In this way, virtue ethics is more observant to the whole person than deontology and utilitarianism, and this is one of the reasons why virtue ethics has gained an increased level of attention in recent decades.

Another common mark of virtue ethics is a concern for a highest end, also known as a telos, highest good, or highest goal.[31] This highest end

---

virtue ethics in its earliest forms but this view is still prevalent in virtue ethics today.

[26] Hursthouse, *On Virtue Ethics*, 3 - 5.

[27] Russell, *The Cambridge Companion to Virtue Ethics*, 1; Hursthouse, *On Virtue Ethics*, 17; Slote, "Virtue Ethics" in *The Routledge Companion to Ethics*, ed. John Skorupski, 478; Christine Swanton, *Virtue Ethics: A Pluralistic View* (Oxford: Oxford University Press, 2003), 1.

[28] Hooft, *The Handbook of Virtue Ethics*, 3.

[29] See especially Hursthouse, *On Virtue Ethics*, 17.

[30] Slote, "Virtue Ethics" in *The Routledge Companion to Ethics*, ed. John Skorupski, 478. For a discussion on the connection between right action and virtue, see Hursthouse, *On Virtue Ethics*, 17.

[31] Some renditions of virtue ethics today do not emphasize seeking a highest end. However, this latter trait is still quite common.

is often described as happiness or eudaimonia. In *The Cambridge Companion to Virtue Ethics* published in 2013, Daniel C. Russell says,

> Eudaimonism dates to ancient Greece, where all the major camps of moral philosophy (Platonists, Aristotelians, Epicureans, and Stoics) were eudaimonists, and their influence in virtue ethics is still strong today... The most influential exposition of eudaimonism is still Aristotle's.[32]

As we observe from these comments, an interpretation of ethics that involves a teleology or seeking a highest end was common in the ancient Western world, and is still quite prevalent in virtue ethics today. According to such a model, pursuing the highest end is the ultimate purpose of ethics, and when such an end (happiness or eudaimonia) is achieved, the virtues are displayed and a person is living a life of activities conducive to his or her health and well-being.

In her book *Virtue Ethics: A Pluralistic View*, published by Oxford University Press, Christine Swanton argues that virtue ethics is indeed a "genus," a general category that refers to a collection of differing portraits.[33] Although the portraits of virtue ethics share some common traits, they have differences. For example, the virtue ethics of Aquinas and Aristotle share much in common, but they have differences. To name one point: Aquinas' virtue ethics is theological, while Aristotle's is not. Both of the virtue ethics of Aquinas and Aristotle differ quite a bit from the virtue ethics of David Hume. All of this is to show that there is diversity within this common genus.

Consistent with Swanton's view, it is certainly possible to have a *theological* version of virtue ethics within the larger genus. In *The Oxford Handbook of Theological Ethics*, Gilbert Meilaender and William Werpehowski share the following statement concerning theological ethics: "Almost any kind of systematic ethical reflection will need to consider the sort of people we ought to be, the goals we ought to seek, and the actions we ought to do."[34] This statement is a strong endorsement of virtue ethics, as this statement emphasizes who a person is, the seeking of goals, and the performance of right action. We also observe the promotion of virtue ethics in theology by figures such as Stanley Hauerwas and D. Stephen Long.[35] Both Hauerwas and Long follow a model of virtue ethics sym-

---

[32] Russell, *The Cambridge Companion to Virtue Ethics*, 8.

[33] Swanton, *Virtue Ethics: A Pluralistic View*, 1.

[34] Gilbert Meilaender and William Werpehowski, editors, *The Oxford Handbook of Theological Ethics* (Oxford: Oxford University Press, 2005), 2.

pathetic to Aristotle and Aquinas. They are concerned with an ethics of teleology or goal-seeking, in which people are to undergo a transformation of character and acquisition of virtues through a spiritual life of practices in a community with rich traditions.

As Hursthouse points out, virtue ethics emerged as a major area of ethics in the second half of the twentieth century.[36] However, this was not its first point of major influence. The rise of virtue ethics in the late part of the twentieth century was not a first emergence but rather a re-emergence. In *The Oxford Handbook of Ethical Theory*, Julia Annas says, "In the tradition of Western philosophy since the fifth century B.C., the default form of ethical theory has been some version of what is nowadays called virtue ethics; real theoretical alternatives emerge only with Kant and with consequentialism."[37] She goes on to say, in reference to virtue ethics: "Its theoretical structure is first clearly stated by Aristotle, but it is wrong to think of it as peculiarly Aristotelian, since it underlies all of ancient ethical theory."[38]

Annas is arguing here that virtue ethics is the default form of ethics in the Western world from the ancient Greeks until the Enlightenment. Even if this is somewhat of an overstatement, there has been substantial work in secondary scholarship that has traced the development of virtue ethics from the ancient Greeks through the medieval Christians.[39] But the prevalence of virtue ethics does not stop at the medieval period.

---

[35] For an account of the virtue ethics of Stanley Hauerwas, see: Glen Pettigrove, "Virtue Ethics, Virtue Theory and Moral Theology" in *The Handbook of Virtue Ethics*, ed. Stan van Hooft (Bristol, CT: Acumen, 2014), 92. For an account of the virtue ethics of D. Stephen Long, see, for example: D. Stephen Long, *John Wesley's Moral Theology: The Quest for God and Goodness* (Nashville: Kingswood, 2005).

[36] Hursthouse, *On Virtue Ethics*, 2.

[37] Julias Annas, "Virtue Ethics" in the *Oxford Handbook of Ethical Theory*, ed. David Copp (Oxford: Oxford University Press, 2005), 515.

[38] Annas, "Virtue Ethics" in the *Oxford Handbook of Ethical Theory*, ed. David Copp, 515.

[39] See, for example, chapters 2 and 4 of Russell, *The Cambridge Companion to Virtue Ethics*. See also Jean Porter, "Virtue Ethics" in *The Cambridge Companion to Christian Ethics*, ed. Robin Gill (Cambridge: Cambridge University Press, 2012). See also Pettigrove's discussion of virtue ethics in Aquinas (Pettigrove, "Virtue Ethics, Virtue Theory and Moral Theology" in *The Handbook of Virtue Ethics*, ed. Stan van Hooft, 88).

The writings of several figures of the seventeenth century that Wesley read exemplify virtue ethics. One of these figures is Gerard Langbaine, a seventeenth century Oxford teacher and Anglican. Langbaine's book *Ethics Compendium* is inspired by Aristotelian ethics. Wesley makes reference to this book in a letter written in 1764: "As to Ethics (or Moral Philosophy) there is full as much of it as you want in Langbain's Compendium."[40] It is also required reading for students at the Kingswood school, a school founded by John Wesley.[41] Wesley's Oxford diaries suggest that Wesley read Langbaine's book on ethics as early as September of 1726.[42] During that same month, his diary records that he also read books on ethics by Henry More and Eustachius A Sancto.[43] Of the three, Langbaine's book seems to be his book of preference but he does make multiple references to More's book.[44]

Like many figures before him, the thought of John Wesley exemplifies the portrait of virtue ethics mentioned above. In Wesley's thought, there is an emphasis on the positive development of character, the heart, and "who the person is" and how this relates to moral action. The preferred character is what comes at the new birth, when a person is born of God and sanctified in the Spirit. There is also an emphasis on teleology. For Wesley, the highest goal is none other than his scriptural doctrine of Christian perfection. This doctrine of Christian perfection is sometimes misinterpreted. What Wesley means by Christian perfection is to obey the greatest commandment of scripture and to love God with one's heart, soul, mind, and strength. Although Wesley's overall thought has some of the common emphases of virtue ethics, it is not identical to every other previous version of virtue ethics. Wesley's virtue ethics is its

---

[40] Wesley, *Letters*, 4:248.

[41] Wesley, 'A Short Account of the Kingswood School,' *Works* (Jackson), 13:287.

[42] This is verified to me through a correspondence with Randy Maddox.

[43] Ibid. The titles of the book are *Ethices compendium* by Lanbaine, *Ethica: sive summa moralis disciplinae, in tres partes divisa*, by Eustachius a Sancto Paulo; and *Enchiridion ethicum: praecipua moralis philosophiae rudimenta complectens, illustrata utplurimum veterum monumentis* by Henry More. It is interesting to note that in both of these books—as in Langbaine's book—, there is an extensive discussion of moral liberty. Henry More, *Enchiridion Ethicum* (London: Benj. Tooke, 1690).

[44] Wesley, 'An Address to the Clergy,' *Works* (Jackson), 10:492. Here More's book on ethics is not mentioned specifically. But More's work as a whole is being referenced.

own species as Swanton would say. In this work, we are calling Wesley's species of ethics "heart ethics."

In the pages that follow, we will examine Wesley's view of ethics. While scholars agree on common emphases in virtue ethics, there is some debate concerning how to give a precise definition of it. In academic works on ethics from the ancient Greeks to the time of Wesley, it is common for there to be a consideration of the various features of the soul and how they relate to each other as a person performs right action and pursues the highest end. In this current work, we will use a meaning of "ethics" that involves an examination of the features of the soul and how they relate to each other as a person performs right action and pursues the highest end. As we examine Wesley's ethics, it will become increasingly clear how Wesley's heart ethics exemplifies a species of virtue ethics. That is, we will observe in depth how Wesley's places a high importance on the heart and who a person is and how these relate to moral action and the pursuit of the greatest goal. At the same time, it will be argued that in Wesley's heart ethics, God's work in the Spirit is the primary force and center of focus.

Introducing Wesley's Ethics

Our examination of Wesley's ethics in this work will involve a careful look at Wesley's view of the soul.[45] For Wesley, the soul is something that has a spiritual nature and includes the natural image of God. God endows each person with understanding, will, and liberty. The part of the soul called the *will* refers to the affections and passions.[46] The part of

---

[45] At times, Wesley seems to use the words "soul" and "spirit" interchangeably. For example, on one occasion, Wesley describes the soul as "a spirit." On another occasion, he describes it as "an immortal spirit made in the image of God, together with all the powers and faculties thereof." He speaks of the soul as having a principle of inward and outward motion and as including affections, passions, and tempers. Wesley, 'The Imperfection of Human Knowledge,' *Works* (BE), 2:576; Wesley, 'The Good Steward," *Works* (BE), 2:284; Wesley, 'Original Sin,' *Works* (BE), 2:175. For this current project, we will use the word "soul" to refer to a person's total consciousness. In chapters 2 – 4, we will engage Wesley's view of the features of the soul in depth.

[46] Wesley, 'The General Deliverance,' *Works* (BE), 2:439 and 2:442; Wesley, 'The End of Christ's Coming,' *Works* (BE), 2:474; Wesley, 'On the Fall of Man,' *Works* (BE), 2:401; Wesley, 'On Divine Providence,' *Works* (BE), 2:540; Wesley, *Letters*, 5:4. It is important to note that Wesley does not use the *will* to refer to choice, and in this way, he differs from many other figures. But it is important to observe the difference between Wesley's use of the "will" in italics versus certain other contexts. On some occasions when Wesley both (1) is not italicizing the word "will" and (2) is not summarizing the features of the

the soul called liberty refers to the power of choice.[47] This meaning of liberty is different from other meanings of liberty that Wesley uses and that are common in the English language.[48]

Wesley's view of moral liberty, understood as moral choosing, plays a key role for his ethics. As Wesley stresses on many occasions, without the power of liberty, it is not possible to have virtue and vice or good and evil.[49] For this reason, according to Wesley, necessitarian models completely undermine virtue and vice altogether, throwing out the possibility of ethics.[50] This is because, according to a necessitarian model, a person must necessarily choose according to what is perceived as the best motive for action. By "libertarian," scholars mean one who holds the doctrine of free will as opposed to the philosophical necessity that is presupposed in absolute predestination.[51] For a libertarian, a human

---

soul, he uses the word "will" as choice. In these contexts, he is often speaking colloquially. See the section below on Wesley's view of the will and liberty.

[47] As will be argued more extensively in chapter 2, Wesley's understanding of this type of liberty is that it is the same as human action, understood as the power of choosing (Wesley, 'The General Deliverance,' *Works* (BE), 2:439 and 2:440; Wesley, 'The End of Christ's Coming,' *Works* (BE), 2:475; Wesley, 'On the Fall of Man,' *Works* (BE), 2:401; Wesley, 'The Original, Nature, Properties, and Use of the Law,' *Works* (BE), 2:6; Wesley, 'God's Approbation of His Works,' *Works* (BE), 2:399; Wesley, 'The General Spread of the Gospel,' *Works* (BE), 2:489). Such action may refer to comparatively neutral human action or action explicitly related to moral matters. It may pertain to action relating to the choice of civil or religious matters (See Wesley, 'Some Observations on Liberty,' *Works* (Jackson), 11:91. It should be noted here that Wesley does not like Richard Price's bringing moral liberty to bear on matters of civil liberty, even though they both involve the power choosing. Wesley is not claiming that the two are unrelated but that their comparison is unhelpful for Price's specific purpose). For a critical response to interpretations of Wesley's view of liberty offered by Albert Outler and D. Stephen Long, see Appendix A.

[48] It must be stressed that Wesley at times intentionally uses other meanings of liberty different from the idea of liberty defined as equivalent to action and choice. One such alternative meaning is when Wesley speaks of the liberty from Romans 8:21, often described as "glorious liberty." Whereas the first type of liberty is applicable to all people at all stages, this second type of liberty is possessed only by children of God. This second type of liberty means freedom from the bondage of sin.

[49] This point is made on numerous occasions and for almost every time that he mentions liberty.

[50] See, for example, Wesley's critique of Edwards and Kames in his essay 'Thoughts Upon Necessity,' (Wesley, 'Thoughts Upon Necessity,' *Works* (Jackson), volume 10).

[51] Exploring the concept of "libertarian" and "necessitarian" is one of the major tasks of James Harris, *Of Liberty and Necessity, The Free Will Debate in*

is free, in at least some cases, to choose for or against the perceived strongest motive. A "necessitarian" is one whose system of thought presupposes that every human choice must be caused by the strongest motive.[52] The theory of absolute predestination is an example of necessitarianism. A "compatibilist" is a necessitarian who argues that moral responsibility is consistent with necessitarianism.

For Wesley, part of what allows a choice to be virtuous is the fact that a person could have chosen otherwise—even against the strongest motive or clearly known greatest good.[53] No one is forced to sin. Sin properly speaking is always a choice. For Wesley, sin properly understood is choosing something known to be evil.[54] Virtue is when someone with a transformed heart chooses to do good. Wesley emphasizes the heart here.[55] Virtue is not right choice alone but it requires right choice (and

---

Eighteenth Century British Philosophy (Oxford: Oxford University Press, 2005). For an account of what is meant by a "libertarian" and "necessitarian," see p. 7 of Harris' book. Also, for more discussion of these ideas, see appendix A.

[52] According to a necessitarian view, if a man chooses to raise his arm at time t_1, then if history were to rewind and playback in a manner that provides the same external conditions, the man must raise his arm at time t_1. This is because every choice is determined by a strongest motive connected to one path of history. Necessitarians believe that the flow of history, including the interaction of all the forces of the universe, only has one trajectory. By contrast, for a libertarian, if history is rewound and played back with the same external conditions, the man is free to lower his arm or perform a different act at t_1. This is because the universe has contingency and choice does not by necessity depend on the strongest motive.

[53] Concerning the point that Wesley believes that a person has the power to choose against the strongest motive and/or clearly-known greatest good, see Wesley, 'Thoughts Upon Necessity,' *Works* (Jackson), especially 10:472. Wesley's comments on conscience reflect his belief that all people have the power to a degree to know accurately what is good and bad (Wesley, 'On Conscience,' *Works* (BE), 3:481), and his comments on liberty reflect his view that one is always free to choose the clearly-known actual bad instead of the clearly-known actual good (see just about any one of Wesley's discussions of liberty after 1774). This is in contrast to Aquinas, for example, who argues that one is not free to choose against a clearly-known actual good. See Henrik Lagerlund and Mikko Yrjonsuuri, *Emotions and Choice: from Boethius to Descartes* (London: Kluwer Academic Publishers, 2002), 14.

[54] There will be more discussion on this matter in the chapters ahead. Wesley says sin is when a person knowingly and voluntarily transgresses a law of God. Wesley, 'The Great Privilege of Those that are Born of God,' *Works* (BE), 1:436.

the corresponding outward actions) that flows from a holy heart.[56] Wesley's emphasis on the importance of inward desires for ethics distinguishes him from ethical figures such as Kant and the pre-modern Stoics.[57]

For Wesley, while the heart is important in the moral life, actions are also important. Choosing to perform fruitful action is something that he encourages for all people regardless of where they are in life.[58] In this way, his ethics places an emphasis on action. Wesley's concern is that any approach to life that ignores the importance of action can lead to Antinomianism (moral laxity) and backsliding. Yet, as implied above, Wesley's ethics is not like the view of a Pharisee. For moral action to have an optimum effect, it must spring from a holy heart of love.

Another key power of the soul concerning ethics is conscience. Conscience involves multiple features of the soul, including an interaction between the understanding and the *will*. Conscience is "a kind of silent reasoning of the mind whereby those things which are judged to be right are approved of with pleasure; but those which are judged evil are disapproved of with uneasiness."[59] The key aspect of conscience concerning Wesley's ethics is that it is a power to a certain degree, to judge whether a past, current, or proposed action is right or wrong. Conscience involves having some knowledge of the moral law. It is not learnable but a degree of it is given by God to every human being. Because of Wesley's under-

---

[55] C.F. Randy Maddox, "John Wesley-Practical Theologian?," *Wesleyan Theological Journal*, 23 (1988): 122 and Randy Maddox, "The Recovery of Theology as a Practical Discipline," *Theological Studies*, 51, no. 4, (1990): 665.

[56] For example, see Wesley, *An Israelite Indeed* (BE), 3:280; Wesley, *Justification by Faith* (BE), 1:192; Wesley, *On Zeal* (BE), 3:320; Wesley, *Upon Our Lord's Sermon on the Mount, Discourse the Fifth* (BE), 1:568; Wesley, *Upon Our Lord's Sermon on the Mount, Discourse the Sixth* (BE), 1:573; Wesley, *Heaviness through Manifold Temptations* (BE), 2:232. Wesley sometimes also uses the word "virtue" to refer to qualities that do not involve choice. See for example, Wesley, *Circumcision of the Heart* (BE), 1:403, in which he uses "virtue" to refer to fruits such as faith and humility.

[57] In general, the Stoics aim to eradicate all emotions, even moderate ones. See Richard Sorabji, *Emotions and Peace of Mind* (Oxford: Oxford University Press, 2000), 17. Emotions and desires are interlinked.

[58] "Fruitful" here means morally preferable. This term will be considered more in chapter 5.

[59] Wesley, *On Conscience* (BE), 3:481.

standing of conscience, Wesley can claim that all people are to some degree morally accountable.

According to Wesley, God plays the main role in ethics. This is because for Wesley, ethics is necessarily theological in nature. In this way, his thought differs from some of the emerging traits of the secular strand of the Enlightenment. Fundamentally, ethics must be understood as involving true Christian faith that is consistent with scripture. Wesley's summarizing account of the views of a Methodist puts this well:

> We believe, indeed, that "all Scripture is given by the inspiration of God;" and herein we are distinguished from Jews, Turks, and Infidels. We believe the written word of God to be the only and sufficient rule both of Christian faith and practice; and herein we are fundamentally distinguished from those of the Romish Church. We believe Christ to be the eternal, supreme God; and herein we are distinguished form the Socians and Arians. But as to all opinions which do not strike at the root of Christianity, we think and let think. So that whatever they are, whether right or wrong, they are no distinguishing marks of a Methodist.[60]

It is clear from this passage, that Wesley sees scripture as a supreme guide for doing ethics. Scripture is not to be discarded in preference for new kinds of scientific or philosophical development.

Note also that in Wesley's ethics, there is no divorce between faith and practice, as is the tendency of some others. An account of Wesley's ethics is by necessity theological ethics. As D. Stephen Long says, "Wesley thought that God and the good, doctrine and ethics, were inextricable."[61] Consistent with this interpretation, Wesley makes the following statement:

> But how great is the number of those who, allowing religion to consist in two branches, our duty to God and our duty to our neighbor, entirely forget the first part, and put the second part for the whole, for the entire duty of man. Thus almost all men of letters, both in England, France, Germany, yea, and all the civilized countries of Europe, extol 'humanity' to the skies, as the very essence of religion. To this great triumvirate, Rousseau, Voltaire, and David Hume, have contributed all their labours, sparing no pains to establish a religion which should stand on its own foundation, independent on any revelation whatever, year, not supposing even the being of a God. So leaving him, if he has any being, to himself, they have found out both a religion and a happiness which have no

---

[60] Wesley, 'The Character of a Methodist,' *Works* (Jackson), 8:340.
[61] Long, *John Wesley's Moral Theology*, 37.

relation at all to God nor any dependence upon him. It is no wonder that this religion should grow fashionable, and spread far and wide in the world. But call it 'humanity', 'virtue', 'morality', or what you please, it is neither better nor worse than atheism. Men hereby willfully and designedly put asunder what God has joined, the duties of the first and second table. It is separating the love of neighbor from the love of God. It is a plausible way of thrusting God out of the world he has made… We know that as all nature, so all religion and all happiness depend on him; and we know that whoever teach to seek happiness without him are monsters and pests of society.[62]

This is a strong and explicit rejection of certain figures of the Enlightenment who attempt to divorce ethics from God. The perceived shortcomings of John Taylor's *Doctrine of Original Sin* also reflect some related concerns. The problem that Wesley sees in Taylor's view is that Wesley thinks it makes doing good possible by a person's own power without needing the assistance of grace provided by Christ's atonement. For Wesley, ethics must be theological. Human beings cannot do anything right on their own because of their total depravity. It is because of Christ's life, death, and resurrection that people may be saved from eternal death, be restored in the image of God, and be capable of performing right action.

Wesley's ethics is teleological: it has a greatest goal. As mentioned in the previous section, Wesley's greatest goal is to love God to one's fullest potential and to love one's neighbor. As one moves towards this greatest end of Christian love, one also undergoes a change in affections, tempers, and desires (components of the heart). In other words, one's affections, tempers, and desires have potential for improvement. One may describe a secular version of this idea as the "education" of the tempers, affections, and desires. Aristotle understood such education to come through repeated practice of good deeds and/or in shadowing the behaviours of one already virtuous.[63] For Wesley the improvement of the tempers, affections, and desires does not come through human-led education but rather by the transformative power of the Spirit. More will be said on this matter in later chapters.

In summary, we have introduced some of the qualities of Wesley's version of ethics. At a preliminary level, we introduced Wesley's view of

---

[62] Wesley, 'The Unity of the Divine Being,' *Works* (BE), 4:69.
[63] For example, see chapter 2, book 2 of Aristotle's *Nicomachean Ethics* (Cambridge, Cambridge University Press, 2000).

the features of the soul. We showed that God plays a leading role in ethics, that Wesley's ethics encourages fruitful action, and that it involves the quest for seeking a greatest end, which is Christian love. All of these points will be explored in more depth in the chapters ahead. Before going further, however, we will highlight some discussions in secondary literature concerning Wesley's ethics.

Recent Scholarship Concerning Wesley's Ethics

So far, there are only a few projects in the secondary literature concerning John Wesley's view of ethics that have aimed to limit their scope of consideration to only Wesley's thought. Most of the projects concerning Wesley's ethics are either constructive in nature (meaning that they modify or expand Wesley's thought) or they opt to explore only limited aspects of Wesley's ethics.

Projects involving Wesley's ethics that are constructive in nature involve work by Leon Hynson, H. Ray Dunning, Theodore Weber, Kevin Twain Lowery, D. Stephen Long, and Timothy Gaines.[64] None of these projects limit the scope of their work to Wesley's thought, but they all draw from Wesley's thought to some degree. Many of them also use sources unknown to Wesley as part of their ethical construction. On the other hand, Manfred Marquardt and Ronald Stone limit their work to information concerning Wesley's life and thought, but the emphasis of

---

[64] Leon Hynson, *To Reform the Nation* (Grand Rapids, Michigan: Francis Asbury Press, c1984), 43; Theodore Weber, *Politics in the Order of Salvation, Transforming Wesleyan Political Ethics* (Nashville TN, Kingswood Books, c2001), 417; Kevin Lowery, *Salvaging Wesley's Agenda, A New Paradigm for Wesleyan Virtue Ethics* (Eugene, Oregon: Pickwick Publications, 2008), especially chapters 7-9; Long, *John Wesley's Moral Theology*; H. Ray Dunning, *Reflecting the Divine Image, Christian Ethics in Wesleyan Perspective* (Downers Grove Ill: Intervarsity Press, 1998); Timothy Gaines, "Can Ethics be Wesleyan?: Moral Theology and Holiness Identity," *Wesleyan Theological Journal*, 51, (2016): 155 - 167. For example, Dunning says, "Wesley did not explore doctrinal themes in full consistency with his central commitments. So to be true to the Wesleyan spirit one must follow those central commitments to their logical conclusions, even if they result in a doctrine that would differ from, even contradict, some of Wesley's own theological comments" (Dunning, *Reflecting the Divine Image*, 22). Also, for example, Gaines says, in reference to the aims of his article: "Though not all these suggestions stem directly from John Wesley's writings, none of them are out of step with his theological trajectory" (Gaines, "Can Ethics Be Wesleyan?," 155 - 156).

these works lies less on Wesley's religious thought and more on either historical occurrences or Wesley's position on specific social issues.[65] Marquardt deals some with theology and religious experience, but most of his book is devoted to exploring social matters such as philanthropy, work in societies, economics, education, slavery, and prison reform. Much of Stone's book involves a historical study of Wesley's life and also explores Wesley's position on ethical issues such as marriage, war, politics, and slavery.

This current project focuses on Wesley's ethics from an approach that is limited to Wesley's own thought, except for the concluding chapter in which the relevance of Wesley's heart ethics for today is considered. It is the assumption of this project that there is a general consistency in Wesley's thought and ethics after 1738, and therefore exploring his ethics is a feasible task.[66] As will be shown, for Wesley, an urgent task of ethics is guiding people to seek God's love and follow the way of salvation, a scriptural roadmap for the Christian life. Following this way of salvation is done by carrying out scriptural practices.

For Wesley, institutional reform and promoting correct forms of government are important priorities, but they are lower priorities than the kind of discipleship that can occur in a smaller context. Achieving institutional reform and influencing government policy are often not easily within one's reach. This is not to deny that to "reform the nation" is one of Wesley's visions for Methodism or that Wesley understands government politics to be related to the salvation and eschatology of the cosmos.[67] Rather, it is to underscore a somewhat prior need for giving attention to the level at which a small group can "work out their own salvation" according to the graces available. In many ways, the success of the secondary concerns (institutional reform, government policy, etc.) depends on the success of people accomplishing by grace the first concern. This current project will explore Wesley's ethics mostly on the level of an individual, local church, and/or small group but touches a little also on those matters that are also important but more out of reach, namely the macroscopic level (institutions, government matters, etc.).

---

[65] Manfred Marquardt, *John Wesley's Social Ethics, Praxis and Principles* (Nashville, TN: Abingdon Press, c1991); Ronald Stone, *John Wesley's Life and Ethics* (Nashville, TN: Abingdon Press, c2001).

[66] See Appendix B, entitled "Consistency in Wesley's Thought."

[67] Wesley, 'Minutes of Some Late Conversations Between the Rev. Mr. Wesley and Others,' *Works* (Jackson), 8:299.

Summary of this Project

In this project, we will be exploring John Wesley's view of ethics in more depth. Earlier, we described "ethics" as a consideration of the features of the soul and how they relate as an agent performs right action and pursues the highest goal of human living.

When exploring Wesley's ethics, an important theme emerges. It is the theme of gift. Over the course of this project, it will be argued that according to the view of John Wesley, a person's pursuit of the greatest end of ethics is an expression of God's gift and that the giftedness of this blessing is illuminated by a critical examination of the work of the Spirit with respect to the active and passive dimensions of a human being. In order to support this thesis, we will take up two tasks. The first task is to clarify the features of the soul.[68] In order to properly understand the graciousness of God in ethics, one must first clearly understand what the features of the soul are and how they work. The second task is to consider in more depth how the features of the soul relate as an agent performs right action and pursues the highest end of ethics. For Wesley, the gospel is foundational for ethics. God plays the leading role in a person's salvific transformation. A person's soul changes depending on where one is along the "way of salvation" (Wesley's roadmap for the Christian journey). Therefore, the second task will require a consideration of Wesley's view of the various stages of the Christian life.

Chapters 2- 4 will assist the first task. In chapter 2, we will clarify what this project means by "active" and "passive." These concepts are at the core of his theology and ethics.[69] It will be shown that these concepts are crucial for clarifying Wesley's view of the soul. As mentioned above, Wesley teaches that a person is endued with the powers of understanding, will, and liberty. In chapter 2, we will begin clarifying Wesley's view of liberty. In chapter 3, we will continue investigating Wesley's view of liberty and also explore his understanding of the will. In chapter 4, we will explore Wesley's understanding of the heart, with its desires, tempers,

---

[68] This task is "first" in the order that it is considered. "First" here does not refer to level of importance.

[69] Examples of places where Wesley does use the terms "active" and "passive" include: Wesley, 'The Good Steward,' *Works* (BE), 2:284 ; Wesley, 'What is Man?,' *Works* (BE), 4:22-24; Wesley, 'Thoughts on Memory,' *Works* (BE), 13:480.

and affections. We will also consider here Wesley's view of practical reason and how it relates to the heart.

In chapter 5, we will begin to consider in more depth how God has the main role in ethics. We will consider the shape of Wesley's theology and show the various ways that the Holy Spirit works in human action. When a person acts in a way that is right, this is "fruitful" action. In chapters 6 and 7, we will explore the relationship between God and person all along the various stages of the Christian life. Chapter 6 will explore the journey from sin to the new birth. Chapter 7 will explore the journey from the new birth to perfect love and the rewards of heaven. In chapter 8, a more detailed account of ethical action will be considered. We will consider the content of Wesley's method for fruitful action. Finally, in chapter 9, we will consider the relevance of Wesley's heart ethics for today. This will involve a consideration of the relevance of Wesley's heart ethics for contemporary theological ethics. It will also involve a consideration of the relevance of Wesley's heart ethics for those not interested in academics but who seek to grow in Christian love.

Chapter 2

Active and Passive

In this chapter, we will begin the task of clarifying John Wesley's view of the features of the soul. However, before doing this, it will be helpful for us to consider what is meant by the concepts of "active" and "passive." As will be shown in this chapter and chapters 3 and 4, these concepts are directly related to how Wesley understands the features of the soul. In order to clarify these concepts of active and passive, we will look at how these concepts were understood in periods before and during Wesley's time. We will also consider some illustrations that will help clarify what these concepts mean. In this chapter, it will also be shown that these concepts of active and passive illuminate John Wesley's understanding of two types of spiritual growth, as well as his understanding of liberty, which is one of his features of the soul.

A Mighty Typology

In order to prepare for a clarification of what is meant by active and passive, it is helpful first to consider the relevance of these concepts to an important debate. The typology of active and passive was at the very core of intense discussions and debates between libertarians and necessitarians in Great Britain in the eighteenth century.[1] This was a debate in which Wesley was involved. Using this typology appealed to many libertarians because they believed it supported a core doctrine of libertarian-

---

[1] See, for example the following sources: Samuel Clarke. *Remarks upon a Book Entituled, A Philosophical Enquiry Concerning Human Liberty* (London: James Knapton, 1717), 8; John Jackson. *A Vindication of Human Liberty* (London: J. Noon, 1730), 8; John Jackson. *A Defense of Human Liberty* (London: J. Moon, 1730), p. 8 and p. 16; Isaac Watts, "An Essay on the Freedom of Will in God and in Creatures," *The Works of the Late Reverend and Learned Isaac Watts* (London: T. and T. Longman and J. Buckland, 1753), 6:399; John Whitehead, *An Essay on Liberty and Necessity: in Answer to Augustus Toplady's Tract* (London: R. Hawes, 1775), 10.

ism. In secondary literature, James Harris explores the concepts of "libertarian" and "necessitarian" in great depth.[2] By "libertarian" is meant one who holds the doctrine of free will as opposed to the philosophical necessity that is presupposed in absolute predestination. For a libertarian, a human is free, in at least some cases, to choose for or against the perceived strongest motive. John Wesley is an example of a libertarian.[3] Yet, in order to be a libertarian, one does not have to believe in God's foreknowledge of human decisions in the same way as John Wesley and Jacob Arminius.[4]

A "necessitarian" is one whose system of thought presupposes that every human choice must be caused by the strongest motive, which many necessitarians believe is the effect of a chain of causes and effects that originates from forces outside of a person.[5] The theory of absolute predestination is an example of necessitarianism. A "compatibilist" is a necessitarian who argues that moral responsibility is consistent with necessitarianism.[6] Libertarianism refers to a belief in free will and rejection of philosophical necessity, also known in some cases as absolute predestination. In this section, we will consider why some libertarians

---

[2] James Harris, *Of Liberty and Necessity, The Free Will Debate in Eighteenth Century British Philosophy* (Oxford: Oxford University Press, 2005). For an account of what is meant by a "libertarian" and "necessitarian," see p. 7 of Harris' book.

[3] See, for example, Wesley, 'Thoughts Upon Necessity,' *Works* (BE), 13:528 – 546. Kenneth Collins, Paul Chilcote, and Laura Bartels Felleman highlight John Wesley's opposition to the doctrine of philosophical necessity. Paul Chilcote and Kenneth Collins, "Thoughts Upon Necessity (1774), An Introductory Comment," *Works* (BE), 13:526; Felleman, "A Necessary Relationship: John Wesley and the Body-Soul Connection," 141.

[4] Stephen Gunter, "John Wesley, a Faithful Representative of Jacob Arminius," *Wesleyan Theological Journal*, 42, (2007): 69.

[5] According to a necessitarian view, if a man chooses to raise his arm at time t_1, then if history were to rewind and playback in a manner that provides the same external conditions, the man must raise his arm at time t_1. This is because every choice is determined by a strongest motive connected to one path of history. Necessitarians believe that the flow of history, including the interaction of all the forces of the universe, only has one trajectory. By contrast, for a libertarian, if history is rewound and played back with the same external conditions, the man is free to lower his arm or perform a different act at t_1. This is because the universe has contingency and choice does not by necessity depend on the strongest motive.

[6] For a discussion of compatibilism, see, for example, Harris, *Of Liberty and Necessity*, 20.

believed this typology was advantageous and how necessitarians tended to respond to it. The typology is "mighty" not because there is a unanimous winner in the debates but because many libertarians found it to be central to the debates.

Many libertarians also preferred using the typology of active and passive because they believed it helped to support a core doctrine of libertarianism. This core doctrine is the idea that human action is not fully caused by the "strongest motive," in which this strongest motive is understood as the effect of a chain of causes and effects that originates from forces external to a person.[7] In disagreement with libertarians, necessitarians hold that human conduct is *entirely* the result of such a strongest motive, something that exists for every situation. Since necessitarians argue this, many libertarians accuse them of making humans out to be purely passive creatures. This is why in libertarian essays, libertarians sometimes charge necessitarians with making humans to be like "clocks" or "stones."[8] For libertarians, the claim that human action is entirely passive is not correct. This is because humans, unlike clocks, have consciousness of self-directed action. Furthermore, many libertarians argue that the consciousness of human action makes it *seem* that a person is the cause of his or her action. Libertarians think it is to their advantage to use a typology of active and passive because they think it helps to accentuate the error in the necessitarian view that human conduct is entirely passive.

For necessitarians, libertarians' use of the typology of active and passive does not succeed in defending libertarianism. For some of them, the libertarian charge of making humans out to be like clocks and stones is

---

[7] According to a libertarian view if a man chooses to raise his arm at time t_1, then if history were to rewind and playback in a manner that provides the same external conditions, the man would be free to lower his arm or perform a different action at time t_1. This is because choice is not determined by a strongest motive connected to one path of history. By contrast, for a necessitarian, every time history is rewound and played back, the man must by necessity perform the same act of raising his arm at t_1. This is because the flow of history, including the interaction of forces, only has one trajectory.

[8] See, for example: Samuel Clarke. *A Demonstration of the Being and Attributes of God* (Cambridge, Cambridge University Press, 1998) 64; Jackson, *Vindication*, 20; Whitehead, *An Essay on Liberty and Necessity*, 23; Joseph Fisher. "A Review of Dr. Priestly's [sic] Doctrine of Philosophical Necessity," *The Arminian Magazine*, 11, (1788):202; Wesley, 'Thoughts Upon Necessity,' *Works* (BE), 13:528 and 13:536.

at some level unfair. Many necessitarians would acknowledge that *in a certain respect*, human beings—unlike stones and clocks— have both an active and passive dimension. What must be emphasized, and what many libertarians tend to fail to acknowledge, is there are two meanings of "passive" that relate to this discussion. For our purposes here, one will be called "the first meaning of passive" and the other will be called the "typeX" meaning of passive.[9] Both of these distinct meanings relate to human consciousness in some way. Diagram 2.1 gives an overview of the various meanings of passive.[10] These meanings will pertain to much of the discussion that follows throughout rest of this project.

Most libertarians and necessitarians seem to *agree* on some of the meanings of passive. For example, both libertarians and necessitarians agree that there is a basic distinction in human consciousness between inclination and choice. If this point is not explicitly stated by every necessitarian, it is at least often implied by the distinctions that are made in related discussions.[11] In accordance with how inclination and choice are perceived differently in consciousness, one could describe the former as "passive" and the latter as "active." It seems that many libertarians and necessitarians would agree that the consciousness of an inclination is passive (see Diagram 2.1). We will call this the first meaning of passive.

While many libertarians and necessitarians agree that there is a dis-

---

[9] The label "typeX" is an arbitrary name given by the author. One could use the name "x" or "y"; it does not matter. The concept to which it refers is readily apparent in eighteenth century discussions.

[10] The page numbers for the diagrams are listed right after the table of contents.

[11] For example, Joseph Priestley makes a clear distinction between an inclination and choice, and Thomas Hobbes seems to do so as well. Jonathan Edwards makes a clear distinction between motive and choice, and it seems that what he means by motive may include an inclination(s). In one instance, Anthony Collins distinguishes between choice and the impressions of passions, appetites, and senses. It seems that these impressions include impressions of inclinations. Of course, Hobbes, Collins, Edwards, and Priestley are all leading necessitarians of their time. See Thomas Hobbes, *A letter about liberty and necessity written to the Duke of Newcastle* (London: J. Grover, 1676); Joseph Priestley. *The Doctrine of Philosophical Necessity Illustrated* (London: J. Johnson, 1777), 27; Jonathan Edwards, *The Works of Jonathan Edwards* (New Haven: Yale University Press, 1957), 141; Anthony Collins. *A Philosophical Inquiry Concerning Human Liberty* (Glasgow: R. Urie, 1749), 70.

tinction in consciousness between inclination and choice, the key point of disagreement between most libertarians and necessitarians is whether or not with respect to consciousness, choice must—by necessity—follow the suggestion of the strongest motive. For necessitarians, every human choice is fully caused by a strongest motive, which in turn is the effect of a chain of causes and effects that fully originates outside of a person. This point itself is one meaning of passive. We will call this view of passive "typeX" (see Diagram 2.1). It is a meaning of passive that necessitarians hold and that libertarians reject. One could devise an experiment in order to attempt to show, using consciousness, which view is correct. However, history has shown that such approaches have failed to produce a unanimous view. Many libertarians argue that consciousness shows that a person may choose against the strongest motive and/or known greatest good.[12] On the other hand, necessitarians argue that consciousness does not show this.[13]

In order to clarify further this well-known debate concerning the typeX meaning of passive, consider the following illustration involving a hungry person. Note that such an illustration of hunger is a somewhat popular source of reference for libertarians and necessitarians in the eighteenth century who are trying to clarify their views.[14] An illustration of a man in an orchard is used both by the necessitarian Joseph Priestley and by the libertarian Joseph Fisher.[15] A man is in an orchard that has peaches and apples. He has an aversion to peaches and a fondness for

---

[12] Harris says, "The libertarian of the eighteenth century is a believer in what philosophers of today call 'agent causation.' In other words, he holds that there is an alternative to regarding motives as the causes of choices and actions." Harris, *Of Liberty and Necessity*, 7.

[13] For example, see Anthony Collins' long discussion of consciousness. Also note that Harris says "Most necessitarians from Hobbes onwards take motives to be causes." Collins, *A Philosophical Inquiry Concerning Human Liberty*, 11; Harris, *Of Liberty and Necessity*, 92 and 7.

[14] Note, for example, the comments of a libertarian defender of John Wesley named John Whitehead. Whitehead uses an illustration of hunger and says, "Being hungry, or tired, is no action, 'tis a mere passive sensation, and can have nothing to do with the freedom of action, being different, *toto genere*, from it." Examples from Joseph Priestley and Joseph Fisher are noted below. Whitehead, *An Essay on Liberty and Necessity: in Answer to Augustus Toplady's Tract*, 23.

[15] Priestley, *The Doctrine of Philosophical Necessity Illustrated*, 27; Fisher, "A Review of Dr. Priestly's [sic] Doctrine of Philosophical Necessity," 11:424 and 11:646.

apples. The fondness for apples here is the strongest motive. The man may choose no more than one piece of fruit. For Priestley, the man must choose to eat the apple. There is no other possibility. For Fisher, the man has the option of choosing to eat either the apple or the peach. For Fisher, the man may choose against the strongest motive, which is in this case the inclination to eat an apple.[16]

What must be emphasized is that in this illustration, both the necessitarian (Priestley) and the libertarian (Fisher) share a clear view of a perceptible difference between inclination and choice. For both, the impression of an inclination—the feeling of hunger to eat— is by its nature passive. In this way, they would both agree on this "first meaning of passive." However, they disagree on whether or not the man is free to choose against his strongest motive. For Priestley, the answer is no. For Fisher, the answer is yes. This concerns the typeX meaning of passive. For Priestley, the choice of eating the apple is itself passive because it is caused by the strongest motive (the inclination to eat an apple). For Fisher, there is no such passiveness. In taking these positions, they both appeal to consciousness and experience. For Fisher—as for Clarke, Jackson, and other libertarians—, it is wrong to claim that something consciously passive (an inclination) causes in a necessary way something that is consciously active (the choice to eat). Necessitarians disagree, and here lies a crucial point of debate for libertarians and necessitarians in the eighteenth century. Harris shows the magnitude of the debate in the eighteenth century and Nicholas Jackson shows the significance of the debate both in the academic discussion and politics in the seventeenth century.[17]

If we put aside for a moment the question of whether there is a typeX

---

[16] For a necessitarian, there are motives other than hunger that can serve as the strongest motive in a parallel situation. Returning to the example of the man in the orchard: suppose a different man comes to the orchard and faces the same situation. After deliberating, he realizes that he has already exceeded the amount of food that he is allowed to eat for that day. In this case, this reason turns out to be the strongest motive and so, this second man does not eat any fruit. The feeling of hunger is disregarded. The point is that for necessitarians, the choice is always caused by the perceived strongest motive—whether it is a feeling of hunger or the result of extensive deliberation.

[17] Nicholas Jackson, *Hobbes, Bramhall and the Politics of Liberty and Necessity* (Cambridge: Cambridge University Press, 2007), 276; Harris, *Of Liberty and Necessity*, 1 – 226.

meaning of passive, we find a distinction that is fairly easy to recognize. This is that there is a fundamental difference with respect to consciousness between choice and other modes of consciousness such as inclination (see again Diagram 2.1). This difference should be fairly obvious for anyone to see. To illustrate this, let us revisit the previous illustration: any person can distinguish between a feeling of hunger to eat apples (an inclination) and the actual choice to eat an apple. *Both* libertarians and necessitarians generally agree on this point. Choice here corresponds to the active power (understood in a certain sense for necessitarians as shown in Diagram 2.1). In this way, there is a clear line of demarcation between active and passive.

Yet, as a goal of this chapter is to prepare to consider the ethics of John Wesley, who is a libertarian himself, the meaning of the active power must also incorporate a more debated element: the doctrine of freedom of choice and the rejection of the typeX meaning of passive. In other words, Wesley's view of action must include: (1) a widely understood notion shared by both libertarians and necessitarians that choosing is active in a certain sense [in contrast to modes of consciousness such as inclination, etc.] and (2) the debated doctrine of freedom of choice that rejects the typeX meaning of passive. This second element is the view that one is free to choose against the suggestion of the strongest motive or clearly-known greatest good. Some opponents of philosophical necessity, such as Ramsay and Burlamaqui, reject this second element for certain cases.[18] Necessitarians reject this second element for all cases. Yet there is evidence that suggests that libertarians such as Clarke, Reid, Fisher, and Wesley view this second element as pertaining to most if not all cases.[19]

In this section, we have considered libertarians' view of the typology of active and passive and why they believe it to support their de-

---

[18] The view of Jean Burlamarqui on this matter resembles a libertarian interpretation of Locke. Jean Burlamaqui, *The Principles of Natural Law* (London: J. Nourse, 1748), section vi-viii, especially p. 19 and p. 22.

[19] H.G. Alexander, *The Leibniz-Clarke Correspondence* (Manchester: Manchester University Press, 1956), 45; Harris says that for Clarke, "We retain the capacity to ignore what the understanding tells us, and to choose the worse thing, while knowing the better." Harris, *Of Liberty and Necessity*, 51; Thomas Reid. "An Essay on the Liberty of Moral Agents," The *Arminian Magazine*, 14 (1791): 60, 61, and 114; Fisher, "A Review of Dr. Priestly's [sic] Doctrine of Philosophical Necessity," 11:202; Wesley, 'Thoughts upon Necessity,' *Works* (BE), 13:544.

fense of libertarianism. For libertarians, it is wrong for what is consciously passive (such as the feeling of hunger) to cause by necessity something that is consciously active (such as the choice to eat an apple). Furthermore, libertarians think that it is wrong to claim that human conduct is entirely passive. Necessitarianism shows agreement at one level with libertarians' typology of active and passive. Both parties accept the passiveness of modes of consciousness such as inclination. However, as mentioned, many necessitarians welcome libertarians' charge of the former, making humans out to be entirely passive. This is with respect to the typeX meaning of passive. Furthermore, such necessitarians believe that the libertarians' typology of active and passive fails to disprove the typeX meaning of passive.

In the upcoming investigation of Wesley's view of the features of the soul, we will show how Wesley's view of the soul relates to a libertarian view of active and passive. But before we take up this task, we will consider more insights from eighteenth century libertarians regarding the concepts of active and passive. This will help clarify further what this project means by active and passive.

Highlights from Eighteenth Century Libertarians

In this section, we will observe more insights from eighteenth century libertarians concerning what is meant by active and passive with respect to human consciousness. No argument will be made that Wesley thinks of himself as inheriting his own views directly from such libertarians. However, it should be noted that these are libertarians that Wesley in fact read.

The typology of active and passive is very important for the eighteenth century libertarian and Anglican Samuel Clarke. Clarke is a leading libertarian during the first part of the eighteenth century. This is a person that Wesley has read.[20] For Clarke, "liberty" and "action" are identical. Also, the idea of choice has close resemblance (if not equivalency) to these two. For instance, Clarke says, "Man is indued with Liberty

---

[20] Through a correspondence with Randy Maddox, it was confirmed that Wesley records in his Oxford diaries that he read *A Demonstration of the Being and Attributes* in September of 1725. He recommends it to clergy in his 'Address to Clergy,' *Works* (Jackson), 10:492. Wesley mentions his reading of the Leibniz-Clarke correspondence in his journal on May 22, 1775. See Wesley, 'Journal,' *Works* (BE), 22:451.

and Choice, which alone is the Power of Acting."[21] He also says, "Whereas the whole essence of *liberty*, consists in the *power of acting. Action* and *liberty* are *identical* ideas."[22] The italics in this statement are from Clarke, and he makes this point on many occasions.

Therefore, for Clarke liberty is defined as action, and so, it must be something that is different from the passive dimension of the soul. For Clarke, as for other libertarians, motives are examples of what is commonly thought to be passive. This is evident in the following statement:

> There is no similitude between a balance being moved by weights or impulse, and a mind moving itself, or acting upon the view of certain motives. The difference is, that the one is entirely passive; which is being subject to absolute necessity: the other not only is acted upon, but acts also; which is the essence of liberty... The motive, or thing considered as in view, is something extrinsic to the mind: the impression made upon the mind by that motive, is the perceptive quality, in which the mind is passive: the doing of any thing, upon and after, or in consequence of, that perception; this is the power of self-motion or action: which in all animate agents, is spontaneity; and, in moral agents, is what we properly call liberty. The not carefully distinguishing these things, but confounding the motive with the principle of action, and denying the mind to have any principle of action besides the motive, (when indeed in receiving the impression of the motive, the mind is purely passive;) this, I say, is the ground of the whole error.[23]

This passage by Clarke is a helpful preparation for the task of this chapter to clarify what is meant by the active and passive dimensions of a person. We observe here an example of the kind of rhetoric that libertarians use in their presentation of the typology of active and passive as a defense against necessitarianism. For Clarke, the necessitarians' approach of making the mind entirely passive is "the ground of the whole mistake." Yet, what is more important for our purpose is Clarke's emphasis that there is a division *in consciousness* between active and passive. For Clarke, the impressions of motives are consciously passive, and the consciousness of action is something different.

---

[21] Clarke, *A Demonstration of the Being and Attributes of God*, 47.
[22] Clarke, *Remarks upon a book, Entituled, A Philosophical Enquiry Concerning Human Liberty*, 15. The italics of this quote are Clarke's.
[23] Alexander, editor, *The Leibniz-Clarke Correspondence*, 97.

What then are these motives that are perceived in a passive way? Clarke does not go in great depth in comparing motives to affections and tempers. In fact, he rarely if ever uses the terms "affections" or "tempers." However, he does make it clear that while passive motives do not cause action, these passive motives do *influence* action. It is precisely for this reason that contemporary scholar James Harris describes Clarke's portrayal of the soul as a "middle view," positioned between necessitarianism on the one side and the doctrine of the liberty of indifference on the other side.[24]

Libertarians after Clarke in the eighteenth century offer opinions as to what is meant by passive motives. For example, as published in the *Arminian Magazine*, Joseph Fisher says, "Our will appears to be in the power of the mind to determine upon action or non-action at pleasure, though love, hatred, fear, &c. are passions or affections of the mind, and the mind so far as influenced by them appears to be wholly passive."[25] Here we observe an explicit reference to the "affections" and the claim that affections influence the mind and appear "wholly passive." Since they influence the mind, presumably the affections are a class of motives. Fisher makes the point explicitly that "an inclination or affection" does not determine by necessity the choice of the mind.[26]

Other eighteenth century libertarians also describe motives as passive. John Jackson makes the following comment: "And tho' the *motives* or *reasons* upon which the mind acts are *out of our power*, and the judgment form'd upon them is *necessary*, yet the *act following* them is not a *necessary* consequence, but matter of *choice*."[27] Some libertarians make judgments out to be passive. Jackson himself holds that the process of reasoning involves action but that many judgments are passive.[28] Others claim that some judgments are active while other judgments are passive. Regardless, it seems that most libertarians of the eighteenth century British context agree that motives (affections, inclinations, etc.) are typically passive.

Many libertarians in the eighteenth century leave out a discussion of

---

[24] Harris, *Of Liberty and Necessity*, 13.
[25] Fisher, "A Review of Dr. Priestly's [sic] Doctrine of Philosophical Necessity," 11:425.
[26] Fisher, "A Review of Dr. Priestly's [sic] Doctrine of Philosophical Necessity," 11:424.
[27] Jackson, *A Defense of Human Liberty*, 100. The italics are Jackson's.
[28] Jackson, *A Vindication of Humane Liberty*, 40.

at least some of the following: affections, tempers, emotions, passions, desires, reasons, judgments, and motives. Many libertarians do not give an extensive account of how these terms overlap, relate, or whether they are all thought to be passive. One point remains true. Many libertarians distinguish between active and passive in some way,[29] and in just about all cases in the eighteenth century, liberty is in some way related to the active dimension of a person.[30] As we will show, Wesley's view has a striking resemblance to Clarke's model.

Our exploration of libertarian views of active and passive has prepared us for considering more illustrations of the active and passive dimension. Some of these illustrations come directly from the writings of libertarians in the eighteenth century. Others do not. The illustrations in the following sections will serve as the basis for *clarifying* what is meant by active and passive for this project. To this matter we now turn.

Approach for Clarifying Active and Passive

The method of this work for clarifying what is meant by active and passive is to draw some from the views of John Wesley's predecessors and contemporaries and to consider also other illustrations.

The meaning of active offered by the following illustrations is compatible with John Wesley's doctrine of freedom of choice. The purpose of this chapter is to clarify a meaning of action in order to prepare for a consideration of John Wesley's thought in the chapters that follow. As we shall see, for Wesley, action and free choosing are inseparable.

In this discussion, we will define "active" and "passive" *from the point of view of human consciousness*. Other meanings of action are not considered here. God's creation of the universe was an action, and this is an important example of action. However, for this project, God's creation of the universe is obviously *not* what we mean by "human action" or the "active dimension of a person." This is because such an action is not active with respect to human consciousness (a human person is not the performer of the action).

[29] For this point in regard to Clarke and Fisher, please see above. See, for example, also: Jackson, *A Vindication of Human Liberty*, 8; Jackson, *A Defense of Human Liberty*, 8 and 16; Watts, "An Essay on the Freedom of Will in God and in Creatures," 6:399; Whitehead, *An Essay on Liberty and Necessity: in Answer to Augustus Toplady's Tract*, 10; cf. Thomas Reid, *Essays on the Active Powers of Man* (Edinburgh: John Bell, 1788), 59-60.

[30] It is hard to find a case where this is not observable.

In order to clarify what this work means by the active and passive dimensions of a person, we will begin by considering some preliminary illustrations. We will then move to some illustrations that will serve more as the centre of focus. As mentioned, some of these illustrations are based on illustrations from libertarians that Wesley has read. In one case, we will revisit the illustration of a hunger, an illustration that was fairly popular in eighteenth century discussions relating to the human mind.

Preliminary Illustrations

In this section, we will consider some preliminary illustrations that will help clarify what is meant by active and passive. We will begin by considering illustrations that help clarify what is meant by the active dimension. Next, we will move to consider illustrations that will help clarify what is meant by the passive dimension.

Illustrations of the Active Dimension

The illustrations that we are about to consider appear to provide the following insights concerning action. Action includes: (a) a power of the human mind to select a final outcome and (b) a power to determine *when* this final outcome is completed.[31] The illustrations that we consider will show that some actions are more complex than others. Many of the following illustrations come from eighteenth century libertarians. For this project, the idea of choice and the idea of action are interchangeable. In other words, there is never an action that is not also in some way a choice. We will now turn to some illustrations to clarify what is meant by action.

An example of a simple action is the power to present a simple image to one's imagination. As Thomas Reid says, "Every man knows that he can turn his attention to this subject or to that, for a longer or a shorter time, and with more or less intenseness, as he pleases. It is a voluntary act and depends upon his will."[32] Consider the following situation, which I will call the "illustration of the purple elephant." A person is free to bring a purple elephant to his mind for contemplation or instead im-

---

[31] For cases when a person believes a final outcome is reachable according to a self-determined time but the attempt is unsuccessful, then part b here is simply: the power to determine *when* the attempt to achieve the final outcome carries on. Note the illustration of the stopped mouth below.

[32] Reid, *Essays on the Active Powers of Man*, p. 80.

agine a yellow house or a black book. This type of action can be performed in almost any situation regardless of external circumstances. This illustration exemplifies both features of the aforementioned description of action: the person elects a final outcome (such as the visualization of a purple elephant) and the person determines when the final outcome occurs.

As should be evident to any reflective person, some actions require the availability of external conditions in one's environment. This is why eighteenth century libertarian Isaac Watts argues that for many kinds of actions to occur, there must be both liberty of choice and liberty of the executive powers.[33] Watts give an example of a man whose mouth is "stopped."[34] In this situation the man's mouth is forced shut but the man does not know it. Such a man has the freedom to choose to speak and does so but when he is unable to produce audible words, he realizes that his mouth is stopped. From this illustration, it is clear that the action of opening the mouth never occurs. However, some action does occur. The choice to open one's mouth (even though the attempt was unsuccessful) was itself an action. A choice to pursue an end that is believed to be in reach is itself an action. One has the power to determine *when* such choice is made. However, given the restricted external environment, the identity of the action in this case was not what was expected.

Consider additional illustrations from eighteenth century British libertarian John Jackson: "Cannot I open or shut my Eyes; sit down, or walk; lie down, or rise; move any of my limbs, or not move them, merely because I will to do so?"[35] Isaac Watts gives similar illustrations: "So I feel myself at liberty, and I chose to stand or walk, I am free, and I choose either to speak or keep silence, to point upward or downward."[36] Similarly, libertarian Jean Burlamaqui says "I find, for instance, that it depends entirely on myself to stretch out or draw back my hand; to sit down or to walk; to direct my steps to the right or left, &c."[37] Here we observe examples of illustrations that allow for both features of action. In each case, one has the power to choose the final outcome to be completed and also to determine *when* the final outcome is complete.

[33] Watts, "An Essay on the Freedom of Will in God and in Creatures," 6:376.
[34] Watts, "An Essay on the Freedom of Will in God and in Creatures," 6:376.
[35] Jackson, *A Vindication of Human Liberty*, 46.
[36] Watts, "An Essay on the Freedom of Will in God and in Creatures," 6:378.
[37] Burlamaqui, *The Principles of Natural Law*, 21.

Not all actions are as simple as these. Consider an illustration where a wealthy merchant decides to buy a horse for an impoverished family in her village.[38] Here, a chain of events must take place for the final outcome to be achieved. The wealthy merchant must give her servant resources and instructions. The servant must then travel a certain number of miles to another village in order to find a horse to purchase. The horse must then be delivered to the impoverished family. Although the chosen action of giving a horse to the needy family is more complex than some of the previous illustrations that we have considered, the wealthy merchant still has enough handle on the situation to determine approximately when the deed will be complete. We may call this action a "complex" action.

Illustrations of the Passive Dimension

Besides offering illustrations to show what is meant by action, we will also consider illustrations to help clarify what is meant by the passive dimension. We will consider three groups of passive perceptions. These groups correspond to the format given in Diagram 2.1. First, there is what this project will call "inclination."[39] The meaning of inclination is illustrated by the aforementioned illustration of a man in the orchard. The inclination in this illustration is *not* the choice in regard to eating the fruit but it is only the feeling hunger. As we will explore in the next section, an inclination may also be a desire of love, such as what Abraham feels for his son Isaac in the Biblical account of Genesis 22. In this case, an inclination is not Abraham's *choice* to sacrifice Isaac by ending his life, but rather it is the feeling of love that Abraham has for his son.

The second group of passive perceptions refers to feelings that sometimes spring from an inclination. Consider, for example, what will be called here the "illustration of the fisherman."[40] A fisherman on a remote island must catch fish or else he dies of hunger. Fish are the only safe

---

[38] There is no source for this illustration. A source is unnecessary here. This illustration is used in order to aid understanding. This is a common approach in any discussion that deals with philosophical writing.

[39] This meaning of "inclination" is no more than what is clarified by the illustrations of hunger and love. Wesley also at times uses the word "inclination," but these instances are rare.

[40] There is no source for this illustration. A source is unnecessary here. This illustration is used in order to aid understanding. This is a common approach in any discussion that deals with philosophical writing.

food source. His inclination is a feeling of hunger, which leads to an inclination to want to try to catch a fish. Yet other feelings emerge based on the fisherman orientation to the target of his inclination, which is his goal of eating fish. Such other feelings emerge in this way. If he catches a fish, he has a feeling of joy. If he fails to catch a fish, then he has a feeling of disappointment. If another fisherman comes along and has more success at fishing, he may have a feeling of jealousy. If, out of spite, his companion intentionally damages his only fishing pole, then he has a feeling of anger. If one day, his older brother promises to give him all the fish he ever needs,[41] then he is likely to have feelings of gratitude. In the various scenarios just considered, it should be evident that feelings of joy, disappointment, jealousy, anger, gratitude, etc. are all passive in nature. These feelings spring from the fisherman's inclination to catch a fish. The second group of passive perceptions may refer to any other temper or feeling that springs in some way from an inclination.

The third group of passive perception simply refers to all remaining kinds of perceptions that are not active in nature. It is not possible to list all these here. They include but are not limited to: feelings of warmness, coldness, all the sensations that come through the five senses, and sensations that come through one's spiritual sense, as felt by the heart or other aspects of the soul.

Illustrations of Focus

Now that we have considered some preliminary illustrations, we are ready to consider some focal illustrations that will clarify further what is meant by active and passive for this project. We will consider four illustrations for this purpose.

The first illustration is the illustration of what will be called "the hungry scientist."[42] Suppose there is a scientist who has learned how to train himself to predict exactly when he will be hungry. He does this by regulating his external environment, including how much food he eats and times for eating. In some sense then, the practice of making himself hun-

---

[41] This point foreshadows, to some degree, our later consideration of God the Father and His gift of salvation.

[42] There is no source for this illustration. A source is unnecessary here. This illustration is used in order to aid understanding. This is a common approach in any discussion that deals with philosophical writing.

gry is in fact an action. He has selected a final outcome (hunger) and determined exactly when this feeling of hunger will emerge.

Yet, what must be emphasized is that while the practice of making himself hungry is an action at one level, the actual feeling of hunger itself is passive, when viewed in its bare sense. It should be evident from common sense that the feeling of hunger in its bare form is an inclination and is something different in its conscious nature from action. In this particular illustration, the emergence of hunger may be caused by action, and it may cease by action (the scientist can end his hunger at any time by simply eating). But during the time that it is allowed to remain, this feeling of hunger imposes itself on human consciousness in a way different from the consciousness of human action. Again, the feeling of hunger is passive with respect to consciousness in a bare sense. Yet, *it is important to observe that this illustration shows a reflexive behaviour*. In a reflexive behaviour—such as if one were to warm oneself with a hot object—, action cannot occur alone. There must be both action and passiveness involved. As it is reflexive, the process of making oneself hungry in this case involves both active and passive elements.

Consider a second illustration, one that does not involve full reflexivity such as in the previous example. This will be called the illustration of Abraham. Consider the story of Abraham and Isaac from Genesis, chapter 22. Abraham believes that God is calling Abraham to sacrifice Isaac. Isaac is Abraham's beloved son and the heir of God's promise. Abraham has a strong affection for his son. This affection is a strong love. It should be self-evident that Abraham's feeling of love involves an inclination that is passive. Nevertheless, Abraham maintains a power to act against his passive inclination of love for his son. Abraham's choice to end Isaac's life is active with respect to Abraham. According to the story, Abraham would have ended Isaac's life, if it were not for the angel who stopped him.

Although Abraham's feeling of love seems to be passive in a bare sense, there is a context in which it may be viewed as "not altogether" passive. The phrase "not altogether" is not to deny that feelings of hunger or love are fully passive in a bare sense. Rather, the phrase "not altogether" here is simply to account for a degree of reflexivity that may apply when viewing the situation in a larger context. It seems that when such feelings are viewed in a context involving reflexive behaviour—and *only* in this context—then at times they may be described as "not altogether" passive or even perhaps active in some cases. The example of the hungry scientist is a case of fully reflexive conduct. In this case, creating feelings of hunger may be called active in accordance to the level that there is *fully* reflexive behaviour. The case of Abraham is different. Abraham cannot rid himself of his strong feelings for his son, but he can to some degree direct his attention away from these feelings by his own power. To some degree (but not to a full-degree), he has the freedom to block out his feelings of love for his son in order to prepare to sacrifice him. He can do this by choosing to try to think about something else. In this way, one may describe Abraham's feelings of love for his son as "not altogether" passive.

It seems that the idea of reflexivity and how it relates to feelings that are passive in a bare sense may help illuminate one of John Wesley's comments. In his essay *Thoughts Upon Necessity*, Wesley says that a person is "not altogether" passive in receiving impressions.[43] Given the nature of active and passive and how such dimensions are verifiable to each and every person's everyday experience, it is reasonable to suggest that Wesley would not deny that some impressions are passive in a bare sense. However, from a larger context, these same impressions are "not altogether" passive. This is due to partial reflexivity, as similarly observed in the illustration of Abraham. In other words, an impression such as Abraham's love for his son, may be passive in a bare sense while also simultaneously "not altogether" passive when viewed from a larger context. From this larger context, for example, one may decrease the impression through reflexive conduct by attempting to direct one's attention away from it. The same appears true for Wesley's understanding of certain impressions.

Consider a third illustration. We will call this the illustration of the flaming dart. A man meets with his pastor and shares that he has never had feelings of love for his neighbor. But the man says he believes such feelings (and the corresponding inclination) are possible, and he hopes to one day have them. The pastor replies that if you maintain a constant resolution[44] for this love, God will definitely give you at a future unknown time the love that you seek. The pastor informs the man that the future time of experiencing this love is unpredictable but that he should expect it as possibly coming now because God can do it now if God

---

[43] Wesley, 'Thoughts Upon Necessity,' *Works*, (BE), 13:544.

[44] Compare this idea of resolution with the resolution to serve God that Wesley encourages all people to have (Wesley, 'On Family Religion,' *Works* (BE), 3:334).

chooses.[45] After meeting with the pastor, and not experiencing God's love now as he initially hoped, the man decides to continue to maintain the resolution. He shows the fruits of this resolution by performing deeds of service for his neighbor whenever he has the opportunity. It should be clear that the resolution is active with respect to the man because it is made (and maintained) at moments *whenever* the man determines. The man has the power to end the resolution at any moment of choice. Clearly the deeds that follow the resolution are also active. Because the man maintains his resolution for love for his neighbor, God appears at an unpredictable time and pricks the man with a flaming dart of love. Upon impact, the effects of the dart are immediately perceived by the man. The impact of the dart changes the man's heart and gives him feelings of true love for his neighbor, including feelings of joy that he has never before experienced! The impact of the dart and its effects are clearly passive in a bare sense with respect to the man. After the encounter, God warns the man that if he chooses to mistreat his neighbors, the man's feelings of love will soon disappear.

While the impact of the dart is clearly passive in a bare sense with respect to the man, there are a number of contexts from this illustration in which the effects of the dart may be described as "not altogether" passive. This is because, again, reflexivity can play a role in the situation. There are at least two courses of action that the man can take in order

---

[45] Compare this point with these comments from Wesley: "God *can* give the end without any means at all; but you have no reason to think he will. Therefore constantly and carefully use all these means which he has appointed to be the ordinary channels of his grace. Use every means which either reason or Scripture recommends as conducive (through the free love of God in Christ) either to the obtaining or increasing any of the gifts of God" (Wesley, 'The Nature of Enthusiasm,' *Works* (BE), 2:59-60). At another time, Wesley says that one should expect Christian perfection by faith and therefore, it cannot hurt to expect it now (Wesley, 'The Scripture Way of Salvation,' *Works* (BE), 2:169). Presumably, the same principle also applies for seeking the first moments of being born of God. This point does not undermine the importance of waiting for God's gifts by performing fruitful actions such as the means of grace, if there is time and opportunity. If such a constant resolution of action is not performed, then God's gifts will likely not come. He says in reference to such fruitful action: "Insomuch that if we willingly neglect either we cannot reasonably expect to be justified at all?" (Wesley, 'Scripture Way of Salvation,' *Works* (BE), 2:162) and "Yea, are not these so necessary that if a man willingly neglect them he cannot reasonably expect that he shall ever be sanctified in the full sense, that is, 'perfected in love'?" (Wesley, 'Scripture Way of Salvation,' *Works* (BE), 2:164).

to alter the effects of the dart. First, the man may choose ahead of time to end permanently his resolution to serve his neighbor. If this is done, the flaming dart of love will never come, and the feelings of love and joy will never be felt. Alternatively, the man can choose to keep the resolution until the dart of flaming love arrives but choose to discontinue the resolution *after* the impact of the dart. In this case, for example, when the man continually mistreats his neighbor, the man therefore loses the feelings of love for his neighbor that had been first given by the impact of the dart. In summary, as the impact of the dart is fully passive from a bare context, it is "not altogether" passive when viewed from a larger context involving a degree of reflexivity. The illustration of the flaming dart is different from an illustration of cupid (or of a dart) that one could use to describe absolute predestination. In such an illustration of cupid, no degree of reflexivity is possible.

Consider a fourth illustration. This illustration will be called the illustration of the fit woman.[46] The fit woman is not fit at first. She begins a practice of exercising while out of shape and with only a small interest in exercising. However, she finds that the more she exercises, day by day and week by week, her inclination for exercising increases and she feels an increased level of pleasure in exercising. This inclination strengthens and builds gradually over time. After a long period of consistent and focused work, exercise becomes a kind of good addiction. Generating an inclination to exercise is something that is largely reflexive. This is because any person can count on the fact that each instance of exercise nurtures the inclination to a small degree. The magnitude of this perceived inclination increases gradually over time. This inclination—in virtue of being an inclination— is in a bare sense passive. However, when viewed in light of reflexive action, the method of building this inclination may be thought of as largely active.

Two Kinds of Spiritual Growth in John Wesley's View of Ethics

John Wesley's understanding of spiritual growth has one important difference from all the illustrations considered in the last section. For John Wesley's understanding of spiritual growth, there is no such thing as *natural* human reflexivity. For Wesley, the *active component* of reflexive be-

[46] Keep in mind that the practice of exercising for the purpose of fitness is as old as humankind. This illustration is not anachronistic.

haviour concerning spiritual growth is only possible by grace. Also, such action is never the human acting alone but rather, it is a co-operating action between God and person. This graciously-empowered reflexivity is a kind of fruitful action, and this will be explored in more depth in chapter 5 of this project.

With this point in mind, we may observe that John Wesley's view of ethics involves two kinds of spiritual growth that in some degree resemble the illustrations that we have considered in this section. The first kind of spiritual growth pertains to a gradual process of growth.[47] It is what commonly occurs as one performs fruitful actions such as practising the means of grace. Such practices are channels through which God's grace flows. This process of gradual growth is comparable[48] to the illustration of the fit woman, as in both cases there is both reflexive behaviour and a gradual nurturing of one's inclination. Important differences should also be noted. For the case of Wesley, the inclination of the heart that develops through the means of grace is more outward directed than in the case of the fit woman. Its object is God and neighbor.

The second kind of spiritual growth evident in John Wesley's thought may also involve the use of fruitful action and the means of grace. This second type of spiritual growth is comparable to the illustration of the flaming dart.[49] On multiple occasions, including one in 1788, Wesley does in fact describe God's giving of love as like the impact of a flaming dart.[50] This second kind of spiritual growth includes what happens at

---

[47] Consider, for example, Wesley's statement in which he says a person knows of the "need he had to be watered of God every moment; so he continued daily in all the ordinances of God, the stated channels of his grace to man: 'in the Apostles' doctrine,' or teaching, receiving that food of the soul with all readiness of heart; in 'the breaking of bread,' which he found to be the communion of the body of Christ; and 'in the prayers' and praises offered up by the great congregation. And thus, he daily grew in grace, increasing in strength, in the knowledge and love of God." Wesley, 'Scriptural Christianity,' *Works* (BE), 1:164. See also: Wesley, 'Sermon on the Mount III,' *Works* (BE), 1:520; Wesley, 'The Original, Nature, Properties, and Use of the Law,' *Works* (BE), 2:19; Wesley, 'The Law Established Through Faith, II,' *Works,* (BE), 2:43; Wesley, 'The Nature of Enthusiasm,' *Works* (BE), 2:60; and Wesley, 'Heaviness Through Manifold Temptations,' *Works* (BE), 2:235.

[48] Obviously, they are not identical. But they are in a sense comparable.

[49] In addition to the evidence given in this paragraph, see the footnotes pertaining to the illustration of the flaming dart.

[50] For example, Wesley says "He darted in to all (I believe, hardly one excep-

the beginning of the new birth and Christian perfection.[51] It is evident that the effects of what occurs at the beginning of the new birth and perfection are not active in nature because, for one, they do not occur according to the time at which a person determines. Their timing is unpredictable. In this way, the second type of spiritual growth is not fully reflexive and is to be distinguished from the first type of spiritual growth, which is fully reflexive. Furthermore, there is a bare context in which the beginning of the new birth and perfection may be viewed as fully passive.[52] This resembles how at one level, in the illustration of the flaming dart, the impact of the dart and the effects of its impact are fully passive in a bare sense.

However, from a larger context, similar to the illustration of the flaming dart, *a degree* of reflexivity does apply even in regard to the onset of the new birth and perfection. Maintaining a constant resolution to serve God by performing fruitful actions such as the means of grace positions one to receive, in an instantaneous manner and at an unknown future time, future blessings such as the new birth and perfection. Without such fruitful actions, these blessings are less likely to occur. From this context, the receiving of gifts such as the new birth and perfection may be viewed as "not altogether" passive.[53] These points will be explored in

---

ted) the melting flame of love, so that their heads were as water and their eyes as fountains of tears" (Wesley, 'Journal,' *Works* (BE), 20:21; see also footnote 94). On several other occasions in his journal, he quotes a poem from the *Hymns and Poems of John and Charles Wesley* in describing what he is observing directly in his ministry: "Dart into all the melting flame Of love, and make the mountains flow" (Wesley, 'Journal,' *Works* (BE), 21:25 and footnote 94; and Wesley, 'Journal,' *Works* (BE), 24:87).

[51] This is considered "growth" because the condition of the heart improves at each of these events. It seems that an instantaneous action does not preclude the possibility of growth in an instant.

[52] Note that Wesley describes the moment of conversion as seeming irresistible. See, for example, Wesley, 'Journal,' *Works* (BE), 19:332; Wesley, 'Thoughts Upon God's Sovereignty,' *Works* (BE), 13:550. Wesley rejects the Calvinist notion of irresistible grace as having by necessity permanently-lasting effects. Rather, he offers that irresistibility is only for one moment. Resistance is possible before and after these moments. See also Wesley, 'The General Spread of the Gospel,' *Works* (BE), 2:489-490. The exception of which Wesley speaks here is "for the time" (longer than a moment). That God works irresistibly at the moment of giving the faith of a child of God seems to be more typical rather than the exception.

[53] Cf. Kenneth Collins, *The Theology of John Wesley, Holy Love and the Shape of*

more depth in chapters 6 and 7.

When exploring John Wesley's two types of spiritual growth in the largest context, the theme of gift in John Wesley's view of ethics becomes increasingly evident. Because of the meritorious work of Christ in His life, death, and resurrection, free grace is offered to all. As we will explore more in chapter 5, the fruitful actions mentioned above (active resolution, etc.) are only possible by God's grace, and they are expressions of God's grace. Also, they are only possible in response to the prior work of God alone in the soul. It is because of the work of the Spirit in the active and passive dimensions of a person that one is able to pursue the greatest end of Christian living and grow spiritually, according to either of the two types of growth. This pursuit itself is an expression of God's gift. These matters will be explored in more depth in the chapters that follow.

What is important to highlight from these illustrations is that John Wesley's portrayal of spiritual growth involves some nuance. Consistent with this point, as Albert Outler and Kenneth Collins have offered, John Wesley's theology is "conjunctive."[54] In this case, we observe the conjunction of two types of spiritual growth in John Wesley's view of ethics.

For Wesley, Liberty is Action

In this chapter, an attempt has been made to clarify what this project means by active and passive. The method for this task has been to provide a consideration of Wesley's libertarian context and explore various illustrations. Illustrations considered include the following: the hungry person, the purple elephant, the stopped mouth, the managing of one's eyes and limbs, the wealthy merchant, the fisherman, the hungry scientist, the story of Abraham and Isaac, the flaming dart, and the fit woman. In each of the illustrations, we observed the following features of action: it involves (a) the selecting of a final outcome and (b) the determination of *when* the outcome is complete. We distinguished the consciousness of action from the consciousness of passive inclinations such as a feeling of hunger or a feeling of love. We also explored the nature of reflexive

---

Grace (Nashville, TN: Abingdon Press, c2007), 163.

[54] One interpretation of the conjunctive nature of Wesley's theology is explored in Kenneth Collins' *The Theology of John Wesley, Holy Love and the Shape of Grace*. See, for example, p. 4. See also Albert Outler, *John Wesley* (New York: Oxford University Press, 1964), viii.

behaviour in certain cases. It is the hope of this author that the illustrations explored here provide to any ordinary person a clear meaning of active and passive, as these concepts will be used in this project.

John Wesley defines "liberty" as the power of choice, which appears quite similar if not equivalent to the active power as clarified using the above illustrations.[55] This meaning of liberty is different from other meanings of liberty that Wesley uses in other contexts.[56] Consider one of Wesley's discussions concerning liberty:

> I am conscious to myself of one more property, commonly called *liberty*. This is very frequently confounded with the *will* but is of a very different nature.[57] Neither is it a property of the will but a distinct property of the soul, capable of being exerted with regard to all the faculties of the soul, as well as all the motions of the body. It is a power of self-determination[58] which, although it does

---

[55] As will be argued more extensively in chapter 2, Wesley's understanding of this type of liberty is that it is the same as human action, understood as the power of choosing (Wesley, 'The General Deliverance,' *Works* (BE), 2:439 and 2:440; Wesley, 'The End of Christ's Coming,' *Works* (BE), 2:475; Wesley, 'On the Fall of Man,' *Works* (BE), 2:401; Wesley, 'The Original, Nature, Properties, and Use of the Law,' *Works* (BE), 2:6; Wesley, 'God's Approbation of His Works,' *Works* (BE), 2:399; Wesley, 'The General Spread of the Gospel,' *Works* (BE), 2:489. Such action may refer to comparatively neutral human action or action explicitly related to moral matters. It may pertain to action relating to the choice of civil or religious matters (See Wesley, 'Some Observations on Liberty,' *Works* (Jackson), 11:91. It should be noted here that Wesley does not like Richard Price's bringing moral liberty to bear on matters of civil liberty, even though they both involve the power choosing. Wesley is not claiming that the two are unrelated but that their comparison is unhelpful for Price's specific purpose). See also Wesley's discussion of free agency and shutting or opening one's eyes here: Wesley, 'The Signs of the Times,' *Works* (BE), 2:531.

[56] It must be stressed that Wesley at times intentionally uses other meanings of liberty different from the idea of liberty defined as equivalent to action and choice. One such alternative meaning is when Wesley speaks of the liberty from Romans 8:21, often described as "glorious liberty." Whereas the first type of liberty is applicable to all people at all stages, this second type of liberty is possessed only by children of God. This second type of liberty means freedom from the bondage of sin.

[57] Wesley's distinction between *will* and *liberty* will be considered in more depth in the next chapter.

[58] This term "self-determination" is quite popular among libertarians. It

not extend to all our thoughts and imaginations, yet extends to our words and actions in general, and not with many exceptions. I am full as certain of this, that I am free with respect to these, to speak or not to speak,[59] to act or not to act,[60] to do this or the contrary, as I am of my own existence. I have not only what is termed a 'liberty of contradiction', a power to do or not to do, but what is termed a 'liberty of contrariety', a power to act one way or the contrary.[61] To deny this would be to deny the constant experience[62] of all human kind. Everyone feels that he has an inherent power to move this or that part of his body, to move it or not, and to move this way or the contrary, just as he pleases.[63] I can as I

---

fits the core doctrine of libertarians that causes of human action do not fully originate outside the self. Necessitarians tend not to use this term. This is because for necessitarians, the first cause of determination is not inside the self but is always outside the self.

[59] In reference to liberty, Watts says it includes a power "to speak or keep silence." Watts, "An Essay on the Freedom of Will in God and in Creatures," 6:378.

[60] Compare this with the following comments from an Anglican libertarian of the Seventeenth Century named John Bramhall in his argument against Thomas Hobbes: "But all this abuse growth from the misunderstanding of liberty. I take it for a power to act or not to act, and he taketh it for an absence of outward impediments." With respect to this subject of liberty, Wesley is closer to Bramhall than Locke. Both Locke and Hobbes share the view that liberty can mean the absence of outward impediments. "Extracts from Locke on Human Understanding with Short Remarks," *The Arminian Magazine*, 5, (1782): 5:415. John Bramhall. *Castigations of Mr. Hobbes* (London: E.T., 1657), 334.

[61] The concept of the "liberty of contradiction" and "liberty of contrariety" go at least as far back as the Scholastics. See, comments by Scotus in John Duns Scotus, *Duns Scotus on the Will & Morality* (Washington D.C.: The Catholic University of America Press, 1997), 150. Boler argues that Scotus is a libertarian. See: Lagerlund and Yrjonsuuri, *Emotions and Choice from Boethius to Descartes*, 129.

[62] Again, drawing from experience is a common approach for philosophers in the eighteenth century. Such a method was especially valued by a libertarian named James Beattie. John Wesley read Beattie's essay on liberty and wrote a positive review of Beattie's larger book at a crucial time in Wesley's own development concerning how to view liberty. This is after the start of the 1770s controversy with the Calvinist necessitarians and before the publishing of "Thoughts Upon Necessity" in 1774. Wesley, 'Journal,' *Works* (BE), 22:321.

[63] The libertarian Jackson speaks of a power to "move any of my limbs, or not move them." Jackson, *A Vindication of Human Liberty*, 46.

choose (and so can everyone that is born of a woman), open or shut my eyes,[64] speak or be silent,[65] rise or sit down,[66] stretch out my hand or draw it in,[67] and use any of my limbs according to my pleasure,[68] as well as my whole body. And although I have not an absolute power of my own mind, because of the corruption of my nature, yet through the grace of God assisting me I have a power to choose and do good as well as evil.[69] I am free to choose whom I will serve, and if I choose the better part, to continue therein even unto death.[70]

As discussed in the footnotes attached to this passage, it is apparent that much of this passage echoes the views of many libertarians before and during the time of Wesley. The illustrations in these comments involve both features of action: (a) determination of final outcomes and (b) the determination of *when* the outcomes are complete. One can speak or not speak, act or not act, open and close one's eyes, rise or sit down, stretch out one's hand or draw it in, or use one's limbs as one wishes. In an environment free of outward restraints, an agent has the power to determine *when* each of these actions occurs. We also observe in this passage a reference to complex action, comparable to the illustration of the wealthy merchant from above. The power to "choose and do good" and to "choose whom I will serve" can involve elaborate schemes of events, such as feeding the needy, attending a society meeting, visiting orphans and those in jail, participating in communion, attending a love feast and watch night service, studying the scriptures, etc. Yet, in regular circum-

---

[64] Both Jackson and Fisher speak of this power to open and shut one's eyes. Jackson, *A Vindication of Human Liberty*, 46; Fisher, "A Review of Dr. Priestly's [sic] Doctrine of Philosophical Necessity," 12:87.

[65] This is Wesley's second reference to "speaking" in this paragraph. Please see the footnote for the first instance.

[66] For a reference to rising or lying down, see Jackson, *A Vindication of Human Liberty*, 46.

[67] Compare this to Burlamaqui's comment regarding Burlamaqui's discussion of liberty: "I find, for instance, that it depends intirely on myself to stretch out or draw back my hand." Burlamaqui, *The Principles of Natural Law*, 21.

[68] Compare to comments by Jackson concerning the movement of limbs: Jackson, *A Vindication of Human Liberty*, 46.

[69] These are the descriptions Wesley often gives concerning liberty. Liberty involves a power of choice and a power to choose between good and evil.

[70] Wesley, 'What is Man?,' *Works* (BE), 4:23.

stances free of restraints, all of these acts are performed more or less *when* the agent chooses to do them.

In the above quotation, Wesley makes an important distinction between "*liberty*" and "*will*." He also makes this distinction about fourteen years earlier in his essay, "Thoughts Upon Necessity."[71] What does Wesley mean by this distinction? How have other libertarians made this distinction? Could this distinction between liberty and will reflect a division between the active and passive dimensions of a person? Answers to these questions will be considered in the next chapter.

In this chapter, we have clarified what this project means by active and passive. We have also introduced two types of spiritual growth in John Wesley's view of ethics. Next, we introduced John Wesley's understanding of liberty, which represents the active dimension of a person. In the next two chapters that follow, we will continue with the first task of the project, which is to clarify John Wesley's understanding of the features of the soul.

---

[71] Wesley, 'Thoughts Upon Necessity,' *Works* (BE), 13:539.

Chapter 3

The Will and Liberty

As we explore Wesley's view of ethics and test the thesis of this project, we begin with the task of clarifying Wesley's view of the features of the soul. Wesley's features of the soul are in fact connected with his understanding of creation. Wesley says, "It was free grace that 'formed man of the dust of the ground, and breathed into him a living soul', and stamped on that soul the image of God."[1] God created human beings in the image of God. Wesley's view of the image of God will be explored more in chapter 6. For now, we will observe that for Wesley, each person has a "natural image" of God. Wesley clearly indicates that after the fall, God restores for all people the part of the natural image that corresponds to having a spiritual nature—a nature that is still endued with understanding, will, and liberty.[2] As shown at the end of the last chapter, Wesley says that the will is often confused with the concept of liberty. For this reason, much of our attention in this chapter will focus on how for Wesley the will compares or contrasts with this power of liberty.

Other Views of the Will

Before clarifying Wesley's view of liberty and will, we will consider briefly several models of the will from figures before and during his time. Such models are chosen based on the degree to which it is judged that their consideration will help clarify Wesley's view of the will.

We will consider first the view of Augustine. For Augustine, one meaning of the will corresponds to what Wesley attributes to the heart. For example, for Augustine, the will (*voluntas*) refers to "appetite, fear, joy, and grief."[3] For Augustine—at least at one stage of his life—, another

---

[1] Wesley, *Salvation by Faith* (BE), 1:117.
[2] Wesley, *Heavenly Treasure in Earthen Vessels* (BE), 4:163.
[3] Richard Sorabji, *Emotions and Peace of Mind* (Oxford: Oxford University Press, 2000), 335.

meaning of will refers to the power of choice, which is, as we observed in the last chapter, something different from passive feelings.[4] This is evident in his discussion of the "free choice of the will" (*liberum arbitrium voluntatis*).[5] As we will consider more below, Wesley's view of the will "properly speaking" does not resemble Augustine's view of the will as the power of choice, but it does resemble Augustine's meaning of the will that refers to fear, joy, etc.[6]

The theology of John Duns Scotus, a scholastic theologian of the thirteenth century, is not the same as Wesley's theology, but there is a degree of similarity in how they use the word "will" (*voluntas* for Scotus) to name passive elements of the soul.[7] Henrik Lagerlund and Mikko Yrjonsuuri offer the following claim: "The first to develop a more systematic way the idea that the will itself has passions in the emotional sense of the term was perhaps John Duns Scotus."[8] Scotus distinguishes between active and passive and claims that the will "is a twofold tendency in the one power, one active, and the other passive."[9] This point is in some degree echoed by Samuel Clarke in the eighteenth century when he states: "As to Willing, this word (as I before observed) has a great ambiguity in it, and signifies two distinct things... The one is entirely pass-

---

[4] Perceptions such as appetite, fear, joy, and grief are not active as defined in this project because one often cannot determine when they occur. For cases in which one may determine the time of these feelings—such as in the illustration of the hungry scientist from chapter 2—, it is because of reflexivity, which is the mutual occurrence of the active and passive powers of mind. Even in this case, it seems that such feelings in their bare sense are only passive.

[5] For more information on Augustine's view of the "will," see the discussion given by the renowned Richard Sorabji. Sorabji makes reference to Augustine's use of the "free choice of the will" on p. 321 of *Emotion and Peace of Mind*.

[6] Also, of course, Wesley would disagree with a Calvinist reading of Augustine that would favour necessity over libertarianism.

[7] Wesley does seem to have some awareness of Scotus' thought as evident from comments in his address to clergy. Wesley, 'Address to the Clergy,' *Works* (Jackson), 10:492.

[8] Lagerlund and Yrjonsuuri, *Emotions and Choice: from Boethius to Descartes*, 18.

[9] William Frank, ed., *Duns Scotus on the Will & Morality* (Washington D.C.: The Catholic University of America Press, 1997), 155. This quote comes directly from Scotus' *Ordinatio* III.17.

ive, belonging to the understanding only and has nothing to do with the question about liberty; the other is truly active."[10]

Presumably, for Scotus, the tendency of the will that pertains to the emotions is the "passive" tendency of the will. As will be discussed below, this passive tendency resembles Wesley's view of the will "properly speaking."[11] Scotus argues that the "active" tendency of the will is that which is "free."[12] Although Scotus' active tendency of the will does not resemble Wesley's view of the will "properly speaking," it does appear to share a similarity with Wesley's (and Clarke's) view of liberty. One reason for this is because for both Scotus and Wesley, a person may use his or her active power to choose against the clearly known greatest good.[13] Consistent with this point, most commentators interpret Scotus' thought to be libertarian.[14] While Wesley's thought differs from that of Scotus, and while Wesley does not openly claim to adopt Scotus' view on any of these points, such resemblances are apparent.

For the purpose of illuminating Wesley's view of the will, it is also helpful to distinguish Wesley's view from the view of an eighteenth century writer from Geneva named Jean Burlamaqui.[15] Like Wesley, Burla-

[10] Clarke, *Remarks upon a Book, Entituled, A Philosophical Enquiry Concerning Human Liberty*, 21-22. On multiple occasions, Clarke clearly claims the following equation: active component of will = liberty = human active power: Clarke, *Remarks upon a Book, Entituled, A Philosophical Enquiry Concerning Human Liberty*, 7-9, 15, 21-22

[11] Wesley, 'What is Man?,' *Works* (BE), 4:22. Wesley, 'Thoughts Upon Necessity,' *Works* (BE), 13:540.

[12] Frank, ed., *Duns Scotus on the Will & Morality*, 155.

[13] Frank, ed., *Duns Scotus on the Will & Morality*, 158. Scotus says the will of a pilgrim "does not of necessity will happiness either in general or in particular." It is assumed here that happiness is the greatest good. Concerning the point that Wesley believes that a person has the power to choose against the strongest motive and/or clearly-known greatest good, see Wesley's essay "Thoughts upon Necessity," especially p. 544 of *Works* (BE).. Wesley's comments on conscience reflect his belief that all people have the power to a degree to know accurately what is good and bad (Wesley, 'On Conscience,' *Works* (BE), 3:481), and his comments on liberty reflect his view that one is always free to choose the clearly-known actual bad instead of the clearly-known actual good (see just about any one of Wesley's discussions of liberty after 1774).

[14] Lagerlund and Yrjonsuuri, *Emotions and Choice: from Boethius to Descartes*, 131.

[15] Wesley read Burlamaqui's *The Principles of Natural Law*. However, it ap-

maqui describes the soul as having the features of "understanding, will, and liberty."[16] Also like Wesley, Burlamaqui holds that there is a meaning of will that refers to "passions" and "inclinations."[17] As mentioned in chapter 2, Wesley differs from Burlamaqui in that the former believes that a human has a power of liberty to choose against the clearly known greatest good, whereas the latter does not.[18] In this way, Burlamaqui, unlike Wesley, must disjoin liberty from action in some cases.[19]

In contexts where they are giving explanations for their views of the features of the soul (understanding, will and liberty), Wesley and Burlamaqui differ in how they define the will. This is the context in which Wesley often italicizes the word "will" and defines it as the affections and passions.[20] This is the will "properly speaking." In this context, for Burlamaqui, the will means more than passive affections: it also includes "an active principle" and is a power whereby a person is "capable to act or not to act."[21] In all contexts where he discusses "understanding, will,

---

pears that the only feedback that Wesley offers for this book is negative. See: Wesley, 'The Unity of the Divine Being,' *Works* (BE), 4:68.

[16] Burlamaqui, *Principles of Natural Law*, 5. Wesley quotes this verbatim. See, for example, Wesley, 'Thoughts Upon God's Sovereignty,' *Works* (BE), 13:548.

[17] Burlamaqui, *Principles of Natural Law*, 14. Wesley, 'What is Man?,' *Works* (BE), 4:22.

[18] Burlamaqui, *The Principles of Natural Law*, section vi-viii, especially 19 and 22. Burlamaqui's view of liberty is somewhat similar to Aquinas' view in that it involves: (a) a freedom to choose between particulars and (b) a freedom to choose between cases where the benefits of options are not clearly evident. See section vi-viii, especially p. 20 and 22. For an analysis of Aquinas' view, see Lagerlund and Yrjonsuuri, *Emotions and Choice: from Boethius to Descartes*, 14.

[19] Since Burlamaqui holds that a person does not have liberty when he or she is presented with two options in which one is clearly a greater good, Burlamaqui must disjoin liberty from the active power in some cases. This is because, in such cases, one must choose (= act) *by necessity (not liberty)* the option that is clearly perceived to be the greater good. In this way, Burlamaqui's view of liberty is different from Wesley's. Yet, as will be shown in the next paragraph, for Burlamaqui, every instance of action is an occurrence of willing, even if it is not an act of liberty in some cases.

[20] Wesley, 'The General Deliverance,' *Works* (BE), 2:439 and 2:442; Wesley, 'The End of Christ's Coming,' *Works* (BE), 2:474; Wesley, 'On the Fall of Man,' *Works* (BE), 2:401; Wesley, 'On Divine Providence,' *Works* (BE), 2:540.

[21] Burlamaqui, *Principles of Natural Law*, 13.

and liberty," Wesley, unlike Burlamaqui, never describes the will as including the active power.[22] Rather, *in these contexts*,[23] Wesley attributes the active power only to the concept of liberty. There is a variety of other discussions of the will in the period preceding Wesley as shown in Herbert McGonigle's discussion of Arminius and the Dutch Remonstrants.[24]

For a significant number of thinkers before and during Wesley's time—which of course include but is not limited to Augustine, Scotus, and Burlamaqui—the word "will" (*voluntas*) refers to a twofold tendency of active and passive, in which the passive tendency corresponds in some way to ingredients of Wesley's view of the heart and the active tendency corresponds to action and the power of choice (Wesley's view of liberty). This convention of using the word "will" becomes somewhat less prevalent in the modern era. Consider the following quotation from the eighteenth century by Thomas Reid:

> In the general division of our faculties into understanding and will, our passions, appetites and affections are comprehended under the will; and so it is made to signify, not only our determination to act or not to act, but every motive and incitement to action.
>
> It is this, probably, that has led some Philosophers to represent desire, aversion, hope, fear, joy, sorrow, all our appetites, passions and affections, as different modifications of the will, which I think, tends to confound things which are very different in their nature.
>
> The advice given to a man, and his determinations consequent to that advice, are things so different in their nature, that it would be improper to call them modifications of one and the same thing. In like manner, the motives to action, and the determination to act or not to act, are things that have no common nature, and therefore ought not to be con-

---

[22] This is different from what Wesley does before 1774, in which he sometimes describes a person as having "understanding, will, and affections" instead of "understanding, will, and liberty." See: Wesley, 'The Doctrine of Original Sin,' *Works* (BE), 12:281; Wesley, *ENNT*, Mark 12:30; and Wesley, 'The Love of God,' *Works* (BE), 4:331. Before using the model of "understanding, will, and affections," Wesley once referenced the typology of understanding, will, and freedom in a sermon from 1730.

[23] Below, it will be shown that there is a separate context in which Wesley uses a different meaning of will for the active power.

[24] See, for example, Herbert McGonigle, *Sufficient Saving Grace*, 17 and 21.

founded under one name, or represented as different modifications of the same thing.

For this reason, in speaking of the will in this Essay, I do not comprehend under that term any of the incitements or motives which may have an influence upon our determinations, but solely the determination itself, and the power to determine.[25]

Thus, for Reid, the will refers to the active power alone.[26] The will does not refer to the passive dimension of the soul, which includes affections, passions, appetites, etc. That is, for Reid, the will does not refer to any of what Wesley sees as ingredients of the heart. Thus, Wesley and Reid differ in that they do not practice the same method for naming the will.[27] And yet, as Wesley is a strong opponent to absolute predestination, Wesley finds Reid's discussion of moral liberty to be a helpful support of this larger cause.[28]

---

[25] Reid, *Essays on the Active Powers of Man*, 60.

[26] See also: Reid, *Essays on the Active Powers of Man*, 37-38.

[27] As mentioned by Maddox, Wesley and Reid also differ on another important matter of ethics, namely regarding how to define virtue and the importance of the affections in the religious life. Reid's ethics is not as holistic as Wesley's. See the last section of Maddox's essay in the book *"Heart Religion" in the Methodist Tradition and Related Movements*, edited by Richard Steele. Reid says, "While a man does what he really thinks wisest and best to be done, the more his appetites, his affections and passions draw him the contrary way, the more he approves of his own conduct, and the more he is entitled to the approbation of every rational being (*Essay on the Active Powers of Man*, 86)." This point stands in direct contrast to Wesley's view of virtue, which presupposes correct choice must flow from the right affections and passions rather than oppose them. See, for example: Wesley, 'Justification by Faith,' *Works* (BE),1:192; Wesley, 'On Zeal,' *Works* (BE) 3:320; Wesley, 'Upon Our Lord's Sermon on the Mount, V,' *Works* (BE), 1:568; Wesley, 'Upon Our Lord's Sermon on the Mount, VI,' *Works* (BE), 1:573; Wesley, 'Heaviness through Manifold Temptations,' *Works* (BE), 2:232.

[28] Wesley puts an extract of Reid's discussion of liberty in volume 14 of the *Arminian Magazine*. Wesley's use of this extract for the purpose of defending free will against absolute predestination is apparent. Wesley says as a preface to this extract, "I do not remember to have ever seen a more strong and beautiful treatise on moral liberty than the following: which I therefore earnestly recommend to the consideration of all those who desire 'To vindicate the ways of God with man.'" Thomas Reid, "An Essay on the Liberty of Moral Agents," *The Arminian Magazine*, 14, (1791): 3.

The Will "Properly Speaking"

From the discussion so far, it should be clear that with regard to describing the will, John Wesley does not entirely follow Reid or any of the other mentioned thinkers. Before giving a more detailed account of Wesley's view of the will, it is helpful to observe that in the English language both in the eighteenth century and today, the word "will" has many different meanings. The *Oxford English Dictionary* gives nine different meanings of "will," with each of many of these meanings having multiple variations.[29] Thus, it should not be surprising that Wesley's view of the will includes more than one meaning. For this project, we will focus on two of Wesley's meanings of will. It will be shown that one of these meanings is passive and the other is active. After 1774, it appears that the will "properly speaking" refers only to the passive dimension. After 1774, Wesley still uses the active meaning of will, even though this meaning is not the will "properly speaking." We will now consider briefly these two important meanings of will that Wesley uses.

The first meaning of will pertains to when Wesley is speaking of the "passions" or "affections," ingredients of the heart. This is the will "properly speaking."[30] Consider the following comments from Wesley:

> This inward principle, wherever it is lodged, is capable not only of thinking, but likewise of love, hatred, joy, sorrow, desire, fear, hope, etc., and a whole train of other inward emotions which are commonly called 'passions' or 'affections.' They are styled, by a general appellation, 'the will.'[31]

When using this meaning of will, Wesley either italicizes the word "will," puts it in quotation marks, or is using it in a context where he is speaking of "understanding, will, and liberty" together. What must be emphasized here is that, unlike Burlamaqui, *there is never an instance in any of these three cases where Wesley describes the will as referring to the active power or power of choice.* On several occasions, falling under one of these three conditions, Wesley does in fact speak of this meaning of will as "exerting itself in various affections and passions."[32] However, it does

---

[29] Simpson and Weiner, *The Oxford English Dictionary* (New York: Oxford University Press, 1989).
[30] Wesley, 'Thoughts Upon Necessity,' *Works* (BE), 13:540.
[31] Wesley, 'What is Man?,' *Works* (BE), 4:22.
[32] Wesley, 'The General Deliverance,' *Works* (BE), 2:439 and Wesley, 'Of Good Angels,' *Works* (BE), 3:6.

not seem that the word "exerting" here exemplifies what this project means by action, as clarified in chapter 2. In centuries preceding Wesley, words such as "movements" and "exertions" were sometimes used to refer to feelings that are passive as understood in this project.[33] These forces may be thought to be active with respect to exterior forces and passive with respect to human consciousness, as by analogy my neighbor's tapping of my shoulder is active with respect to my neighbor and passive with respect to me.

Near the end of the previous chapter we highlighted the following comments from Wesley in 1788: "I am conscious to myself of one more property called *liberty*. This is very frequently confounded with the *will* but is of a very different nature. Neither is it a property of the will but a distinct property of the soul."[34] Notice here that the word "will" is in italics, which as mentioned above, is common when Wesley is using will to refer to the affections and passions of the heart. The distinction between liberty and will in this passage is not a reflection of the distinction between liberty and will found in Locke or Burlamaqui, nor is it a reflection of the distinction between liberty and will found in Reid.[35] It seems most likely that this statement is simply distinguishing the human active power (liberty) from the components of the heart such as the passions and affections (what Wesley describes as the italicized will). Indeed, it seems that Wesley is speaking here of a dividing line between active and passive: the line between liberty and will. Although the will does

---

[33] Cf., for example, Augustine's comments (Richard Sorabji, *Emotions and Peace of Mind*, 335). Cf. also, for example, Hirvonen's analysis of Ockham. Lagerlund and Yrjonsuuri, *Emotions and Choice: from Boethius to Descartes*, 158.

[34] Wesley, 'What is Man?,' *Works* (BE), 4:23.

[35] For the reasons why this differs from Locke, please see Appendix A. For reasons why this differs from Burlamaqui, see the discussion above. For Reid, there are several distinctions between liberty and will: (1) Liberty is what gives humans a power that animals do not have (Reid, *Essays on Active Powers of Man*, 205-206 and 308, in which Reid claims that liberty requires reason). Like humans, animals have the power of willing but unlike humans, they cannot reason. Unlike Reid, Wesley does not require that liberty involve human reason. Thus, for Wesley, even animals have a degree of liberty (Wesley, 'The General Deliverance,' *Works* (BE), 2:440), and (2) Certain kinds of choice that follow from the force of habit are not examples of liberty (Reid, *Essays on Active Powers of Man*, 270). By contrast, Clarke and Wesley hold that, under normal circumstances, liberty pertains to all instances of choice (action). For Wesley, one has the liberty to follow or choose against the force of habit.

not constitute the entire spectrum of human passive experiences, it seems that the occasions of the will—hatred, joy, sorrow, etc.—are passive in nature. In the above paragraph where he distinguishes between liberty and will, Wesley goes on to give various illustrations of what he means by liberty as the active power: opening and shutting one's eyes, rising and sitting, etc. Such illustrations reinforce the point that for Wesley, liberty is the active power. It is no surprise that Wesley also calls liberty a "self-moving," "self-governing," and "self-determining" principle.[36]

Free Will

In addition to the meaning of the will just considered—i.e. the will "properly speaking," Wesley has a second important meaning of the will.[37] This meaning tends to be used when Wesley is speaking more colloquially. In contrast to the first meaning of will, this meaning never involves the use of italics, and it is never used in discussions of "understanding, will, and liberty." Interestingly enough, this meaning of will appears to be similar if not identical to Wesley's understanding of liberty as the power of choice. It also appears to refer to that which this project means by active, as developed in chapter 2. Both of Wesley's meanings of will considered so far are distinguished in the following comments: "Whereas we do not properly 'take up our cross' but when we voluntarily suffer what is in our power to avoid; when we willingly embrace the will of God, though contrary to our own; when we choose what is painful because it is the will of our wise and gracious Creator."[38] Clearly in this passage, we observe an active meaning of the will in the use of the phrase "willingly embrace." The passage indicates that it is "in our power" to avoid or embrace the will of God. Here, the choice of the active will may work contrary to the inclination of the passive will. The passive will is the first meaning of will that we have considered in this section. It deals with the passions and affections. The passive will here is referenced by the phrase "our own."

[36] Wesley, 'Heavenly Treasure in Earthen Vessels,' *Works* (BE), 4:163. The original statement is in *The Arminian Magazine*, 15, (1792): 119. Wesley also describes liberty as a power of "self-determination" (Wesley, 'The General Spread of the Gospel,' *Works* (BE), 2:489; Wesley, 'What is Man?,' *Works* (BE), 4:24; and Wesley, 'Thoughts Upon Necessity,' *Works* (BE), 13:539).

[37] "Second" here does not mean chronologically. This adjective is a way of distinguishing one meaning of "will" from the other meaning discussed.

[38] Wesley, 'Self-Denial,' *Works* (BE), 2:244.

Another example of using will to refer to the active power is apparent in the following comments from Wesley: "By a single act of my will I put my head, eyes, hands, or any part of my body into motion."[39] *Notice here that the word "will" is not italicized or put in quotes.* It is clear from these comments that the will is referring to the active power here because a person has the power to determine *when* to put such body parts into motion. There are other instances of Wesley's use of the word will to refer to action that will not be observed here.[40] However, we will consider the following comments from Wesley:

> To say every man can believe to justification or sanctification *when* he will is contrary to plain matter of fact. Every one can confute it by his own experience. And yet if you deny that every man can believe *if* he will, you run full into absolute decrees. How will you untie this knot? I apprehend very easily. That every man may believe if he will I earnestly maintain, and yet that he can believe when he will I totally deny.[41]

From this passage we may make a number of observations. First, it is clear that *Christian belief* is itself *not* active in the sense that is clarified in chapter 2 of this project. One reason why this is clear is because a person cannot determine *when* this believing occurs. Although Christian believing is not active, the *will*[42] to believe *is* active. Believing must be distinguished from the will to believe. It should be evident to any person's experience that the will to believe is active. This is because one may will to believe, or not will to believe, at any time one chooses.

For Wesley, willing an openness that invites God to give Christian belief is not possible by natural means but is only possible through prevenient grace.[43] This act of willing (choosing) is an example of moral liberty. As mentioned in chapter 1, for Wesley, liberty is identical to the

---

[39] Wesley, 'What is Man?,' *Works* (BE), 4:23.

[40] See, for example, the following places in Outler, editor, *Works* (BE): 3:432, 3:435, 2:189, 4:26, 4:69, 4:226, 3:85, 3:220, 3:284, 3:372.

[41] Wesley, *Letters*, 6:287.

[42] These are my italics, not Wesley's. When Wesley italicizes the word "will," he is using the other meaning of will.

[43] For a discussion of grace that is necessary for free will, see: Wesley, 'Predestination Calmly Considered,' *Works* (BE), 13:287 and Wesley, 'Some Remarks on Mr. Hill's "Review of all the Doctrines Taught by John Wesley",' *Works (*BE), 13:460 and for a discussion of grace that is necessary for liberty, see for example, Wesley, 'The General Deliverance,' *Works* (BE), 2:489 and Wesley, 'What is Man?,' *Works* (BE), 4:24.

power of choosing. Some acts of choosing, such as opening or closing one's eyes, may be thought as more neutral. Other kinds of choosing, such as that which deals with the choice regarding spiritual matters or regarding the choice of good or evil, is moral choosing which is moral liberty. For Wesley, it seems that this moral liberty is identical to his notion of "free will."[44] The will in this sense, refers to the human active power—Wesley's second meaning of will— that is made possible only by grace with regard to moral matters.[45] For Wesley, free will is only possible by free grace. This is one way in which we may observe that for Wesley, the language of free will is compatible with the language free grace.[46] "Free will" describes that of which Wesley speaks in the above quotation[47]: one is free to will that God gives Christian faith or not will it.

---

[44] Since, as it seems, free will is identical to moral liberty, free will must be understood as a power by grace to choose between good and evil, including the power to choose for God to give Christian faith or reject it. (Several important examples of Wesley's discussion of this power of choosing are found here: Wesley, 'The General Deliverance,' *Works* (BE), 2:489 and Wesley, 'The Important Question,' *Works* (BE), 3:197). One of Jonathan Edwards' comments shows that Edwards believes that many opponents of necessity equate "free will" with "liberty." The title of one of the major parts of Edwards' book on free will speaks of the "Freedom of Will, as that wherein Arminians Place the Essence of Liberty of All Moral Agents." If Wesley does in fact equate free will with liberty, as it seems that he does, he is taking a position that appears common among Arminians. Wesley speaks of free will and liberty in Wesley, 'Predestination Calmly Considered,' *Works* (BE), 13:290 (see also 13:287 - 288). See also his comments on free will in his review of Mr. Hill (Wesley, 'Some Remarks on Mr. Hill's Review,' *Works* (BE), 13:460). Without some role of the active power in salvation (Wesley's second meaning of will, i.e. free will), grace would be eternally irresistible. Please see chapter 5 for a more detailed account of how Wesley understands the relationship between grace and the human active power.

[45] For a more detailed account of Wesley's view of how grace relates to the active power, please see chapter 5.

[46] Wesley does not hold a doctrine of free grace in a purely Calvinist sense, but he does give his own view of free grace that is compatible with free will. Concerning his view of grace and free will, Wesley says: "Natural free-will, in the present state of mankind, I do not understand: I only assert, that there is a measure of free-will supernaturally restored to every man, together with that supernatural light which 'enlightens every man that cometh into the world." Wesley, 'Predestination Calmly Considered,' *Works* (BE), 13:287.

[47] Wesley, *Letters*, 6:287.

In the passage above, Wesley makes it clear that he avoids the doctrine of "absolute decrees."[48] This is because not only some but any person, by grace, is free to will to believe. Such an act of willing is certain to precede some future unknown time in which God gives the person Christian belief. This freedom to will to believe is "free will." It is free because *any person* can choose heaven or hell. This is different from Jonathan Edwards' view of the soul, in which a person may not choose against the strongest motive.[49] The result of such a premise in Edwards' view is that some people are forced to hell and have not freedom to choose against this fate. Edwards' view that some people are not free to choose heaven is in direct contrast to Wesley's view of free will. For Wesley, if there is no liberty—that is, if there is no free will—, then there is no power of choosing good or evil, no virtue or vice. For Wesley, Edwards' attempt to reconcile the power of performing virtue and vice with a system of necessity is a failure.[50]

Thus, we have observed two different meanings that Wesley uses for the word "will." The first meaning we observed refers to the affections and passions, which appear to be passive. The second meaning refers to the power of choosing, the exercise of liberty, which is an active power. To some, such a practice for using the word will may seem a bit confusing. In one place in his writing, Wesley is strongly distinguishing between liberty and will, such as in the cases where "will" is italicized.[51] In other cases, such as in his discussion of "free will," Wesley seems to be making the will to be identical to liberty. Why would Wesley not opt to follow Reid and simply confine his meaning of will to the power of choosing, thus separating the word "will" from the affections and passions? Although there is no certain answer, there is one strong possible answer. As we will now explore, one possible answer to this question concerns Wesley's response to Edwards in 1774.

Responding to Edwards?

For a period of time in his life, Wesley did in fact summarize his view of the soul in a manner more like Reid. At least once in 1733, twice in the

---

[48] Wesley, *Letters*, 6:287.
[49] Edwards, *The Works of Jonathan Edwards*, 142.
[50] Wesley, 'Thoughts Upon Necessity,' *Works* (BE), 13:539.
[51] Wesley, 'What is Man?,' *Works* (BE), 4:23; Wesley, 'Thoughts Upon Necessity,' *Works* (BE), 13:539.

1750s, and once in 1760, Wesley would describe a person as having "understanding, will, and affections."[52] It seems that Wesley does not often modify this practice until 1774, at which time he begins using on a more regular basis the language of "understanding, will, and liberty." In his writing of *Thoughts Upon of Necessity*, first published in 1774, it seems that Wesley needed a way to respond effectively against Edwards' system of necessity and absolute predestination. Secondly, on the other hand, according to scholar Richard Steele, it is evident that he admired at some level Edwards' view of the affections.[53] These factors together could be part of why we observe in 1774 the use of "understanding, will, and liberty" instead of "understanding, will, and affections."

In response to Edwards in 1774, Wesley says, "there can be no moral good and evil, unless they have liberty as well as will, which is entirely a different thing. And the not adverting to this seems to be the direct occasion of Mr. Edwards's whole mistake."[54] In this response to Edwards, Wesley's opposition to the doctrine of necessity is not new. However, what appears different here is that Wesley is now using the word "liberty" to describe one of the three major features of the soul. It seems that the introduction of the language of "liberty" is useful to Wesley because it provides a more overt way to contrast himself from necessitarians such as Edwards in regard to how to describe the human active power. For Edwards, "the will" includes the active power, the power of choice.[55] In 1774, Wesley transitions from using the "will" as the name for his formal definition of the active power to using "liberty" as the name for his formal definition of the active power. For Wesley, it may be that he thinks that the word "liberty" helps observers more easily recognize the view—

[52] Wesley, 'The Doctrine of Original Sin,' *Works* (BE), 12:281; Wesley, *ENNT*, Mark 12:30; and Wesley, 'The Love of God,' *Works* (BE), 4:331 and 'The New Birth,' *Works* (BE), 2:188. In one instance, he speaks of "understanding, freedom of will, and various affections" (Wesley, 'The New Birth,' *Works* (BE), 2:188).

[53] Wesley published an extract of Edwards' treatise on the affections not more than two years before the publishing of *Thoughts Upon Necessity*. See Richard Steele, *"Gracious Affection" and "True Virtue" According to Jonathan Edwards and John Wesley* (London: The Scarecrow Press, 1994), 218.

[54] Wesley, 'Thoughts Upon Necessity,' *Works* (BE), 13:539.

[55] Edwards, *The Works of Jonathan Edwards*, 137 (from Edwards' book on free will). Edwards also calls the affections "modes of the exercise of the will." Edwards, *The Works of Jonathan Edwards*, 309. In this way, Edwards seems to have a twofold tendency of will that includes affections and choice.

contra Edwards— that a person is free to choose against the strongest motive and that one is free from the constraints of necessity. However, like Edwards, Wesley now uses the "will" to refer to the affections.

In the same section of *Thoughts Upon Necessity* Wesley goes on to make a revealing comment. Wesley provides insights regarding how his practice of naming has changed:

> It seems, they who divide the faculties of the human soul into the understanding, will, and affections, unless they make the will and affections the same thing; (and then how inaccurate is the division!)[56] must mean by affections, the will, properly speaking, and by the term will, neither more nor less than liberty.[57]

This point is interesting because Wesley appears to be referring at least to himself, namely his prior practice of describing a person as having "understanding, will, and affections."[58] With respect to those later occasions when Wesley is summarizing the features of the soul (starting in 1774), Wesley's new use of the word "liberty" is the same as his old meaning of "will." The following comment should make this clear: "by the term will, neither more nor less than liberty." Also, Wesley's new meaning of will is the same as his old meaning of the affections.

Although Wesley reveals this change in how to name the soul in 1774, he still maintains in more colloquial contexts the second meaning of "will," the active power of choosing.[59] Now in 1774, however, such an active meaning is no longer the will "properly speaking." The will "properly speaking" is the first meaning of will that we considered in this section. It refers only to the passions and affections, components of the heart. The *idea* of "free will," the power for any person to choose good or evil

---

[56] What Wesley appears to be saying here is that if one were to use the model of "understanding, will, and affections," and make will and affections the same thing, then the model would be in effect: "understanding, affections, and affections." Thus, Wesley comments, how this would be an "inaccurate division!"

[57] Wesley, 'Thoughts Upon Necessity,' *Works* (BE), 13:540. Notice that the italics here are Wesley's.

[58] In most such cases, Wesley speaks of "understanding, will, and affections." In one case, he speaks of "understanding, freedom of will, and various affections" (Wesley, 'The New Birth,' *Works* (BE), 2:188).

[59] See, for example, Wesley, *Letters*, 6:287 and his comment in 1788: "By a single act of my will I put my head, eyes, hands, or any part of my body into motion." Wesley, 'What is Man?,' *Works* (BE), 4:23.

and the power to choose for God to give Christian faith, remains in Wesley's thought, but the *name* of "free will" is not as important after 1774, and this name is rarely used during this period. After 1774, Wesley most often uses the *name* of "liberty" in order to describe this moral power of choosing.[60] For a summary of Wesley's view of the will and how it compares to the aforementioned thinkers, please see diagram 3.1.

We have now concluded our investigation of Wesley's view of the will. For Wesley, the will "properly speaking" includes the affections and passions. This meaning of the will is used in contexts in which Wesley italicizes the word "will" or discusses together the three features of a person—understanding, will, and liberty. This meaning of the will is passive in nature and something very different from liberty, which is the active power. However, Wesley also uses a second meaning of will. He uses this meaning more often in contexts that are less formal. This meaning of will is the power of choosing or "free will." It seems to be equivalent to Wesley's meaning of liberty.

So far, for the first task of the project, we have looked at Wesley's view of liberty and will. We will now turn to a consideration of Wesley's view of the heart. As we have shown, the will properly speaking is part of the heart. Yet in the next chapter, we will consider the heart in more depth.

---

[60] As noted in noted in chapter 1, this is a different meaning of liberty from another meaning that Wesley uses when he speaks of the "glorious liberty" of the sons of God as in Romans 8:21.

Chapter 4

The Heart

Our first task in exploring Wesley's view of ethics is simply to examine and clarify the features of the soul. This has been the focus for chapters 2 and 3. In chapter 2, we clarified what is meant in this project by active and passive, and we began exploring Wesley's view of liberty. In chapter 3, we examined Wesley's view of liberty and the will. As we have shown, the feature of "liberty" is equivalent to the active power. The will "properly speaking" refers to the affections and passions and is passive in nature. There is also a second meaning of the will which refers to the power of choosing, which is the same as what is meant by "free will" and is equivalent to liberty.

In this chapter, we will consider in more depth Wesley's understanding of the heart. The heart will be examined in light of the concepts of active and passive. This will involve a number of steps. We will begin by considering Wesley's view of the desires of the heart. Then we will consider the relationship of the heart to the pursuit of happiness. Next we will explore Wesley's understanding of the tempers, dispositions, and affections. After this, we will consider the significance of Wesley's eyewitness accounts of those people who experience "fire" and "flames" in their heart and how these experiences exemplify passive experiences, involving the work of God alone. Finally, we will consider briefly Wesley's understanding of reason and its role in ethics.

After concluding our examination of the heart and reason in this chapter, we will have completed the first task of the project. This will prepare us for the second task of the project: exploring how the features of the soul relate as an agent performs right action and pursues the highest end of ethics. Such a move will lead us to defend the thesis of this project that for Wesley, the pursuit of Christian love, including the performance of fruitful action, is an expression of God's gift.

For now, we will focus our attention on Wesley's view of the heart. We will begin by taking a look at what Wesley means by the desires of the heart.

Desires of the Heart

In chapter 2 of this project, we used the word "inclination" to describe a feature of the passive dimension of a person, and we used a number of illustrations in order to clarify what is meant by inclination. Examples of inclinations include but are not limited to: a feeling of hunger for food, such as in the illustration of the man in the orchard or a feeling of love that a parent may have for a child, such as in the illustration of Abraham and Isaac. Many analysts of ethics throughout the history of academic thought have identified pleasure and pain as essential features of an inclination.[1] In its essence, an inclination involves the conscious feeling of pleasure and/or pain depending on how a person is in relationship to the goal (the target of the inclination). The foreseen prospect of experiencing pain or pleasure is metaphorically the "springs" of human action and the impetus for driving a person to seek the inclination's goal. As will be discussed more below, for Wesley, the idea for how a holy heart is a "spring" for virtuous action is crucial for his view of ethics.[2]

To help clarify how pain and pleasure are the springs of inclination, consider some examples from chapter 2. For a hungry person, the goal is to eat. The fulfilment of the goal, in this case eating, brings a vivid perception of pleasure. The unfulfilling of the goal, in this case not eating, leads to a vivid perception of pain and uneasiness. Thus, a hungry person is impelled to eat. A person is not forced by necessity to eat, but resisting this inclination will result in pain and uneasiness. Similarly, for a child in a healthy family, the goal of the child is to live in the presence of the parents. The fulfilment of this goal brings pleasure and happiness for the child. The unfulfilling of this goal brings pain and uneasiness (a

---

[1] See, for example, Aristotle's *Nicomachean Ethics* and many books on ethics that follow.

[2] For examples of Wesley's use of the metaphor of a "spring" in reference to the heart, see for example: Wesley, 'Address to the Clergy,' *Works* (Jackson), 10:498; Wesley, 'On Zeal,' *Works* (BE), 3:320; Wesley, 'What is Man?,' *Works* (BE), 4:22.

child often cries in the absence of his or her parents). Thus, a child is internally impelled and driven to be in the presence of the parents.

This idea of inclination, as clarified by this project, is apparent in Wesley's understanding of the heart. First, this idea appears consistent with his actual use of the term of "inclination."[3] Additionally, this idea is evident in his use of other terms that pertain to the heart. It appears that an enduring form of an inclination, as clarified in chapter 2, is similar if not equivalent to what Wesley means by "desire" in the context of when he is speaking of the force that rules the heart. The question then is how does this inclination/desire relate to the idea of love? Although Wesley at times may portray the idea of love as something more than merely a passive desire/inclination, it is clear that he understands a passive desire/inclination to be a key part of his idea of love.[4] In this project, there will be times when discussing "love," we speak of only the passive component of love. This is something that Wesley himself sometimes does.[5] For the discussion that follows, the context clues of "desire" and/or "inclination" should make it clear when this is being done. When speaking of love as referring to a "desire" or "inclination," we are speaking of the passive component of love.

For Wesley, a human being may be subject to one of either two ruling desires: the love of God and neighbor or the love of the world.[6] Such a

[3] In one instance, he contrasts "inclination" with "choice" (Wesley, 'The Doctrine of Original Sin,' *Works* (BE), 12:257). In another piece, he seems to equate it with impulse and desire, in a manner that makes it appear passive. Here, the Spirit is the giver of the feeling of inclination. Wesley, 'A Letter to a Person Lately Joined with the Quakers,' *Works* (Jackson), 10:181.

[4] For clear evidence that Wesley at times speaks of love in a passive sense, see: Wesley, 'The Doctrine of Original Sin,' *Works* (BE), 12:277, 12:338, and 12:339 (especially 12:277). Concerning Wesley's view of how love and desire compare, a number of observations may be made. In 1737, Wesley says: "What is it to love God but to delight in him, to rejoice in his will, to desire continually to please him, to seek and find our happiness in him, and to thirst day and night for fuller enjoyment of him?" Wesley, 'On Love,' *Works* (BE), 4:383. As we will show, Wesley continues to portray love as including desire, as evident in his 1766 publication (and 1789 publication) of *A Plain Account of Christian Perfection*. Wesley, 'A Plain Account of Christian Perfection,' *Works* (Jackson), 11:418. On some occasions, it is useful to cite the Jackson edition of this treatise since, unlike the bicentennial edition, the former edition quotes the whole text.

[5] See, for example, Wesley, 'The Doctrine of Original Sin,' *Works* (BE), 12:277.

[6] For a clear statement of how these two ruling loves are exclusive of each other, please see Wessley, "Address to the Clergy," *Works* (Jackson), 10:498. For

desire is a key ingredient of Wesley's view of the heart. For Wesley, the heart may be defined as that which includes one of these two ruling desires *and* all the passive elements—tempers, affections, dispositions, etc.—that may accompany it.[7] With regard to these two ruling desires: at one end of the spectrum is a perfected person's love for God. Wesley describes a perfected person as follows: "I know many that love God with all their heart. He is their one desire, their one delight, and they are continually happy in him. They love their neighbors as themselves. They feel as sincere, fervent, constant a desire for the happiness of every man, good or bad, friend or enemy, as for their own."[8] Just as a child finds pleasure and happiness in the presence of a parent, so does a perfected person find pleasure and happiness in the presence of God. A perfected person also has a desire for the happiness of one's neighbor.

The alternative ruling desire of the heart is love of the world. Wesley derives this view of evil love from his reading of 1 John 2:16: "Love not the world, neither the things that are in the world: if any one love the world, the love of the Father is not in him. For all that is in the world, the desire of the flesh, and the desire of the eye, and the pride of life, is not of the Father, but is of the world."[9] This love of the world serves as part of what Wesley means by "original sin."[10] This scripture shows that the love of the world includes three desires, and each of these desires has a corresponding pleasure. In this regard, Wesley's own teaching follows this scriptural teaching.[11] The "desire of the flesh" seeks the "pleasure of

---

places where Wesley distinguishes between Christian love and love of the world, see for example: Outler, editor, *Works* (BE), 2:88, 2:158, 2:194, 2:132, 2:481, 3:174.

[7] As will be shown below, the ruling desire of Christian love is itself a temper but it is not the only holy temper. There are other holy tempers as well.

[8] Wesley, 'A Plain Account of Christian Perfection,' *Works* (BE), 13:187 directs you to 13:100 - 101. These comments were included in the 1766 publication (and 1789 publication) of 'A Plain Account of Christian Perfection.'

[9] Wesley, *ENNT Notes*, 1 John 2:16. Wesley says elsewhere: "For whenever we are not aiming at God we are seeking happiness in some creature. And this, whatever that creature may be, is no less than idolatry. It is all one whether we aim at the pleasures of sense, the pleasures of the imagination, the praise of men or riches; all which St. John comprises under the general expression, 'the love of the world.'" Wesley, 'A Single Eye,' *Works* (BE), 4:123.

[10] Wesley, 'Original Sin,' *Works* (BE), 2:179.

[11] Wesley makes references to these desires and pleasures fairly frequently. See Wesley, 'The Way to the Kingdom,' *Works* (BE), 1:226.

sense," which pertains to overindulgences of eating, drinking, smelling, feeling, and/or any kind of the inferior appetites.[12] The "desire of the eye" seeks the "pleasure in imagination," which is an inordinate taste for new and beautiful things such as beautiful horses, elegant furniture, delightful gardens, music, collecting curious items, splendid places, favourite animals and/or an inordinate taste for learning such as relating to poetry, history, art, science, etc.[13] The "pride of life" leads to seeking too strongly the pleasure that comes from gaining the honour and esteem of other people and produces shame in things for which one should feel good.[14]

Like Christian love, love of the world inclines a person to seek a highest end. For both love of the world and Christian love, this highest end is thought to be happiness. Each of the differing loves corresponds to a different vision of what happiness is. To this subject of happiness we now turn.

Happiness

As a goal must serve as the target for an individual inclination, the concept of happiness[15] (a goal in itself) must serves as the target for the ruling inclination/desire of one's heart. As Wesley says, "The desire of happiness is inseparably [bound] to our nature, and is the spring which sets all our faculties a-moving."[16] As we will show, a desire for Christian happiness is given by grace. A desire/love for the world is from a person's corrupt nature, owing to the fall. As we have shown in previous chapters, for Wesley, there is a power of liberty to choose against the strongest desire, strongest motive, and/or clearly known greatest good. In other words, one is free to choose against a clearly-perceived option for happiness. However, as will be shown more in the chapters that follow, the motivational impact of a person's inclination for true happiness is an indispensable and key ingredient for Wesley's view of ethics.[17]

[12] Wesley, 'On God's Vineyard,' *Works* (BE) 3:516; Wesley, 'Sermon on the Mount, VII,' *Works* (BE), 1:599; Wesley, 'Spiritual Idolatry,' *Works* (BE), 3:105.

[13] Wesley, 'On Riches,' *Works* (BE), 3:525; Wesley, 'The Repentance of Believers,' *Works* (BE) 1:338; Wesley, 'Spiritual Idolatry,' *Works* (BE), 3:107.

[14] Wesley, 'An Israelite Indeed,' *Works* (BE), 3:284; Wesley, 'On Riches,' *Works* (BE), 3:526; Wesley, 'On Family Religion,' *Works* (BE), 3:339.

[15] The word "happiness" is used frequently in Wesley's writings. It is often described as involving holiness and sanctification.

[16] Wesley, 'Death and Deliverance,' *Works* (BE), 4:209.

For now, we will highlight some important features of Wesley's view of happiness. First, the idea of happiness as a highest goal is presupposed in the idea of the heart. This is because the heart is understood to include the sum of one's inclinations, and these inclinations must by their essence have a net target, which is the goal that is understood to be happiness.[18] Second, while happiness, as a general idea is a single goal, it relates to a web of other goals that serve the larger purpose. In the case of Christian happiness, such goals include but are not limited to the practice of the "means of grace." Such practices, as they are performed by grace, are a means for an end: they promote the larger goal of loving God and neighbor.

Third, Christian happiness involves feelings of pleasure. For example, Wesley says in reference to Psalms 16:11 and 36:8, concerning one who is born of God: "He knows there can be no happiness on earth, but in the enjoyment of God, and in the foretaste of those 'rivers of pleasure which flow at his right hand for evermore.'"[19] Fourth, Christian love and happiness are inseparable.[20] Fifth, as may be evident from the fourth point, seeking happiness is primarily outward-focused rather than self-focused. In seeking happiness, one's mindset is primarily on seeking the love of God and neighbor. As Wesley says: "Singly aim at God. In every step thou takes, eye him alone. Pursue one thing: happiness in knowing, in loving, in serving God."[21] In this way, happiness is outward-focused.

---

[17] This inclination is of course Christian love. Contrast this point with the views of Reid and Kant that place less importance on inclinations for virtue.

[18] As to happiness being the highest end, Wesley says, for example, "Now the best end which any creature can pursue is happiness in God." Wesley, 'The Righteousness of Faith,' *Works* (BE), 1:213. See also Wesley, 'Spiritual Worship,' *Works* (BE), 3:100 and Wesley, 'Sermon on the Mount, VIII,' *Works* (BE), 1:615.

[19] Wesley, 'Journal,' *Works* (BE), 19:17. Wesley also says, "God shall satisfy them with the blessings of his goodness, with the felicity [happiness] of his chosen"... "He shall give them to drink of his pleasures, as out of the river which he that drinketh of shall never thirst—only for more and more of the water of life." Wesley, *Sermon on the Mount, II*, 1:497. I add the word "happiness" in brackets.

[20] Wesley says, "And according to the degree of our love is the degree of our happiness." Wesley, 'An Israelite Indeed,' *Works* (BE), 3:283. See also, for example, Wesley, 'The Unity of the Divine Being,' *Works* (BE), 4:67; Wesley, 'On Laying the Foundation of the New Chapel,' *Works* (BE), 3:585; and Wesley, 'Sermon on the Mount IX,' *Works* (BE), 1:635; Wesley, 'An Earnest Appeal to Men of Reason and Religion,' *Works* (BE), 11:45.

[21] Wesley, 'On Dissipation,' *Works* (BE), 3:123.

As the heart includes either the inclination of Christian love or the inclination of worldly love, a person is subject to pursuing one of two differing views of happiness. Those who are not yet born of God often believe that happiness is fulfilling the inclination to love the world.[22] The alternative version of happiness, which is the superior of the two options, is the love of God and neighbor.[23] Owing to original sin, each person begins life with an inclination to love the world. It is only by the work of the Spirit, the work of God alone, that one is able to receive a new heart, in which the ruling inclination for love of the world is replaced with a ruling inclination to love God and neighbor.[24] This transformation is performed in a manner that is passive with respect to a person. Scriptures that Wesley frequently cites in reference to this include but are not limited to: Romans 5:5 and John 3:1-8.[25] In this transformation, which takes place at the new birth, Christian love is now for the first time the ruling inclination of the heart such that the person has power over sin.[26]

Wesley believes that many people who are not born again are deceived about happiness. They are deceived because they wrongly believe that the fulfilling of their love of the world will bring happiness.[27] They are also deceived because they mistakenly believe that religion itself is misery.[28] Wesley acknowledges that there are pleasures in fulfilling the love of the world but claims that these are short lasting.[29] He argues that in a manner that is quite opposite to the expectations of most unbelievers, fulfilling the love of the world actually leads to pain and misery.[30] On

---

[22] For evidence of this point, see, for example: Outler, editor, *Works* (BE): 3:524, 3:351, 3:147, 4:123, 3:110.

[23] See above for evidence for how Wesley views that the love of God and happiness are inseparable.

[24] See Wesley, 'On Patience,' *Works* (BE), 3:174. See also, for example: Outler, editor, *Works* (BE), 4:67, 2:158, 8:41, 1:273. This point will be explored in more depth in chapter 6 and 7.

[25] See, for example: Outler, editor, *Works* (BE), 3:500 (Romans 5:5); 4:36 (Romans 5:5); and sermon 45, "The New Birth" (John 3:1-8).

[26] This point will be explored in more depth in chapter 6.

[27] See Wesley, 'The Important Question,' *Works* (BE), 3:192 and Wesley, 'The Unity of the Divine Being,' *Works* (BE), 4:65.

[28] Wesley, 'The Important Question,' *Works* (BE), 3:189.

[29] Wesley, 'The Important Question,' *Works* (BE), 3:193. The point is implied: Wesley, 'The Unity of the Divine Being,' *Works* (BE), 4:71.

[30] This point is emphasized here: Wesley, 'The Important Question,' *Works*

the other hand, the pleasures of true happiness, which involves love of God and neighbor, are stronger and long-lasting.[31] For Wesley, there is no true happiness (and feeling of fulfilment), except through the love of God and neighbor.[32] Although suffering—as in bearing one's cross—is sometimes a part of the Christian life, such suffering actually helps to build true happiness.[33]

The Language of Tempers, Dispositions, and Affections

Before we continue with the task of examining Wesley's view of the heart, let us take a moment to retrace some of the steps already taken. In chapter 2, the author clarified what is meant in this project by active and passive. An example of a passive experience includes but is not limited to the feeling of an inclination. Earlier, in this chapter, it was claimed that this project's meaning of inclination is apparent in John Wesley's view of the heart. It was claimed that this meaning of inclination is similar if not identical to Wesley's understanding of a ruling desire of the heart, as exemplified either by the love of the world or Christian love.[34] After this, we went on to analyze further the nature of inclination by examining happiness, which is, for a Christian, the target of the sum of the inclinations of the heart.

Yet, although we have begun looking at Wesley's view of the ruling inclinations of the heart and his understanding of happiness, our task of examining Wesley's view of the heart is not complete. In order to serve our greater purpose of the first task of this project, which is to clarify Wesley's view of the features of the soul, we must clarify further other aspects of what Wesley means by the heart. In his discussions of the

---

(BE), 3:197.

[31] See, for example, Wesley, 'The Important Question,' *Works* (BE), 3:197.

[32] Wesley, 'An Israelite Indeed,' *Works* (BE); Wesley, 'The Unity of the Divine Being,' *Works* (BE), 4:67; Wesley, 'On Laying the Foundation of the New Chapel,' *Works* (BE), 3:585; Wesley, 'Sermon on the Mount, IX,' *Works* (BE), 1:635; Wesley, 'An Earnest Appeal to Men of Reason and Religion,' *Works* (BE), 11:45. Cf. Wesley, 'Spiritual Worship,' *Works* (BE), 3:100, where he says being a Christian and true happiness are inseparable.

[33] See, for example, Wesley, 'The Important Question,' *Works* (BE), 3:190-192; Wesley, 'God's Love to Fallen Man,' *Works* (BE), 2:428.

[34] Again, we are speaking here of only the passive components of the love of the world and the love of God.

heart, Wesley often uses the language of "tempers," "dispositions," and "affections." Thus, one question for consideration is: how does each one of these terms— temper, disposition, and affection—compare and contrast with the others? Another important question is: how does each of these terms compare and contrast with what we have described so far as a "ruling inclination/desire?" Based on Wesley's writings, we cannot give exhaustive answers to these questions, but we can give partial answers. It will be shown that what can be said helpfully assists our larger purpose.

We will begin by considering the second question. Instead of considering each of the terms together—affection, disposition, and temper—, we will first consider only the idea of a temper. Some of how these other terms relate may be inferred. So then how does Wesley's view of a ruling inclination/desire relate to his understanding of a temper? As should be clear, the ruling desire for a Christian is Christian love.[35] On multiple occasions, Wesley describes this love itself as a temper.[36] In his sermon "On Charity," Wesley speaks of "love" as the "ruling temper of my soul."[37] Yet, it is also clear from his discussions that love (a temper) is not identical to other tempers. This is evident from the illustration of concentric circles that he gives in his sermon "On Zeal."[38] According to this illustration, the temper of love is in the centre, while the other tempers—longsuffering, gentleness, meekness, goodness, fidelity, temperance— are implied to be different and are thus identified in a circle exterior to love.[39] Wesley speaks of these other tempers on many occasions.[40] The scriptures on which Wesley bases these tempers include but

---

[35] Note that we are speaking here of the passive component of love. Concerning Wesley's view of how love and desire compare, see above and also Wesley, 'On Love,' *Works* (BE), 4:383. For evidence that Wesley believes that for a Christian, love rules all other tempers, see: Outler, editor, *Works* (BE), 3:453, 1:495, 4:71. Jackson, editor, *The Works of Wesley*, 9:85, 12:445, 8:198.

[36] Outler, editor, *Works* (BE), 3:301, 3:422, 3:77; and Wesley, 'Address to the Clergy,' *Works* (Jackson), 10:498.

[37] Wesley, 'On Charity,' *Works* (BE), 3:301.

[38] Wesley, 'On Zeal,' *Works* (BE), 3:313.

[39] Wesley, 'On Zeal,' *Works* (BE), 3:313.

[40] See, for example, Outler, editor, *Works* (BE), 4:147, 3:75. When discussing the tempers, Wesley does not always give exactly the same list. Other tempers include but are not limited to: joy, peace, and patience (Wesley, 'On Perfection,' *Works* (BE), 3:75 and Wesley, 'A Farther Appeal to Men of Reason and Religion,' *Works* (BE), 11:269).

are not limited to "the fruits of the Spirit" from Galatians 5:22-23 and some of the beatitudes from Matthew 5.[41] Love and these other holy tempers exemplify what Wesley means by "virtues."[42]

The same distinction between the temper of the ruling inclination and other separate tempers is also true in the case of evil. For one not born of God, the ruling desire is love of the world. This produces other evil tempers of "anger, hatred, malice, revenge, envy, jealousy, evil surmisings."[43] It seems that Wesley bases these unholy tempers on at least Galatians 5:20 and Colossians 3:5-8.

The distinction between the temper of Christian love and the other holy tempers is also made in contexts where Wesley is speaking of the latter as "springing" or "flowing" from the former.[44] It seems that each of these other tempers—long suffering, gentleness, meekness, goodness, fidelity, temperance, etc.—is the fruit of love and describes a loving person, but each of these tempers by itself is not identical to love. Although the temper of love and these other tempers are not identical, they come in a package. They are given by God at the new birth and strengthened by God in various ways throughout the rest of the Christian life. As will be discussed more below in this section, these other holy tempers, like the passive component of love, are often passive.

We have shown that for Wesley, the ruling desire of the heart is a temper and that a temper may refer to other forms of consciousness such as long-suffering, meekness, etc. The other question of this section is: how does each one of these terms— temper, disposition, and affection—compare and contrast with the others? As to this question, our focus will begin with considering how Wesley's view of tempers compares with his view of affections. In some cases, Wesley appears to make a distinction between a temper and affection. In reference to a remark

---

[41] Pertaining to "fruits of the Spirit," see for example, Wesley, 'On Perfection,' *Works* (BE), 3:77. Pertaining to beatitudes, see for example, Wesley, 'Sermon on the Mount, I,' *Works* (BE), 1:475.

[42] See, for example, Wesley, 'Circumcision of the Heart,' *Works* (BE), 1:403. As we will discuss more in the chapters ahead, virtue may also involve the active power. Virtue is not confined to passive qualities.

[43] For the point that many of these are tempers, see Wesley, 'The Important Question,' *Works* (BE), 3:194. For the point that these spring from the love of the world (the desire of the flesh, the desire of the eye, and the pride of life), see Wesley, 'The Way to the Kingdom,' *Works* (BE), 1:227.

[44] See, for example, Outler, editor, *Works* (BE), 3:453, 1:495, 4:71. Jackson, editor, *The Works of Wesley*, 9:85, 12:445, 8:198.

in scripture concerning friends' devotion of love (1 Thessalonians 2:17), Wesley describes a temper as a "fixed posture of the soul," something different from "transient" affections.[45] Consistent with this point, in another piece, Wesley offers tentatively that a temper is a "state," something that is a "lasting sensation" and is "rooted."[46] He describes it as something that is not "fleeting" but something that we "habitually feel."[47] Yet, his comments on this matter are scarce, and he does not give a thorough explanation.

Consider now one possible interpretation of Wesley's view of how tempers compare with affections that is consistent with the last point that tempers have a "lasting" nature. The key point of this interpretation is that "affection" is a broader term than "temper." Under such a view, all tempers are affections but not all affections are tempers.[48] In other words, all the lasting and firmly rooted affections are tempers, but all the short-lived affections are not tempers. There are some clues in Wesley's writings that suggest that he could allow for such an interpretation.[49] Yet, one point remains clear: regardless of what Wesley may

[45] Wesley, *ENNT*, comments on 1 Thessalonians 2:17.

[46] Wesley, *Letters*, 5:200.

[47] Wesley, *Letters*, 5:200. Wesley also says here that he does not think that he has the authority to distinguish between a frame of mind and a state. His statement is tentative.

[48] For clarity, consider the truth: all rabbits are animals but not all animals are rabbits.

[49] Clues that support this possibility include those places in Wesley's writings where he uses "temper" and "affection" to refer to the same idea. For example, he indicates that both "love" and "joy" are both tempers and affections (he calls "love" a temper here: Outler, editor, *Works* (BE), 3:301, 3:422; 3:77; Wesley, 'Address to the Clergy,' *Works* (Jackson), 10:498; he calls "love" an affection here: Outler, editor, *Works* (BE), 2:420, 2:474, 4:22; he calls "joy" a temper here: Wesley, 'On Perfection,' *Works* (BE), 3:77; he calls "joy" an affection here: Wesley, 'What is Man?,' *Works* (BE), 4:22). Interestingly, in one case, Wesley speaks of love as a "filial affection from which spring every good temper, and word, and work" (Wesley, 'On Predestination,' *Works* (BE), 2:420). This is an example of how for Wesley, an "affection" may sometimes refer to a lasting state rather than a transient feeling. This Christian love is both an affection and a temper. That tempers are affections is also apparent in his comment that the "affections" are the "*only* spring of action" (Wesley, 'What is Man?,' *Works* (BE), 4:22). If it is true that the affections are the "only springs of action," then affections must include tempers. This is because Wesley elsewhere says tempers are springs (see, for example, Wesley, 'On Zeal,' *Works* (BE), 3:320). From this

think, he does not emphasize on many occasions any distinctions between tempers and affections. We will not consider in as much depth how Wesley's view of tempers compares with his view of dispositions. However, we will observe that leading Wesleyan scholars agree that for Wesley, tempers may be thought of as dispositions.[50] Please see diagram 4.1 for a summary of Wesley's view of the heart.

Although Wesley does not often give a thorough account for how to distinguish between tempers, affections, and dispositions, the following point is in fact clear. Wesley frequently makes the point that all of these elements—tempers, affections, and dispositions—apply to the inward dimension, *not* the outward dimension of the person.[51] This leads to the question of whether Wesley thinks of tempers, affections, and dispositions as passive, as clarified in chapter 2 of this project.

While it may be a stretch to claim that all tempers and dispositions are passive in their entirety, it seems that for Wesley it is generally the case that tempers and dispositions are passive, as clarified in chapter 2 of this project. Evidence for this is found in Wesley's critical dialogue with John Taylor, most notably represented in Wesley's longest published work, *The Doctrine of Original Sin*. Please consider the following comments from this work:

> What is holiness? Is it not, essentially love? The love of God and of all mankind? Love producing 'bowels of mercies, humbleness

---

evidence, it appears that "affections" sometimes refer to tempers (lasting inclinations and/or feelings) and other times refer to certain transient conditions.

[50] Collins, Kenneth, "John Wesley's Topography of the Heart," *Methodist History*, 36, (April 1998): 165; Randy Maddox, *Responsible Grace* (Nashville, TN: Kingswood Books, 1994) , 69; Clapper, Gregory, "John Wesley's Language of the Heart," *Wesleyan Theological Journal*, 44, (2009): 97.

[51] Wesley speaks of all three—tempers, dispositions, and affections—as inward and contrasts them from action here: Wesley, 'Sermon on the Mount, VI,' *Works* (BE), 1:572. Another occasion in which he speaks of all three together as inward is where he makes the comment regarding God's judgment of the "inward working of every human soul: every appetite, passion, inclination, affection, with the various combinations of them, with every temper and disposition that constitute the whole complex character of each individual." (Wesley, 'The Great Assize,' *Works* (BE), 1:363) (It appears that he is listing here together many commonly-understood ingredients of the heart, regardless of overlap in meaning among at least some of them). Other occasions include the mention of inward tempers (Outler, editor, *Works* (BE), 1:304, 1:339, 2:317, 3:424) and inward dispositions (Wesley, 'Sermon on the Mount, V,' *Works* (BE), 1:568).

of mind, meekness, gentleness, long-suffering'? And *cannot* God shed abroad this love in any soul without his concurrence? Antecedent to his knowledge or consent? And supposing this to be done, will love change its nature? Will it be no longer holiness? This argument can never be sustained—unless you would play upon the word 'habits'. Love is holiness wherever it exists. And God *could* create either men or angels, endued from the very first moment of their existence with whatsoever degree of love he pleased.

You 'think, on the contrary, it is demonstration, that we cannot be righteous or holy, we cannot *observe* what is right, without our own free and explicit choice'. I suppose you mean, *practice* what is right. But a man may *be* righteous before he *does* what is right, holy in heart before he is holy in life. The confounding these two all along seems to be the ground of your strange imagination that Adam 'must choose to be righteous, must exercise thought and reflection before he *could* be righteous'. Why so? 'Because righteousness is the right *use and application* of our powers.' Here is your capital mistake. No, it is not. It is the right *state* of our powers. It is the right *disposition* of our *soul*, the right *temper* of our *mind*.[52]

Wesley is making a clear distinction in these comments between active and passive. The temper of love and the other holy tempers—bowels of mercies, humbleness of mind, meekness, gentleness, longsuffering—are passive because they do not require the "concurrence of one's active power" or one's "explicit choice." Tempers and dispositions are "states."[53] They are something different from the power of choosing, as this choosing is action as defined in chapter 2 of this project.

Later, in the same treatise, Wesley makes additional comments that argue this same point that tempers and dispositions are often passive. He says,

Nay, 'Righteousness is *right action*.' Indeed it is not. Here (as we said before) is your fundamental mistake. It is a *right state of mind*,

---

[52] Wesley, 'The Doctrine of Original Sin,' *Works* (BE), 12:277. All italics are Wesley's.

[53] Cf. Aristotle's view of a "state" in *Nicomachean Ethics*, book II, chapters 1-3.

which differs from right action as the cause[54] does from effect. Righteousness is properly and directly *a right temper* or *disposition of mind*, or a complex of all right tempers.[55]

And cannot God by his almighty power infuse any good tempers into us? You answer: 'No. No being whatever can do for us that which *cannot be at all* if be not *our own choice*, and the effect of *our own industry* and exercise. But all good tempers are the effect of *our own* industry and exercise. Otherwise they *cannot be at all*.'

Nay then, it is certain they *cannot be at all*. For neither lowliness, meekness, long-suffering, nor any other good temper, can ever be the effect of *my own industry* and *exercise*. But I verily believe they may be the effect of God's Spirit, working in me whatsoever pleaseth him."[56]

In the first paragraph, Wesley clearly distinguishes tempers and disposition from "action." In the second and third paragraph, Wesley is once again distinguishing tempers from one's "own industry and exercise" and from "choice." One's own industry and exercise is active, and one's power of choice is also active. Tempers are something different from this. Tempers are passive. Holy Tempers are given by the work of God alone, that is, by the Spirit.

We have illuminated Wesley's view of the heart, as we explored his understanding of the ruling desire of the heart, as well as tempers and affections. We will now turn our attention to accounts of how Wesley observed the work of the Spirit in the hearts of people participating in the life of the church.

[54] Notice the phrase "cause does from effect." Wesley does not mean by this comment that tempers cause choice in a fashion that exemplifies necessity. If this were true, he would be guilty of a philosophical necessity that he spends all of his essay "Thoughts Upon Necessity" arguing against. What Wesley probably means here is that because of the motivational impact of tempers—as they involve pains and pleasures—, human choice usually (not by necessity) follows the suggestion of the ruling temper. This point underscores the holistic nature of Wesley's view of ethics. Compare this point to Samuel Clarke's idea of "moral necessity" discussed in chapter 1.

[55] Wesley, 'The Doctrine of Original Sin,' *Works* (BE), 12:338. All italics are Wesley's.

[56] Wesley, 'The Doctrine of Original Sin,' *Works* (BE), 12:339. All italics are Wesley's.

The "Fire" and "Flames" of the Heart

In his journal, Wesley frequently gives an account of heart-felt experiences in the life of the Methodist revival. As A. Skevington Wood argues, the "burning heart" was a central idea in Wesley's ministry.[57] Wesley often describes these kinds of heart-felt experiences that he observes in himself and others by using the terms "fire" and/or "flame." Such experiences took place in various forms of religious social practice, such as in society meetings, band meetings, love feasts, preaching, praying, and/or other kinds of religious contexts. For Wesley, some of these observable feelings were often fleeting and not as lasting tempers. On the other hand, often such feelings marked a person's experience of the new birth or Christian perfection, and in this way, they marked the arrival of lasting Christian tempers.

In 1744, around five years after the start of the revival, Wesley gives the following report: "In the society, God did sit upon his people as a refiner's fire. He darted into all (I believe hardly one excepted) the melting flame of love; so that their heads were as water, and their eyes as fountains of tears."[58] Clearly from these comments, we observe the work of the Spirit with respect to a person's passive dimension. That is, we observe here the work of God alone, something separate from the concept of human action, as clarified in chapter 2. God is touching powerfully the hearts of those in Christian community as a "melting flame." The presence of God is something that is clearly and powerfully felt.

In 1749, after about a decade of the Methodist revival, Wesley makes the following report: "At the meeting of the Select Society, such a flame broke out as was never there before. We felt such a love to each other that we could not express."[59] Once again, Wesley is using the language of "flame" to describe the passive experience of God's love in the human heart. In February of 1761, Wesley gives an account of a remarkable occasion of God's work. He says, "After preaching at the Foundery in the evening, I met the Bands as usual. While a poor woman was speaking a few artless words out of the fullness of her heart, a fire kindled, and ran, as flame among the stubble, through the hearts of almost all that hear: So, when God is pleased to work, it matters not how weak, or how mean,

---

[57] See, for example, A. Skevington Wood, *John Wesley: The Burning Heart* (Grand Rapids, Michigan: Eerdmans, 1967), 68 – 69.

[58] Wesley, 'Journal,' *Works* (BE), 20:21.

[59] Wesley, 'Journal,' *Works* (BE), 20:307 - 208.

the instrument."⁶⁰ Here Wesley is speaking of "fire" to describe the passive feelings of God in the hearts of those at the band meeting. Once again the Spirit is acting alone on human hearts. The human participants are active in their decision to gather and have a band meeting, but the actual touching of the heart itself is something that is passive in a bare sense.

Wesley's use of the language of "fire" and "flame" to describe human perceptions of God in the heart is something that continues on a regular basis in his journals throughout his life, including his later years. Indeed, the elderly Wesley speaks of the "fire" and "flame" of the Spirit in the heart on a number of occasions. In 1784, at the age of 81, John Wesley gives the following account: "After preaching to an earnest congregation at Coleford, I met the society. They contained themselves pretty well during the exhortation; but when I began to pray, the flame broke out. Many cried aloud, many sunk to the ground, many trembled exceedingly; but all seemed to be quite athirst for God, and penetrated by the presence of his power."⁶¹ Note that Wesley says, "the flame broke out." He is speaking once again of the passive feeling of God's love in the human heart. In this particular instance, the effects were rather dramatic: people cried aloud and trembled, etc. In 1787, Wesley described the testimony of a woman in a religious class meeting as follows: "her words were as fire, conveying both light and heat to the hearts of all her heard."⁶² This "heat" is no doubt something that is felt in a passive way.

On occasions of giving pastoral counsel, Wesley comforted those seekers who did not in fact experience the love of God in a dramatic way. Although he believed the passive feelings of the Spirit were typical for the Christian life, he did acknowledge that the Spirit worked in a variety of way in regard to how the Spirit is felt. In 1785, he wrote to one inquirer:

> There is an irreconcilable variability in the operations of the Holy Spirit on the souls of man, more especially to the manner of justification. Many find Him rushing upon them like a torrent, while they experience 'The o'erwhelming power of saving grace.' This has been the experience of many; perhaps of more in this late visitation than in any other age since the times of the Apostles. But

---

⁶⁰ Wesley, 'Journal,' *Works* (BE), 21:301.
⁶¹ Wesley, 'Journal,' *Works* (BE), 23:331.
⁶² Wesley, 'Journal,' *Works* (BE), 24:8.

in others He works in a very different way: 'He deigns His influence to infuse, Sweet, refreshing, as the silent dews.' It has pleased him to work the latter way in you from the beginning; and it is not improbable He will continue (as He has begun) to work in a gentle and almost insensible manner.[63]

For Wesley, the Christian life must involve in some degree a passive experience of God's love in the heart. Yet, as he explains here, there is variation in how this is felt. In some, the experience is calm and not dramatic. In other cases, it is as a strong fire. Nevertheless, in general, whether strong or faint, there is an experience that is in some degree *felt*. Regardless of the degree of feeling, Wesley frequently makes observation of the Spirit working as "fire" and "flame." There are dozens of such instances in his journals throughout his entire ministry after the start of the revival in the late 1730s.

Therefore, for Wesley, the heart is something that has a ruling desire, with happiness as the target. It is also the locus of other forms of consciousness, involving the feeling of tempers and affections. Many of these are passive in nature. The heart is a cherished dimension of how human beings sense and perceive God. By touching the heart, God gives many sincere seekers feelings of fire and flames of love, which include feelings of joy and pleasure.

Practical Reason and the Heart

Wesley places less emphasis on reason than on the heart for the attainment of what he calls "true religion."[64] In this way, one who is unintelligent and uneducated has just as equal access to true religion and Christian salvation as one who is educated, highly intelligent, and privileged. This is because all people—whether poor, rich, smart, unintelligent, or whatever else—may receive just as easily the gift of Christian faith and the transforming tempers of the heart, the result of the work of God alone. Wesley is clear to state that reason alone cannot produce any of the following: Christian faith, hope, the love of God, virtue, and

---

[63] Wesley, *Letters*, 7:298.

[64] Wesley, 'The Way to the Kingdom,' *Works* (BE), 1:220. There are many occasions in which Wesley emphasizes the importance of the heart for true religion. It is hard to miss them. Several examples include: Outler, editor, *Works* (BE), 2:530, 3:448 and Wesley, 'An Earnest Appeal to Men of Reason and Religion,' *Works* (BE), 11:45.

happiness.⁶⁵ Yet Wesley gives much value and importance to reason. He sees it as having an important role in the Christian life.⁶⁶

Wesley says that reason is "much the same with understanding."⁶⁷ It exerts itself in three ways: simple apprehension (the barely conceiving of something in the mind), judgment (determining whether conceptions agree or disagree with one another), and discourse (the motion of progress of the mind from one judgment to another).⁶⁸ Reason appears to involve at least some role for the active power, as clarified in chapter 2 of this project. This is especially evident in the aforementioned idea of discourse. One is generally free to determine *when* to begin this discourse of reason, and one is generally free to determine how long to continue it. For Wesley, choosing to use it as much as possible is the preferred option. Moreover, reason should be used as much possible because it is part of what it means to love God with all of one's mind, as commanded in scripture.

Consistent with this point, Wesley sees reason as important for matters of ethics. This is practical reason. In a person's pursuit of the greatest end of Christian living, Spirit-empowered reason works not alone but in conjunction with the Spirit-empowered heart.⁶⁹ As mentioned above, the heart provides the "spring" of action. This spring derives in large part from the motivational impact of pleasures and pain.

---

⁶⁵ Wesley, 'The Case of Reason Impartially Considered,' *Works* (BE), 2:593-598.

⁶⁶ In regard to reason, Wesley describes himself as using "a middle way" (Wesley, 'The Case of Reason Impartially Considered,' *Works* (BE), 2:600). He is not one to deny any value of reason, but he is also one not to give it exclusive privilege in matters of religion. Reason is valuable in religion for explaining the scriptures and for keeping conscience void of offense (Wesley, 'The Case of Reason Impartially Considered,' *Works* (BE), 2:592). Also, he makes it clear in his *Address to the Clergy* that he has high expectations for clergy to use their reason by means of studying (Wesley, 'Address to Clergy,' *Works* (Jackson), 10:492). His high regard for reason is evident in the curriculum he helps establish for the Kingswood school and in the advice that he gives to Methodists.

⁶⁷ Wesley, 'The Case of Reason Impartially Considered,' *Works* (BE), 2:590. Wesley claims to take this model of reason from Aristotle. See Wesley, 'Remarks Upon Mr. Locke's "Essay on Human Understanding",' *Works* (Jackson), 13:456.

⁶⁸ Wesley, 'The Case of Reason Impartially Considered,' *Works* (BE), 2:590.

⁶⁹ For an example of how Wesley thinks that the Spirit works in human reason, see Wesley, 'A Letter to a Person Lately Joined with the Quakers,' *Works* (Jackson), 10:181.

The spring of the heart points a person towards the ultimate end, which is happiness in the love of God and neighbor. Thus, without the heart, reason is aimless. A person may know the greatest end and reason well concerning the greatest end, but without the holy tempers of the heart, one is weak and powerless in pursuit of it.

Practical reason is the faculty whereby one may effectively determine the means to the greatest end of Christian love. In this way, practical reason for Wesley involves the planning and execution of what he calls the "means of grace."[70] These are practices from which one waits[71] in order to receive the grace that leads to the highest end of loving God and neighbor. Many of the means of grace are active in nature, and they are instances of using one's power of liberty. Practical reason involves calculating when to use these practices and how frequently to use them. It also involves calculating how to budget one's time and resources for the purpose of performing various kinds of means of grace.[72]

In some cases, knowing how to use and apply the means of grace are not immediately clear. In many such cases, it is important to use practical reason. Consider Wesley's comments as follows:

> You seem not to have observed, that the Scripture, in most points, gives only general rules; and leaves the particular circumstances to be adjusted by the common sense of mankind. The Scripture, for instance, gives that general rule, 'Let all things be done decently and in order.' But common sense is to determine, on particular occasions, what order and decency require. So, in another instance, the Scripture lays it down as a general, standing direction: 'Whether ye eat or drink, or whatever ye do, do all to the glory of God.' But it is common prudence which is to make the application of this, in a thousand particular cases. 11. 'But these,' said another, 'are all man's inventions.' This is but the same objection in another form. And the same answer will suffice for any reason-

---

[70] Wesley says in regard to the means of grace, "But we allow that the whole value of the means depends on their actual subserviency to the end of religion." Wesley, 'The Means of Grace,' *Works* (BE), 1:381.

[71] Wesley teaches that one must "wait" for grace in the means of grace. Wesley, 'The Means of Grace,' *Works* (BE), 1:384.

[72] See, for example, Wesley's comments in his sermon "The More Excellent Way," sermon 89 in Outler's *Works* (BE) and his sermon "The Good Steward," sermon 51 of Outler's *Works* (BE).

able person. These are man's inventions. And what then? That is, they are methods which men have found, by reason and common sense, for the more effectually applying several Scripture rules, couched in general terms, to particular occasions.[73]

In this passage, Wesley stresses how it is impossible for scripture to give instructions for every specific occasion. Quite often, the scripture will give a "general rule" or principle of conduct, and it will be up to each person to use common sense and reason to the best of his or her ability in order to know how to apply such rules and principles. This is prudence, a kind of practical reasoning. Also, as we see from these comments, there is never an idle moment. By grace, one may always use one's prudence to determine how best to use one's time and resources for whatever situation one faces. In harmony with this point, Wesley says, "Use every means which either reason or Scripture recommends as conducive (through the free love of God in Christ) either to the obtaining or increasing any of the gifts of God."[74]

For Wesley, another power of the soul related to practical reasoning is conscience. Conscience involves multiple features of the soul, including an interplay between practical reasoning and the heart. Conscience is "a kind of silent reasoning of the mind whereby those things which are judged to be right are approved of with pleasure; but those which are judged evil are disapproved of with uneasiness."[75] In this way, we see that conscience involves both reasoning and a regard for feelings of pleasure and uneasiness in the heart. The key aspect of conscience concerning Wesley's thought is that it is a power to a certain degree, to judge whether a past, current, or proposed action is right or wrong. Much of conscience is not given by intentional learning. God gives a degree of conscience to every human being.[76] Because of Wesley's understanding of conscience, Wesley can claim that all people are to some degree morally accountable.

---

[73] Wesley, 'A Plain Account of the People Called Methodists,' *Works* (BE), 9:263.

[74] Wesley, 'The Nature of Enthusiasm,' *Works* (BE), 2:59.

[75] Wesley, 'On Conscience,' *Works* (BE), 3:481.

[76] Wesley, 'On Conscience,' *Works* (BE), 3:481

Responding to Secondary Literature: Clapper, Maddox, and Collins on the Affections

Gregory Clapper, Randy Maddox, and Kenneth Collins have all proposed interpretations of John Wesley's view of the affections and tempers of the heart. In *Responsible Grace: John Wesley's Practical Theology* published in 1994, Randy Maddox says that Wesley "traded on a slight but significant distinction between affections and tempers."[77] Maddox says that for Wesley, a temper is a "habitual disposition of a person."[78] Collins, like Maddox, agrees that there must be a distinction between the tempers and affections. They both use Wesley's comments in reference to 1 Thessalonians 2:17 as support for this claim. In these comments, Wesley speaks of "transient affections of holy grief, desire, or joy" on the one hand, and he speaks of "calm standing tempers" as a "fixed posture of the soul" on the other hand.[79] This leads Collins to conclude that "The affections, on the other hand, as well as the 'passions' which constitute intensified affections, are less enduring and habituated than the tempers."[80]

In the essay "John Wesley's language of the heart" published in 2009, Gregory Clapper responds to Maddox and Collins. Clapper says in reference to them: "Two recent interpreters of Wesley have asserted that there is an important difference in the way that Wesley uses the terms 'affections' and 'tempers.'"[81] He summarizes the claims made by Maddox and Collins and observes how they use Wesley's comments on 1 Thessalonians 2:17 in support of their claims. Clapper then says in reference to their comments on Wesley's view of 1 Thessalonians 2:17: "I think, however, it is problematic to lay so much conceptual weight on this one quote, especially since 'calm' and 'standing' are not fixed characterizations of 'temper' in Wesley's work, as 'transient' is not a fixed characterization of 'affection' in his usage."[82] In other words, Clapper is rejecting the point shared by Maddox and Collins that Wesley distinguishes the

---

[77] Maddox, *Responsible Grace*, 69.

[78] Maddox, *Responsible Grace*, 69

[79] Wesley, *ENNT Notes*, 1 Thessalonians 2:17.

[80] Collins, Kenneth, "John Wesley's Topography of the Heart," *Methodist History*, 36, (April 1998): 171.

[81] Gregory Clapper, "John Wesley's Language of the Heart," *Wesleyan Theological Journal*, 44, (2009): 95.

[82] Clapper, "John Wesley's Language of the Heart," 95.

meanings of temper and affection on a regular basis. Clapper explores some passages in Wesley's writings and then concludes at the end of the essay that there is a "rough equivalence of the terms 'affections' and 'tempers' in Wesley's usage."[83]

All of these contributors offer helpful insights in regard to Wesley's view of the tempers and affections, and it might be possible to reconcile them. As mentioned above, the best solution may be simply to recognize a broader range of meanings to which the term "affection" refers. Wesley says (as noted by Maddox and Collins), "affection" refers to "transient" or short-lasting effects such as grief, joy, etc. But in other contexts, Wesley describes an "affection" as something that is more fixed and longer-lasting. For example, Wesley describes love as an "affection."[84] He also describes love as a "temper."[85] The fact that he describes love as both an affection and a temper gives support to Clapper's argument that a temper and affection are sometimes equivalent. Such equivalency is also apparent in Wesley's comment that the "affections" are the "*only* spring of action."[86] If it is true that the affections are the "only spring of action," then affections must include tempers. This is because Wesley elsewhere says tempers are springs.[87]

But this is not to reject the insights offered by Collins and Maddox. Collins is correct in pointing out that there can also be a distinction between a temper and a short-lasting affection. How is this possible? The solution here is simply to recognize that the concept of an "affection" refers to a broader range of meanings than temper. In other words, the point is that all tempers are affections but not all affections are tempers. The affections that are fixed postures and longer-lasting are tempers and the affections that are transient and short-lasting are something different. Again, it is unfortunate that Wesley does not give much discussion of this point. However, such an interpretation appears possible.

---

[83] Clapper, "John Wesley's Language of the Heart," 101.

[84] Outler, editor, *Works* (BE), 2:420, 2:474, 4:22.

[85] Outler, editor, *Works* (BE), 3:301, 3:422; 3:77; Wesley, 'Address to the Clergy,' *Works* (Jackson), 10:498.

[86] Wesley, 'What is Man?,' *Works* (BE), 4:22

[87] See, for example, Wesley, 'On Zeal,' *Works* (BE), 3:320.

Summarizing the First Task of this Project

As we have reached the end of this chapter, we have completed the first task of this project. That is, we have completed our quest to clarify Wesley's understanding of the features of the soul. In chapter 2, we clarified what this project means by active and passive. It was also shown that for Wesley, there is a meaning of liberty that is equivalent to the human active dimension. In chapter 3, we explored Wesley's view of the will properly speaking and contrasted it with his view of liberty. The will properly speaking is the composite of the passions and affections of the heart. This is passive and not active like liberty. "Will" may be used in a second sense that is equivalent to liberty. Such a meaning of the will is the same as free will or the power of choosing. This meaning of the will is active.

In chapter 4, we explored Wesley's view of the heart. Carlton Young describes the religion of the heart as a key element of the Methodist sensibility during Wesley's time.[88] It was shown that the heart is passive in nature. For Wesley, the will properly speaking is part of the heart. The heart includes a ruling desire, along with other tempers, dispositions, and affections. In the final section of chapter 4, we briefly considered Wesley's view of the understanding, particularly his view of reason. Reason has an active element. A person generally may regulate when and how long to use reason. The correct use of reason is possible when reason works in conjunction with the motivating spring of the heart. Practical reason involves the planning and execution of the means of grace conducive to the end of loving God and neighbor. It involves prudence, knowing how to effectively apply general rules and principles from scripture to particular circumstances. It is also involved in the operation of one's conscience.

Thus, in summary, for Wesley a person is endued with understanding, will (part of the heart), and liberty. The understanding includes the power of reason. The understanding pertains to all matters of consciousness and so must also relate to the consciousness of the will properly speaking and liberty. The will properly speaking includes one's passions and affections. It includes the feelings of inclinations/desires and other tempers of the heart. Liberty is one's active power. It is the power of choosing. It may determine such tasks as rising and sitting down, opening or closing one's eyes, the will to believe or not to believe, choosing

---

[88] Carlton Young, *Music of the Heart, John & Charles Wesley on Music and Musicians* (Carol Stream, IL: Hope Publishing Company, 1995), ix.

to follow God's commandments or rejecting them, or anything that is active in nature. It is only by grace that liberty may be used for moral matters. In reference to such moral liberty Wesley says, "I have not an absolute power over my own mind, because of the corruption of my nature, yet through the grace of God assisting me I have a power to choose and do good as well as evil. I am free to choose whom I will serve, and if I choose the better part, to continue therein even unto death."[89]

In the chapters that follow, we will embark on the next task of this project: explore more how the features of the soul relate as an agent performs right action and pursues happiness. This will involve more of a consideration of Wesley's account of true Christianity, how God has a leading role in Wesley's view of ethics, and how the Spirit works in human action. The pursuit of happiness, seeking the highest form of perfect Christian love, continues but is not the same at all points in the Christian life. For this reason, in the second task of this project, we must consider John Wesley's roadmap for the Christian life. Wesley's roadmap is the "way of salvation." This roadmap is central and indispensable for understanding Wesley's view of ethics. However, before treating Wesley's roadmap, it is helpful to first consider Wesley's understanding of the role of the Holy Spirit with respect to the human active power. We will consider this point in the next chapter.

---

[89] Wesley, 'What is Man?,' *Works* (BE), 4:24.

CHAPTER 5

FRUITFUL ACTION AND THE HOLY SPIRIT

In the last 3 chapters, we performed the first task of this project by clarifying Wesley's view of the features of the soul. For the second task of this project, we will consider more how these features relate with regard to the performance of right action and the pursuit of the highest end of ethics, which is loving God and neighbor to one's full potential. For Wesley, this second task necessarily requires a consideration of God's leading role in ethics. This is because Wesley's species of ethics is theological. The thesis of this project is that according to John Wesley, a person's pursuit of the greatest end of ethics is in fact an expression of God's gift and that the giftedness of this blessing is illuminated by a critical examination of the work of the Spirit with respect to the active and passive dimensions of a human being. Although the role of the Spirit in both passive and active dimensions will be considered in this chapter, this chapter will devote special attention to the role of the Holy Spirit in human action (the active dimension of a person). As we will show, exploring in more depth the role of the Spirit in human action illuminates the gracious nature of fruitful human action in John Wesley's heart ethics.

In order to show Wesley's view of the role of the Spirit in human action, we will take a number of steps. First, we will consider a general overview of Wesley's theology. Second, terminology will be defined. We will consider what is meant by the terms "fruitful action" and "passive operation." These terms will guide us in considering Wesley's view of the work of the Holy Spirit in ethics with regard to the active and passive dimensions of a person. Third, we will explore in more depth the work of the Spirit with respect to the active dimension of a person. This will involve an investigation of the features of Wesley's view of fruitful action and how these features are important for Wesley's ethics. Fourth, we will explore the nature of fruitful action by considering how it is consistent with Wesley's view of free-will. Next, we will consider a brief comparison of Wesley and Luther. Last, we will consider how the work of this chapter has bearing on the thesis of this project.

The Shape of Wesley's Theology

A primary focus of Wesley's theology is the love of God and neighbor. This is the "true religion"[1] of the heart and "faith [Christian faith] working by love."[2] This is the greatest end of Christian living. It is also the fulfilment of the greatest commandment of the Bible. This true religion of the heart requires the bearing of outward fruit (the performance of good action or limitedly good action), if there is time and opportunity. Without this "religion of the heart," a commitment to Christian orthodoxy—correct doctrines and opinions—falls short.[3] Indeed, Wesley speaks of this "'Christianity'; not as it implies a set of opinions, a system of doctrines, but as it refers to men's heart and lives."[4] For Wesley, a poor, uneducated, mentally-disabled person who has Christian faith working by love has a better theology than a person who is a wealthy and highly intelligent expert of Christian doctrine but who lacks Christian love.

For Wesley, having the religion of the heart is more important than whether one is Presbyterian, Moravian, Lutheran, Quaker, Methodist, Anglican, Catholic, etc.[5] In this way, Wesley's theology may be viewed as ecumenical in a Christian sense. For Wesley, it would be preferable to be

---

[1] He says "that true religion, the very essence of it, is nothing short of holy tempers" (Wesley, 'On Charity,' *Works* (BE), 3:306). In a letter in 1790, the mature Wesley says in regard to religion: "the greatest thing of all— religion. I do not mean external religion, but the religion of the heart" (Wesley, *Letters*, 8:218). Yet, this religion of the heart must involve the performance of good action lest it not have authentic love. For the point that this true religion in its highest form involves loving God and neighbor with all one's capacity, see: Outler, editor, *Works* (BE), 3:585, 4:106 and Wesley, 'The Principles of a Methodist Farther Explained,' *Works* (BE), 9:229.

[2] This is a common expression for Wesley.

[3] For an example of how Wesley cautions against having only orthodoxy of belief without the religion of the heart, see: Wesley, 'The Way to the Kingdom,' *Works* (BE), 1:220.

[4] Wesley, 'Scriptural Christianity,' *Works* (BE), 1:161.

[5] See, for example, Wesley, 'The Catholic Spirit,' *Works* (BE), 2:90.

a Calvinist with Christian faith working by love than to accept all of John Wesley's views without such love. Wesley affirms the theology of *any* human being who has Christian faith working by love and describes him or her as "a companion in the kingdom" and a "joint-heir of his [Christ's] glory."[6] Although Wesley believes that having Christian faith working by love (the religion of the heart) is more important than whether one is Presbyterian, Lutheran, Quaker, Moravian, Anglican etc, he still believes that the Church of England is preferable to the rest.

In 1777, Wesley gives a helpful overview of his theology.[7] He begins by indicating that his theology focuses on the love of God and neighbor. Consistent with this point, he gives three main sources for his theology. First, he mentions the Bible. In one context, he says, "We believe, indeed, that 'all Scripture is given by the inspiration of God;' . . . We believe the written word of God to be the only and sufficient rule both of Christian faith and practice."[8] Second, he mentions the "religion of the primitive church," and he gives a list of names that he sees as authoritative.[9] Third, he mentions the religion of the Church of England.[10] Of course, there is much overlap in all three. We will now consider in a bit more depth the last source—the religion of the Church of England.

Wesley's theology is basically orthodox Anglican. In 1777, Wesley says that he believes the Church of England to "come nearer the scriptural and primitive plan than any other national church upon earth."[11] During the beginning stage of Methodism, "orthodox" is Wesley's own self-description. In reference to the early Methodists, Wesley said: "They were all orthodox in every point; firmly believing not only the three creeds, but whatsoever they judged to be the doctrine of the Church of England, as contained in her Articles and Homilies."[12] During the remainder of his life, Wesley remains a devoted and loyal Anglican priest.[13] However,

---

[6] Wesley, 'The Catholic Spirit,' *Works* (BE), 2:90. Another example of this view is how Wesley regards the Calvinist Methodist George Whitefield. Cf. Wesley, 'On the Death of George Whitefield,' *Works* (BE), 2:331

[7] Wesley, 'On Laying the Foundation of the Chapel,' *Works* (BE), 3:585.

[8] Wesley, 'The Character of a Methodist,' *Works* (BE) 9:34.

[9] Wesley, 'On Laying the Foundation of the New Chapel,' *Works* (BE), 3:586.

[10] Wesley, 'On Laying the Foundation of the New Chapel,' *Works* (BE), 3:586.

[11] Wesley, 'On Laying the Foundation of the New Chapel,' *Works* (BE), 3:590.

[12] Wesley, 'On Laying the Foundation of the New Chapel,' *Works* (BE), 3:582.

[13] Baker, *John Wesley and the Church of England*, p. 318-320.

near the end of his life, Wesley's sympathies decline for what are perhaps some of the less-important doctrines of Anglicanism.[14]

During the later stages of his life, Wesley maintains faithfully what is basically *the core* of orthodox Anglican theology. For example, in his Sunday service sent to the American Methodists in 1784, he recommends with esteem the Nicene and Apostles' Creeds, the doctrine from the Council of Chalcedon, much of the Book of Common Prayer, and most of the Anglican Articles of Religion. From this package, it is clear that he is continuing to recommend doctrines upholding the authority of scripture for matters of salvation, the Trinity, the virgin birth, the Person of Christ (including the resurrection, Incarnation, and the atonement), the Person of the Holy Spirit, original sin, free will, baptism, the Lord's Supper, the nature of the sacraments, the doctrine of justification by faith alone, and more. Wesley maintains *at least* all of these commitments throughout the rest of his life. Apparently, trimming Anglican Articles of Religion for American Methodists is something that Wesley would not have normally performed for anyone had it not been for the extraordinary circumstances regarding the American Revolution.[15] However, what took place reflected his preferred Anglican doctrines.

Consistent with his commitment to the Bible, the primitive church, and Anglican theology, he also sees his standard sermons (*Sermons*), *Explanatory Notes Upon the New Testament* (*ENNT*), and Large Minutes of the Conference (*Minutes*) as authoritative for theology. Through the "model deed" established in 1763, Wesley prohibited the preachers of his movement from preaching any doctrine other than what is contained in his *Sermons* and *ENNT*.[16] Also, in a letter to the American Methodists in 1783, he instructed them to follow the doctrine and discipline as found in Wesley's *Sermons*, *Minutes*, and *ENNT*.[17]

Wesley's theological commitments led him to hold the doctrine of the Trinity in esteem, despite the difficulties of some Anglican theolo-

---

[14] This is evident in 1784 when he revises the Anglican Book of Common Prayer and sends this to the Methodists in North America. For more information on Wesley's preparing of the Sunday Service, see Heitzenrater, *Wesley and the People Called Methodists*, 289.

[15] Heitzenrater, *Wesley and the People Called Methodists*, 290.

[16] Wesley, 'Minutes of Several Conversations between the Rev. Mr. Wesley and others,' *Works* (Jackson), 8:331. See also Heitzernater, *Wesley and the People Called Methodists*, 213.

[17] Heitzenrater, *Wesley and the People Called Methodists*, 285.

gians of this time period regarding the doctrine of the Trinity. As Jason Vickers points out, some theologians working on the doctrine of the Trinity adopted some terms for discussion that led to conceptual confusion, and so this type of theological discourse lost some momentum.[18] However, in the practical life of the church, especially among the Methodists in some contexts, the language of the Trinity functioned well.[19] In regard to his practical doctrine of assurance, John Wesley makes the comment:

> But I know not how anyone can be a Christian believer till 'he hath' (as St. John speaks) 'the witness in himself'; till 'the Spirit of God witnesses with his spirit that he is a child of God.' —that is, in effect, till God the Holy Ghost witnesses that God the Father has accepted him through the merits of God the Son—and having this witness he honours the Son and the blessed Spirit 'even as he honours the Father'.[20]

The witness of the Spirit here is John Wesley's doctrine of assurance. It is integral to Wesley's understanding of Christian faith. This statement shows how for Wesley, Christian faith is interwoven with knowledge of the Trinity. Wesley cautions against the danger of assenting to the Trinity while forgetting and/or neglecting the true religion of the heart. Nonetheless, Wesley describes the Trinity as having "close connection with vital religion."[21] The economic Trinity is certainly discernible in Wesley's theology of love. He says in reference to those who are perfect in love: "Ye have known both the Father and the Son and the Spirit of Christ in your inmost soul."[22]

---

[18] Jason Vickers, *Invocation and Assent* (Cambridge: Eerdmans Publishing Company, 2008), 101.

[19] For example, it appeared prevalently in the hymns, sermons, and prayers of Charles Wesley. These were fairly widespread in the Methodist movement. See Vickers, *Invocation and Assent*, 171.

[20] Wesley, 'On the Trinity,' *Works* (BE), 2:385.

[21] Wesley, 'On the Trinity,' *Works* (BE), 2:376.

[22] Wesley, 'Christian Perfection,' *Works* (BE), 2:105. He also says that such people have known "the eternal Three-One God" (Wesley, 'On the Discoveries of Faith,' *Works* (BE), 4:37). Also, Wesley frequently uses Trinitarian language in his discussion of the new birth when he quotes Galatians 4:6: "'God has sent forth the Spirit of his Son into your hearts, crying, Abba, Father'" (See, for exam-

For this chapter, we will be exploring John Wesley's view of the role of the Holy Spirit in human action. Thus, one could describe what will be done here as falling under the category of pneumatology. According to orthodox theology—to which Wesley adhered—, *all* pneumatology is in fact Trinitarian. This is because, according to the creeds held by both Wesley and the Church of England, the Spirit never acts apart from the Father and the Son. This point is especially important in regard to human salvation. Due to the fall, humankind suffers from sin and death and a condition of total depravity, with a carnal nature of corrupt affections and tempers. Without God's grace, humankind is separated from God and cannot do anything right. It is for the sake of Christ's life, death, and resurrection that God the Father lovingly offers salvation to humankind through the Spirit. In every instance in which "God" or the "Spirit" is mentioned in this project we are presupposing that the Trinity is at work.

For the first task of this project, we clarified Wesley's view of the features of the soul.[23] We distinguished between active and passive dimensions, as clarified in chapter 2. It was shown that the desires, tempers, and affections of the heart and the will properly speaking pertain to the passive dimension and liberty pertains to the active dimension. As the understanding is thought to pertain to all instances of consciousness, one may infer that the understanding pertains to both active and passive dimensions. For this current chapter, we will focus on the work of the Spirit mostly with respect to the active dimension—which is different from but intimately related to the passive dimension. As we have shown in previous chapters, Wesley has a meaning of 'liberty' that is equivalent to the human active power. "Fruitful action"[24] is a subcategory of exercising one's liberty.[25] That is, liberty (understood as the power of choosing) is a broader category than fruitful action. Not all actions, exercises of one's liberty, are fruitful. An example of this is sinful action. *As we will show, when the Holy Spirit works with respect to the active dimension of a person, this and only this is fruitful action.*

---

ple, Wesley, 'On the Discoveries of Faith,' *Works* (BE), 4:36).

[23] It is "first" in the sense of order considered, not in the sense of priority.

[24] What is meant by this phrase and how it relates to Wesley will be considered more below.

[25] Virtue involves both holy tempers and correct choice flowing from these holy tempers. Yet, "fruitful action" of a child of God refers only to the active component of virtue.

Active and Passive Work of the Spirit

Our focus on the work of the Spirit leads us to Wesley's view of grace. For Wesley, grace is a relational idea that includes how the Spirit impacts a human being. Grace involves the empowering presence of the Holy Spirit. Its effects include how the Spirit impacts the forensic part of salvation (what God does for us) and also in regard to the features of the soul, including the understanding, will, and liberty (what God does in us). Wesley says:

> By 'the grace of God' is sometimes to be understood that free love, that unmerited mercy, by which I, a sinner, through the merits of Christ am now reconciled to God. But in this place it rather means that power of God the Holy Ghost which 'worketh in us both to will and to do of his good pleasure'. As soon as ever the grace of God (in the former sense, his pardoning love) is manifested to our soul, the grace of God (in the latter sense, the power of his Spirit) takes place therein. And now we can perform, through God, what to man was impossible.[26]

The effects of Christ's merits go beyond only pardoning for past sins. As the merits of Christ take effect, the Spirit of God is manifest to one's soul (including understanding, will, and liberty) in other perceivable manners, as the Holy Spirit works in a person "both to will and to do of his good pleasure."[27] Thus, for Wesley, the meaning of grace includes the empowering presence of the Holy Spirit.

Over the course of the next three chapters, as we conduct the second task of this project, we will explore how the Spirit works with regard to the features of the soul. For this purpose, we will use two terms to assist the discussion. We will use the phrase "passive operation" to refer to John Wesley's understanding of the work of the Spirit with respect to the passive dimension of a person (including the heart and the will properly speaking), and we will use the phrase "fruitful action" to refer to John Wesley's understanding of the work of the Spirit with respect to the active dimension of person (the exercise of one's liberty or the act of choosing).

---

[26] Wesley, 'The Witness of Our Own Spirit,' *Works* (BE), 1:309.
[27] This is in reference to Philippians 2:12-13. One of Wesley's key sermons on these verses is "On Working Out Our Own Salvation," sermon 85 of Outler, editor, *Sermons*, volume 3.

The phrases "passive operation" and "fruitful action" are rooted in Wesley's own language. Notice Wesley's use of the word "operations" in the following comment.

> 'By feeling, I mean, being inwardly conscious of. By the operations of the Spirit, I do not mean the manner in which he operates, but the graces which he operates in a Christian.' And again: 'We believe that love, joy, peace, are inwardly felt, or they have no being; and that men are satisfied they have grace, first by feeling these, and afterwards by their outward actions.'[28]

From these comments, it is clear that for Wesley, operations of the Spirit produce "feeling," which includes the feelings of love, joy, peace, etc. In these comments, Wesley is clearly distinguishing these feelings from "outward actions." Indeed, these feelings are passive, as clarified in chapters 2-4 of this project. It is *not* clear from Wesley's writings that he *limits* such operations of the Holy Spirit to *only* the passive dimension (the aforementioned feelings, etc.). Nevertheless, for this project, when we speak of "passive operation," we are speaking only of the passive aspect of such operations. The adjective "passive" should make this clear. "Passive operation" includes but is not limited to the Spirit's production of the feelings of desires, tempers, and affections of the heart. It also includes the Spirit's giving of conscience and anything else that is done passively with respect to a person.

The phrase "fruitful action" is directly inspired by Wesley's own language. Fruitful action is action that brings forth "fruits meet for repentance."[29] It is possible only by grace. For Wesley, this concept is inspired by Isaiah 1:16-17, Matthew 3:8, and Luke 3:9.[30] Consider the following comments from *The Principles of a Methodist Farther Explained*. Wesley says that he means "by 'fruits meet for repentance,' forgiving our brother, ceasing from evil, doing good, using the ordinances of God, and in gen-

---

[28] These comments are a direct quote from Wesley's letter to Dr. Rutherforth (*Works* (Jackson) 14:355). This quote includes pasted comments from Wesley's earlier work *A Farther Appeal to Men of Reason and Religion* and also comments from a letter to the Rev. Mr. Downes. See Jackson, editor, *The Works of Wesley*, 8:78 and 9:104. In the second sentence of the above quote, Wesley is distinguishing between the operations of the Spirit that are beyond human understanding versus the operations of the Spirit that are perceivable by a person.

[29] Wesley, 'The Scripture Way of Salvation,' *Works* (BE), 2:162.

[30] Wesley, 'The Scripture Way of Salvation,' *Works* (BE), 2:163; Wesley, 'Letter to the Rev. Dr. Horne,' *Works* (Jackson), 9:111.

eral, obeying him according to the measure of grace which we have received."[31] Notice that fruitful action is active, as clarified in chapter 2 of this project. Notice also that "ceasing from evil, doing good, using the ordinances of God" are the same as following Wesley's *General Rules*.[32] Also, Wesley says here that fruitful action refers to "in general, obeying him according to the measure of grace which we have received." Presumably, this refers to obeying all the moral commandments of scripture as much as possible and using the means of grace as much as possible.[33] Therefore, in summary, fruitful action refers to doing all of the following as much as possible (when there is time and opportunity): follow the *General Rules*, obey all moral commandments of scriptures, and practice any other remaining means of grace. Andrew Thompson and Henry Knight show that Wesley's view of the means of grace refers to a wide range of activities.[34] For Wesley, fruitful action is any morally preferable action. It is exercising one's liberty, one's power of choosing, to do what is right.

Wesley makes further clarifications regarding fruitful action. He says explicitly in regard to fruits meet for repentance before the new birth: "'These I cannot as yet term good works, because they do not spring from faith and the love of God.' Although the same works are then good, when they are performed by 'those who have believed.'"[35] In this sense, fruitful action has two types. The first type is fruitful action that is performed *before* the new birth and justification. This is not good works (or good action) properly speaking. However, as we shall show in the next chapter, such action is good in a limited sense. The second type of fruitful action is right action that is performed *after* the new birth. Wesley clearly identifies this second type.[36] This is virtue properly speaking.[37] It

[31] Jackson, editor, *The Works of Wesley*, 8:428. C.F. 8:47, 8:288 and 9:111.

[32] Wesley, 'The Nature, Design, and General Rules of the United Societies,' *Works* (BE), 9:69 - 73.

[33] For an example of how Wesley links "fruits meets for repentance" with some specific examples of means of grace, see: Wesley, 'The Scripture Way of Salvation,' *Works* (BE), 2:166.

[34] Andrew Thompson, *John Wesley and the Means of Grace: Historical and Theological Context* (Ph.D. Diss., Duke University, 2012), 138; Henry Knight, *The Presence of God in the Christian Life: John Wesley and the Means of Grace* (Metuchen, NJ: Scarecrow Press, 1992), 3.

[35] Wesley, 'The Principles of a Methodist Farther Explained,' *Works* (BE), 9:176. There are quotes within quotes because Wesley is quoting himself.

[36] For Wesley's discussion of fruitful actions after the new birth, see Wesley,

is action that flows from a loving heart. This includes good works (or good action) properly speaking. Wesley consistently maintains this point after 1738,[38] and it allows him to remain consistent with article 13 of the Articles of Religion of the Church of England, "Of Works Done Before Justification."[39]

For Wesley, it seems that even if one is not yet justified or born of God, and even if one cannot yet do good works properly speaking, one is always by grace capable of "doing good." In other words, there is a distinction between "good works" and "doing good." The former refers to the action in itself and the latter refers to the effects of an action. That is, Wesley makes a distinction for how some actions are not "good in themselves" on the one hand but are still "good and profitable to men" on the other hand.[40] All people can by grace do good, but only those who are born of God can do "good works," actions that are good in themselves. Good works are both good in themselves and have positive effects. For those who are not yet justified and born of God, only the latter applies to doing good. For this reason, one who is not yet justified cannot do good works but can "do good," as stated in the *General Rules*.[41] This point will be discussed more in chapters 6 and 8. In either case, whether before the new birth or after, the action that is performed is fruitful action.

'The Scripture Way of Salvation,' *Works* (BE), 2:166.

[37] See Wesley, 'An Israelite Indeed,' *Works* (BE), 3:280 and the relevant footnotes from chapter 1 of this project.

[38] See the appendix entitled, "Consistency in Wesley's Thought."

[39] Wesley, 'A Farther Appeal to Men of Reason and Religion,' *Works* (BE), 11:113. The distinction between good works properly speaking and action that is good in a limited sense helps Wesley avoid a contradiction regarding his use of scripture (Wesley, 'Some Remarks on Mr. Hill's "Farrago Double-Distilled",' *Works* (BE), 13:509 and 10:523). In his sermon "Justification by Faith" Wesley focuses on Romans 4:5, which he translates: "To him that worketh not, but believeth on him that justifieth the ungodly, his faith is counted to him for righteousness (Wesley, 'Justification by Faith,' *Works* (BE), 1:182)." Here one "worketh not" in the sense that one is not capable of performing any good works "strictly speaking" (Wesley, 'Justification By Faith,' *Works* (BE), 1:192). In other words, one who "worketh not" is one who still should perform fruitful action (the first type mentioned above) as much as possible, if there is time and opportunity.

[40] Wesley, 'Justification By Faith,' *Works* (BE), 1:192.

[41] We know that it was in fact Wesley's expectation for those who are not yet justified to follow the *General Rules*.

These concepts of passive operation and fruitful action are crucial for Wesley's theology and view of ethics. The concepts that these terms represent are that which Wesley clearly recognizes, frequently uses, and highly values.[42] A consideration of the pneumatological dimensions of passive operation and fruitful action will help to clarify Wesley's "way of salvation," his practical roadmap for Christian living. We will show how it helps to distinguish the roads from the landmarks so to speak.

There is difference between passive operation and fruitful action on the one hand and the two types of spiritual growth mentioned in chapter 2 on the other hand. Each of these two types of spiritual growth have elements of both fruitful action and passive operation. At the same time, the type of spiritual growth comparable to the fit woman described in chapter 2 has a larger degree of fruitful action and the type of spiritual growth analogous to the flaming dart typically has more noticeable effects of passive operation. The illustrations in chapter 2 concerning the two types of spiritual growth should help make this clear.

As we will show, the concepts of active and passive provide clarity that helps to underscore the thesis of this project. To restate this thesis: for Wesley, the active pursuit of the highest end of Christian living is an expression of God's gift and the giftedness of this blessing is illuminated by a critical examination of the work of the Spirit with respect to the active and passive dimensions of a human being. This important emphasis in Wesley's practical thought is often misinterpreted or missed altogether when Wesley's view of passive operation and fruitful action are confused, improperly mixed together, misunderstood, and/or overlooked.

Key Features of Fruitful Action

For Wesley, in order for a human action to be a fruitful action, it must involve the work of the Holy Spirit.[43] Fruitful action is always the effect of God's grace. For this project, fruitful action is defined so as to describe the largest category regarding Wesley's view of any action that has posi-

---

[42] Wesley does not use the words "passive operation" often but he uses the concept often. One may handle a concept without using specific words.

[43] For two of Wesley's most extensive discussions of the co-working nature of God and person, see: Wesley, 'Predestination Calmly Considered,' *Works* (BE), 13:288, and Wesley, 'On Working Out Our Own Salvation,' *Works* (BE), 3:199.

tive moral value.⁴⁴ It refers to all such actions that have a positive moral value. Fruitful actions include all righteous actions and all good actions. Any human action that is not fruitful must either be sinful or neutral in nature.

It is evident from Wesley's writings that his view of fruitful action includes the following important features: (1) it may occur only in response to the motivational force of affections⁴⁵ of the heart that have received the transforming work of the Holy Spirit alone (passive operation) in some way during a previous occasion, (2) human effort *alone*—even in response to the work of the Spirit on the heart — is *not* enough for fruitful action to occur, and (3) the Holy Spirit and the person always act simultaneously from the beginning of a fruitful action until the end.

Consider now the first feature of Wesley's view of fruitful action: it may occur only in response to the motivational force of affections that have received the transforming work of the Holy Spirit alone (passive operation) in some way during a previous occasion. That is, although fruitful action itself is completely distinct from the passive operation of the Spirit, it may only occur only in response to the effects of passive operation of the Spirit. This view is apparent in many of Wesley's theological discussions, including his discussion of Phil 2:12-13 in his sermon, "On Working Out Our own Salvation." Here Wesley says, "God worketh in you; therefore you can work—otherwise it would be impossible."⁴⁶ He is also clear that for people who are not yet born of God, any fruitful action must be preceded by and flow from the spiritually affected desires produced by prevenient grace and repentance.⁴⁷ For those already born of God, such fruitful action must be preceded by and flow from the transformed heart of the new birth.

The Holy Spirit's previous work alone on the affections is an important precondition for there to be any fruitful action in part because of the motivational impact that this work provides. For Wesley, the affections of the heart are different from human action but are intimately related to it. Unlike the view of absolute predestination (or necessitar-

---

⁴⁴ Please see the discussion of fruitful action above.

⁴⁵ It is assumed here that affections include tempers. Please see the diagram of the heart from chapter 4.

⁴⁶ Wesley, 'On Working Out Our Own Salvation,' *Works* (BE), 3:206.

⁴⁷ Jackson, editor, *The Works of Wesley*, 8:428. C.F. Jackson, editor, *The Works of Wesley*, 8:47, 8:288 and 9:111. See also chapter 6 for an account of how Wesley understands prevenient grace to affect the desires of every person.

ianism), for Wesley, affections do not necessitate a particular human action. However, they do provide motivational impact. This is to say that the affections of the heart make certain actions easier or more difficult. As observed in chapter 4, an enduring inclination (a temper or kind of affection) makes doing a certain action easier by bringing pleasure to a person who completes the suggested action. Such an inclination makes doing a contrary certain action more difficult by bringing uneasiness or pain to the person who completes this action. This is how the person's perception of holy affections is different from but intimately related to fruitful action. This helps to show why the heart is a key to Wesley's view of ethics and a centrepiece for Wesley's view of "true religion." For Wesley, without the prior perception of Spirit-empowered affections of the heart (passive operation), the performance of fruitful works is impossible.

A second feature of fruitful action is as follows: human effort alone[48]—even in response to the work of the Spirit on the heart— is not enough for a fruitful action to occur. Wesley believes "all power to think, speak, or act right is in and from the Spirit of Christ."[49] If one's right action is "in" Christ, then it seems that it is not being performed alone. Wesley speaks of one's "utter inability to do all good unless he [God] 'water thee every moment.'"[50] From this, it is clear that fruitful action cannot exist without uninterrupted watering of the Spirit. This second feature of fruitful action refers even to people who have not gone through the heart-changing effects of the new birth and perfection. Although such people cannot perform good works properly speaking, they are still able to "do good" because the Spirit is "watering thee every moment."[51]

The second feature of fruitful action also applies to those who have received either the new birth or perfection. Suppose that one were to try to argue that a Christian could in fact do fruitful action alone. According to such an argument, God transforms the tempers of the heart at the

---

[48] The meaning of "alone" here is somewhat contextual. By "alone," I mean that during the moment of an act, the action is a purely human action. It is possible to imagine that a purely human action may occur even after God transforms the heart and makes it holy. As we will show, Wesley rejects this model.

[49] Wesley, 'On the Death of George Whitefield,' *Works* (BE), 2:342.

[50] Wesley, 'Sermon on the Mount, XIII,' *Works* (BE), 1:696.

[51] See the discussion above concerning the distinction between good works and doing good.

new birth, and a person is then able to respond by acting alone in the performance of good works. This in fact is a version of semi-Pelagianism. Wesley is clearly not a semi-Pelagian in this sense, and it is also evident that he would reject that a human (even one who is born of God and perfected) is ever capable of doing fruitful action alone in this sense. That Wesley believes a person who is born of God is never capable of doing a fruitful action alone is evident from the following comment. Wesley speaks of "our helplessness, of our inability to think one good thought, or to form one good desire; and much more to speak one word aright, or to perform one good action but through his free, almighty grace, first preventing us, and then accompanying us every moment."[52] Notice here the phrase "accompanying us every moment." It is not enough for the Holy Spirit only to "prevent" or work on the heart before a person acts. The semi-Pelagians claim this point. For Wesley, *in order for a fruitful action to take place*, the Holy Spirit must both act before the action by means of touching the heart (passive operation) *and* accompany *during* the entire action.

This point leads to the third feature of fruitful action: the Holy Spirit and the person act simultaneously from the beginning of the act until the end. Wesley says, "Whatsoever good is in man, or is done by man, God is the author and doer of it."[53] If God is the doer of a fruitful act done by man, there does not seem to be any opportunity for this act to be done by the human alone. God and the human must be acting during the entire time. Wesley also says "no good is done, or spoken, or thought by any man without the assistance of God, working together in and with those that believe in him."[54] Here, Wesley uses the phrase "working together in and with." During a fruitful action, God is "working together in and with" the human. Each one is never alone during a fruitful action. Human action and God's action are simultaneous during the entire fruitful act. In his sermon "On Working Out Your Own Salvation," Wesley says that God does the work of "preventing, accompanying, and following."[55] Consider here the phrase "accompanying." This underscores the simultaneousness of the active partnership between God and the person during the fruitful act.

---

[52] Wesley, 'The Scripture Way of Salvation,' *Works* (BE), 2:166.
[53] Wesley, 'Free Grace,' *Works* (BE), 3:545.
[54] Wesley, 'Of Evil Angels,' *Works* (BE), 3:24.
[55] Wesley, 'On Working Out Your Own Salvation, *Works* (BE), 3:209.

Wesley says that God will "'prevent them that believe in all their doings, and further them with his continual help', so that all their designs, conversations, and actions are 'begun, continued, and ended in him.'"[56] The important phrase here is "continual help." This "continual help" implies that there is never a moment when the human acts alone in a fruitful act; God's active role is continuous and unbroken. An emphasis on God's involvement during the entire time frame of the fruitful act is evident from the phrase "begun, continued, and ended." In other words, there is no taking turns when it comes to a fruitful act. During the entire time frame of a fruitful action, from the beginning until the end, God is acting and the person is acting simultaneously.[57]

Given the co-working nature of fruitful action, involving both the agency of God and the person, it is helpful to now consider the question of how Wesley can hold such a view of fruitful action while also rejecting absolute predestination. If God is involved in all fruitful action, how is such action not a matter of necessity?

Fruitful Action and Free Will

One could raise an objection to Wesley's view of fruitful action by asking how such a view may be consistent with Wesley's doctrine of free will. In other words, how can the claim that God is the doer of human fruitful action avoid the consequence of absolute predestination? Could it be that Wesley is contradicting himself?

Perhaps there are multiple ways of showing how absolute predestination (or necessitarianism) is not a necessary consequence of Wesley's view of fruitful human action. One possible solution could draw on an analogy of mules used by a contemporary philosopher in his analysis of the view of John Duns Scotus on human causation.[58] However, what will be offered here is just to claim that if Wesley's two views (the co-working nature of fruitful action and the doctrine of free will) are capable of existing in harmony, an explanation of this harmony is in some ways beyond human understanding. Throughout history and even in the scientific

---

[56] Wesley, 'The Repentance of Believers,' *Works* (BE), 1:349.
[57] See also: 'Wesley, Sermon on the Mount, XIII,' *Works* (BE), 1:696.
[58] William Frank, "Duns Scotus on Autonomous Freedom and Divine Co-Causality," Medieval Philosophy and Theology, 2, (1992). As shown in chapter 3, most interpreters of Scotus offer that Scotus is a libertarian, a proponent of free will.

world today, intellectuals believe that it is logical that some things exist while at the same, these same things are not capable of having an explanation. These phenomena must have some mystery. In such a universe, the mysterious nature of co-working fruitful action and free will existing together is one example among many cases of mystery. Claiming mystery is not in every case simply a retreat from a mistake, a sign of inconsistency or the failure to solve a solvable problem. Claiming mystery is sometimes the best and only logical move. As it stands, Jerry Walls claims that Wesley's view of freedom is "widely shared."[59] See Diagram 5.1 for an illustration of how Wesley's view of fruitful action contrasts with his understanding of a necessitarian view.

Although Wesley would argue that his view of free will is superior to the view of absolute predestination, he would admit it is difficult to explain free will fully. The subject of free will v. absolute predestination is one that has been fiercely debated by leading intellectuals for centuries. Even for those who adhere strongly to one side, mystery is often acknowledged. Wesley describes his discussion of this subject as a "clumsy way of cutting the knot which we are not able to untie."[60] Yet, taking the side of free will is not arbitrary for Wesley, but is of high importance since he believes the character of God as love (something that is offered to all people) is at stake.[61] Even as he acknowledges limitations to his view of free will, Wesley would admit that his view of free will is different from some in the Reformed tradition. One example of someone with a different view is Martin Luther.

Wesley versus Luther

An exhaustive comparison of Wesley and Luther regarding grace and action is far beyond the scope of this project. Nevertheless, a moment will be taken to highlight some key differences. We will first contrast Luther

---

[59] Jerry Walls, "Wesley on Predestination and Election" in *The Oxford Handbook of Methodist Studies*, ed. William Abraham and James Kirby (Oxford: Oxford University Press, 2009), 625.

[60] Wesley, 'The General Spread of the Gospel,' *Works* (BE), 2:489.

[61] For Wesley, if there is no free will, then some people are destined for hell, regardless of their effort. For Wesley, this undermines the character of God as loving. If God is love as the Bible says, then God would not allow for the creation of human beings who are destined to hell from their birth. See for example, Jackson, editor, *The Works of Wesley*, 10:227 and 10:473.

with Erasmus. This will prepare for a clearer comparison of Wesley and Luther.

During the sixteenth century, Luther debated Erasmus on the subject of free will. Erasmus defended free will and sided closer with the teachings of the Catholic church while Luther opposed free will and defended a view more compatible with his own version of the doctrine of justification by faith, which served as a foundational doctrine of the Reformation. In one regard, Erasmus' concern with Luther's doctrine of grace was similar to Wesley's concern with the doctrine of predestination held by the Calvinists of his time. Erasmus says,

> Those who deny any freedom of the will and affirm absolute necessity, admit that God works in man not only the good works, but also evil ones. It seems to follow that inasmuch as man can never be the author of good works, he can never be called the author of evil ones. This opinion seems obviously to attribute cruelty and injustice to God, something religious ears abhor vehemently.[62]

During the sixteenth century, arguments of philosophical necessity had not reached the same level of sophistication that they would reach in the eighteenth century. Nonetheless, Erasmus believed that Luther's theology showed that there is only one possible trajectory of history. According to Erasmus' reading of Luther, whatever sin occurs is unavoidable, and whatever good occurs is unavoidable. Thus, as we observe in the above quote, the result for Erasmus is that Luther's theology makes God to be the author of evil and therefore contrary to what the scriptures teaches about a loving and just God.

For Erasmus, multiple trajectories of history are possible. Each person has the power to choose salvation or reject it so that either path is an option.[63] In addition to this point, Erasmus goes a step further in his difference from Luther. For Erasmus, there is a greater role in salvation for the active power of the soul. In this way, Erasmus view of free will is more closely suitable to the theology of the Catholic church. For salvation to occur, a person must "continue and not withdraw from divine

---

[62] Erasmus, Desiderius, 'The Free Will,' *Erasmus and Luther, Discourse on Free Will*, (New York: Continuum, 2007), 75.

[63] Erasmus, 'The Free Will,' 17.

grace."⁶⁴ Erasmus would not want to claim a form of Pelagianism that gives all merit to human works but hopes that his view of free will "ascribes total salvation to divine grace."⁶⁵ At the same time, he speaks of two causes in the same work, grace as the principal cause and a person's will as the secondary cause.⁶⁶ He makes it clear that he believes that it is grace that makes free will possible in the first place and that grace is necessary for the completion of salvation. He also describes the role of the will as the middle part of a three-step process, with grace alone being applied at the beginning and end, the first and third steps.⁶⁷

Luther, on the other hand, rejects Erasmus' position on free will and holds that it is not possible to argue for free will while also claiming that God deserves full merit and glory for human salvation. For Luther, there is only one cause of salvation, and it is God. He is different from Erasmus in that Luther would deny any role (no matter how small) of willing in human salvation. Luther says in his commentary on Galatians 4:7:

> Whoever is a son must be an heir as well. For merely by being born he deserves to be an heir. No work and no merit brings him the inheritance, but only his birth. Thus he obtains the inheritance in a purely passive, not in an active way; that is, just his being born, not his producing or working or worrying, makes him an heir. He does not do anything toward his being born but merely lets it happen. Therefore we come to these eternal goods—the forgiveness of sins, righteousness, the glory of the resurrection, and eternal life—not actively but passively. Nothing whatever interferes here; faith alone takes hold of the offered promise.⁶⁸

Luther is saying that one receives the inheritance of eternal goods: forgiveness of sins, righteousness, etc. in a way that is purely passive. For Luther's view of the forgiveness of sins and spiritual inheritance, Eras-

---

[64] Ibid., 73.
[65] Ibid., ix and 73.
[66] Ibid., 73.
[67] Ibid., 73.
[68] Martin Luther, 'Lectures on Galatians,' *Luther's Works on C.D. Rom, American Edition*. Editors Jaroslav Pelikan and Helmut T. Lehmann (Fortress Press and Concordia Publishing House, 2004), volume 26, comments on Galatians 4.

mus' view of two causes does not hold. God alone is the author of it without human cause.

How does Luther then differ from Wesley? Consider first Erasmus and Wesley. One could argue that in comparison to Erasmus, Wesley sees a greater role for grace in the active power of the soul. For Wesley, unlike Erasmus, there is not a three step process in the same sense. This is because God never, at any degree, withdraws from what is going on. God is the full doer of fruitful action, not a partial doer of it. God is not only assisting the fruitful act of the will, God is performing the full act of the will itself. Again, he says, "Whatsoever good is in man, or is done by man, God is the author and doer of it."[69] In this way, for Wesley, God is fully deserving of merit and glory, in all ways, at all times, in all contexts.

Luther might respond to Wesley by saying that such an argument has internal conflicts. If God is the full doer of any fruitful action of the will, then how can one resist God? This view does not seem to leave room for the possibility of different trajectories of history. In other words, Luther might argue, it is not logically possible to have free will on the one hand and God being the full doer of fruitful action on the other hand. Therefore, for Luther, Wesley's view has an internal conflict. Wesley might reply that the way to reconcile the two points is beyond human understanding. The author of this project is not taking sides but simply highlighting differences.

With respect to their theology of action, Wesley and Luther have some points of agreement. Like Wesley, Luther speaks of an expectation of good works flowing from grace after justification. Mirsolav Volf describes Luther's view of these good works as follows: "We are not simply the final destinations in the flow of God's gifts. Rather, we find ourselves midstream, so to speak. The gifts flow unto us, and they flow on from us. From Christ, gifts flow to us, each one of us; and from us, they flow to those in need."[70] Volf highlights Luther's image of the conduit. People are conduits or channels of God's gifts to others.[71] In this way, Wesley and Luther share the idea of how God first transforms a person and how from this transformation, God's grace flows forth in the good working of the transformed person. Even with this point of agreement, Wesley

---

[69] Wesley, 'Free Grace,' *Works* (BE), 3:545.
[70] Miroslav Volf, *Free of Charge* (Grand Rapids, Michigan: Zondervan, 2005), 50.
[71] Ibid.

and Luther do not see works after justification in exactly the same way. As we will show in the upcoming chapters, Wesley emphasizes that a justified person can backslide and lose justification if good works are not carefully practiced and maintained. For Wesley, unlike Luther, the choice to continue doing good works properly speaking and being a Christian is under the control of one's free will.

As we will explore in more depth in the next chapter, Wesley accepts the doctrine of justification by faith alone. He even shares with Luther some core elements of a doctrine of imputed righteousness. Wesley describes his own view of imputed righteousness as the sense that "all believers are forgiven and accepted, not for the sake of anything in them, or of anything that ever was, that is, or ever can be done by them, but wholly and solely for the sake of what Christ had done and suffered for them."[72] He sees this view as not being shared by the Roman Catholic church.[73] As we will explore, Wesley is concerned with emphasizing how imputed righteousness is not a free pass to sin or live an apathic life.

Further Analysis

Over the course of this chapter, we showed Wesley's view of the role of the Spirit in human action. In order to do this, we took a number of steps. First, we considered a general overview of Wesley's theology. Wesley is committed to the teachings of the Bible, teachings of the primitive church, and the doctrines of what is basically orthodox Anglicanism. Most importantly, for him, theology is not possible without a "true religion" of the heart, a religion that requires the bearing of outward fruit if there is time and opportunity. This consideration of the shape of Wesley's theology helps to provide context for exploring the role of the Holy Spirit in regard to Wesley's view of ethics, particularly in regard to human action. Later, terminology was defined. We considered what is meant by the terms "passive operation" and "fruitful action." Passive operation is the work of the Holy Spirit with respect to the passive dimension of a person, and fruitful action is the work of the Holy Spirit with respect to the active dimension of a person. After this, we explored the various features of fruitful action. It was shown how Wesley's use of these features is evident from a consideration of his writings and his treatment of scripture. Next, we explored the nature of fruitful action

---

[72] Wesley, 'The Lord Our Righteousness,' *Works* (BE), 1:455.
[73] Wesley, 'The Lord Our Righteousness,' *Works* (BE), 1:460.

by considering how it is consistent with Wesley's view of free-will. Last, we compared some of Wesley's views with Luther. Now we will begin to consider some of the practical implications of the discussion.

Our discussion of Wesley's understanding of the role of the Spirit with respect to the active dimension is significant for several reasons. First, it is helpful to the extent that it protects against a common misunderstanding that in the thought of John Wesley, there are moments when a human acts alone in the performance of fruitful action. Wesley's view of salvation is not a dynamic interplay of God acting alone and the human responding alone. The Holy Spirit plays a role in all positive transformations of the heart (passive operation) as well as in all fruitful action that a person does. There is never a moment of fruitful action in which a human acts alone.

Second, this discussion is significant for how one is to view the glory of God. The view that a human may do fruitful action alone diminishes the glory of God. One could argue that it is impossible for God to have the whole glory if at any point after God alone begins the work of human salvation, a person may do fruitful work alone in response. Since for Wesley, there is never a moment when a human may do a fruitful action without the simultaneous assistance of the Spirit, it is easier for him to make an argument that God deserves the whole glory. For Wesley, the character of a divine human-interaction where God first acts alone and afterwards the person acts simultaneously with the Spirit to perform an active response represents a model that is sufficient for God deserving the whole glory.[74] Whether one may direct a criticism against this point or not, it is clear in Wesley's own mind. To the degree that the clarification in this chapter protects against a misreading of Wesley that holds that a person may at times do fruitful work alone, the argument of this chapter underscores the importance of the glory of God for Wesley and offers insight for the practical benefit of any follower of Christ.

Fruitful action is distinct from passive operation and yet, as we have shown it is intimately related to it. Passive operation concerns the work of the Spirit on the human heart, which is a central focus for John Wes-

---

[74] To see an example of Wesley's portrayal of this principle, please see his comments on Phillipians 2:13: Wesley, *On Working Out Our Own Salvation*, 3:202. Note also, that for Wesley, one may understand God to deserve the whole glory for human salvation in this way without needing to presuppose absolute predestination. See for example paragraph 46 and 47 of Wesley, 'Predestination Calmly Considered,' *Works* (BE), 13:288.

ley's view of ethics. The love of God shed abroad in the heart is the premier condition of the Christian life and is the only source of virtuous action, but the Spirit can work in human action before such love is given. As shown above, fruitful action also applies to actions before both justification and the new birth. These actions flow from a spiritually-affected heart of a lower magnitude. In each instance of fruitful action (before or after the new birth), God acts before the act (in the form of passive operation on the desires and affections of the heart) and during the act. Our work in previous chapters that clarifies what is meant by active and passive and what is meant by the features of the soul positions us now to see this point vividly. Because of what the Trinitarian God has done through Christ's life, death, and resurrection, and through the restoring work of the Spirit in salvation in both active and passive dimensions of a person, Wesley can claim that God deserves the whole glory for each fruitful action, and it also for this reason, the theme of gift emerges mightily in the center of view. The performance of fruitful action and the pursuit of the highest end of Christian living *is itself* an expression of God's gift. For Wesley, free will and choice are not opponents to grace, as some interpreters of theology worry. When used for fruitful action, the act of choosing is the *embodiment* of God's gift.

Chapter 6

From Sin to New Birth

For the next two chapters, we will consider Wesley's ethics for each stage along the way of salvation, his roadmap for the Christian life. For each stage, we will consider how right action, i.e. fruitful action, is performed (or not performed) and how the highest end is pursued. It will be argued that regardless of the stage, according to the view of John Wesley, a person's pursuit of the greatest end of ethics is an expression of God's gift and that the giftedness of this blessing is illuminated by a critical examination of the work of the Spirit with respect to the active and passive dimensions of a human being.

The approach taken here will continue to regard God's foundational role in ethics. This will require a consideration of the work of God in both active and passive dimensions of the soul. For Wesley, "the way of salvation" is a phrase that describes the entire path on which God initiates and assists one's growth in holiness of heart and life. Please see diagram 6.1 for a portrayal of Wesley's way of salvation. The way of salvation is composed of a progression of stages, often moving sequentially in time in this order: servant of God, newborn child, perfected child, and inhabitant of heaven. For this chapter, we will start off by considering Wesley's view of an "impenitent sinner," a stage prior to salvation. After this, we will begin exploring the early stages of Wesley's way of salvation, including the servant of God and the child of the new birth.

The Impenitent Sinner

For John Wesley, the least preferable stage of human existence during life on earth is being an "impenitent sinner."[1] In regard to impenitent sinners, Wesley says: "I entirely agree that hell was designed only for stubborn, impenitent sinners."[2] In general, an impenitent sinner refers to

---

[1] Examples of Wesley's discussions of "impenitent sinners" include: Wesley, '*Of Hell,*' *Works* (BE), 3:43; Wesley, *Letters*, 2:133.

those who fully resist the grace that God has given in order to grow in salvation. This person does not have the faith of either a servant of God or child of God. He or she does not at the minimum fear God and work righteousness.

Many—if not all—people are impenitent sinners at some period in their life. For Wesley, this stage even refers to some of those people who have already been baptized. Wesley indicates that many people who are baptized, either as infants or later in life, lose some of the effects of their baptism. He says "Lean no more on the staff of that broken reed, that ye were born again in baptism. Who denies that ye were then made 'children of God, and heirs of the kingdom of heaven'? But notwithstanding this, ye are now children of the devil; therefore ye must be born again."[3]

The Image of God

In order to explore Wesley's view of an impenitent sinner, it is helpful to first consider Wesley's view of the image of God. Wesley teaches that before the fall, humankind possessed the image of God. This image of God includes three components: the natural, moral, and political image. The natural image means that each person has a human spirit. For Wesley, the essence of a spirit is being endued with understanding, will, and liberty.[4] Thus, Wesley links the natural image of God with understanding, will, and liberty.[5] The moral image means that a person has righteousness and holiness.[6] The political image means that humankind is given the power to govern the planet, including the animals that inhabit it.[7]

---

[2] Wesley, *Letters*, 2:133.

[3] Wesley, 'The Marks of the New Birth Works,' *Works* (BE), 1:430.

[4] See, for example, Wesley, 'On Attending the Church Service,' *Works* (BE), 3:474 and Wesley, 'Thoughts Upon Necessity,' *Works* (BE), 13:539. In one instance, Wesley lists "freedom of the will" in place of liberty (Wesley, 'The New Birth,' *Works* (BE), 2:188). Please see chapter 3 for an account of the equivalence between liberty and free will in Wesley's thought.

[5] See, for example, Wesley, 'The End of Christ's Coming,' *Works* (BE), 2:474-475.

[6] Wesley, 'The End of Christ's Coming,' *Works* (BE), 2:475.

[7] Wesley, 'The New Birth,' *Works* (BE), 2:188.

Wesley teaches that owing to the fall, there is death and that humankind faces the "entire corruption of our nature."[8] For all humankind after the fall—including impenitent sinners, the moral image (righteousness and holiness) is fully lost and the natural image is partly lost.[9] Wesley indicates that after the fall, God provides for all people (including impenitent sinners) the part of the natural image that corresponds to having a spiritual nature—a nature that is still endued with understanding, will, and liberty.[10]

Prevenient Grace

Wesley holds to the doctrines of original sin and total depravity, which mean that it is impossible for any person after the fall to have a holy heart or to perform any level of right action by his or her own natural power.[11] But after the fall, no person suffers a purely natural[12] state, a condition of inescapable corruption. Wesley says, "For allowing that all the souls of men are dead in sin by *nature*, this excuses none, seeing there is no man that is in a state of mere nature; there is no man, unless he has quenched the Spirit, that is wholly void of the grace of God."[13] By His free grace, God gives to all people after the fall certain spiritual gifts that help to direct them towards God and the highest goal of Christian living. Such gifts are the effect of what Wesley calls "prevenient grace."[14] This prevenient grace takes effect because of Christ's atonement.[15] It is only because of prevenient grace that all people after the fall—including impenitent sinners—continue to possess part of the natural image of God that is free of total corruption.[16]

[8] Wesley, 'The New Birth,' *Works* (BE), 2:190.
[9] Wesley, 'On the Fall of Man,' *Works* (BE), 2:410.
[10] Wesley, 'Heavenly Treasure in Earthen Vessels,' *Works* (BE), 4:163.
[11] See, for example, his sermon *Original Sin* (Wesley, 'Original Sin,' *Works* (BE), volume 2) and his treatise *The Doctrine of Original Sin* (Wesley, 'The Doctrine of Original Sin,' *Works* (BE), volume 12).
[12] The word "natural" here does not refer to the image of God but to the totally-depraved state of humankind that must manifest if there is no assisting grace.
[13] Wesley, 'On Working Out Our Own Salvation,' *Works* (BE), 3:207.
[14] See, for example, 'On Working Out Our Own Salvation,' *Works* (BE), 3:207 and Wesley, *Letters*, 6:239.
[15] See, for example, Wesley's comments on Romans 5:18. Wesley, *Letters*, 6:239.

Wesley bases the doctrine of prevenient grace on his interpretation of John 1:9 that says the following in reference to Christ: "This was the true light, who lighteth every man that cometh into the world."[17] For Wesley, some of the effects of prevenient grace include the passive operations of the Spirit.[18] The passive nature of such occasions of prevenient grace is evident from the following comment explicitly in reference to prevenient grace: "Every man has a greater or less measure of this, which *waiteth not for the call of man*."[19]

For Wesley, such passive operations of prevenient grace include the giving of "conscience," the slight touching of the desires of one's heart, and at times the giving of a slight conviction of having done wrong.[20] Prevenient grace also allows a person to use his or her active power in a manner that is free from the necessity of sin. That is, because of prevenient grace, all people have a power of liberty, which is a power of free will.[21] Without this prevenient grace, due to total depravity, all people would be necessitated to act only according to sin. It is because of this liberty, enabled by prevenient grace, that an impenitent sinner is capable of performing at some level fruitful actions, including actions that are good in *a limited sense*.[22]

---

[16] In regard to how prevenient grace affects the natural image (understanding, will, and liberty): God's giving of conscience relates to the understanding; God's touching on the desires relates to the will properly speaking; furthermore, God provides the power of liberty. This will be explored more below.

[17] This is the English translation of John 1:9, as it appears in Wesley's 1788 *ENNT*. Places where Wesley associates this verse with prevenient grace include but are not limited to: Wesley, 'On Working Out Our Own Salvation,' *Works* (BE), 3:207 and Wesley, 'Predestination Calmly Considered,' *Works* (BE), 13:288.

[18] For more of a discussion of the passive operations of the Spirit, see chapter 5 of this project.

[19] Wesley, 'On Working Out Our Own Salvation,' *Works* (BE), 3:207. Italics are added by me.

[20] This point will be explored more below.

[21] Wesley, 'Free Grace,' *Works* (BE), 3:560; *Works* (Jackson), 10:392 and 10:229. For an account of the equivalence of liberty and free will in Wesley's thought, see chapter 3.

[22] Wesley makes it clear that all human beings have liberty, and thus all human beings—even impenitent sinners— are capable of action that is in *a limited sense* good (Outler, editor, *Works* (BE), 4:163 and 1:192). Below, it will be shown how this action that is limitedly good contrasts with good action strictly speaking.

Every person is given the gift of conscience.[23] Wesley defines conscience as follows:

> Conscience, then is that faculty whereby we are at once conscious of our own thoughts, words, and actions, and of their merit or demerit, of their being good or bad, and consequently deserving either praise or censure. And some pleasure generally attends the former sentence, some uneasiness the latter.[24]

From these comments, it is clear that conscience includes the power to know correctly what is good and what is bad. That is, it involves some knowledge of the moral law. It also involves the passive experience of pleasure and pain that arises in consequence to one's perception of whether a proposed action is good or bad.

Wesley also indicates that prevenient grace touches an impenitent sinner's desires. In regard to prevenient grace, Wesley says that "everyone has sooner or later good desires, although the generality of men stifle them before they can strike deep root or produce any considerable fruit."[25] In another place, Wesley says that prevenient grace produces "the first wish to please God."[26] To the extent that a wish is a desire, one may see clearly from these comments that the Holy Spirit through prevenient grace touches in a small degree the desires of everyone. Also, through prevenient grace, God gives a slight conviction of having done wrong.[27]

---

[23] Wesley, 'On Conscience,' *Works* (BE), 3:481.

[24] Wesley, 'On Conscience,' *Works* (BE), 3:481.

[25] Wesley, 'On Working Out Our Own Salvation,' *Works* (BE), 3:207. This desire is different from those of one who is "born of God." God works on the desires and affections of all people, even those people who are impenitent sinners.

[26] Wesley, 'On Working Out Our Own Salvation,' *Works* (BE), 3:203.

[27] Wesley, 'On Working Out Our Own Salvation,' *Works* (BE), 3:203. Also, Wesley makes the following comment that seems to apply to many impenitent sinners: "As the Spirit of God does not 'wait for the call of man', so at some times he *will* be heard. He puts them in fear, so that for a season at least the heathen 'know themselves to be but men'. They feel the burden of sin, and earnestly desire to flee from the wrath to come. But not long. They seldom suffer the arrows of conviction to go deep into their souls; but quickly stifle the grace of God, and return to their wallowing in the mire" (Wesley, 'The Spirit of Bondage and Adoption,' *Works* (BE), 1:265). Impenitent sinners often reject the passive operations of the Spirit.

For Wesley, an impenitent sinner does not have the power to perform good works strictly speaking. However, such a person does have the power to perform fruitful actions that are in a limited sense good. In answer to a question of how a person may do good before he or she is justified, Wesley says,

> If it is objected, 'Nay, but a man, before he is justified, may feed the hungry, or clothe the naked; and these are good works,' the answer is easy. He may do these, even before he is justified. And these are in one sense 'good works'; they are 'good and profitable to men'. But it does not follow that they are, strictly speaking, good in themselves, or good in the sight of God. All truly 'good works' (to use the word of our Church) 'follow after justification', and they are therefore 'good and acceptable to God in Christ', because they 'spring out of a true and living faith'.[28]

For Wesley, an impenitent sinner has the power to feed the hungry or clothe the naked, etc. However, such action is not "truly 'good works'" and are not "properly good."[29] As shown in the last chapter, Wesley makes a distinction between "good works" and "doing good." An impenitent sinner can do the latter without having the capability of the former. Yet, even when an impenitent sinner is "doing good," such action is in "one sense" good. The limited degree of goodness of such action is only possible because of the power given to *all people* by prevenient grace. As mentioned above in this section, prevenient grace gives an impenitent sinner a Spirit-affected desire and a conviction of wrong doing from which such fruitful action flows.[30]

However, it seems that Wesley would not allow that this action is "acceptable of God" in the same manner as the works of righteousness that are performed by a servant of God, which we will explore below. Much less does this action of an impenitent sinner meet the standard of virtue, which is only the fruit of one who has experienced the new birth. The key difference between good action properly speaking and good action that is in a limited sense good is that good action properly speaking

---

[28] Wesley, 'Justification By Faith,' *Works* (BE), 1:192.
[29] Wesley, 'Justification By Faith,' *Works* (BE), 1:192 and 1:193.
[30] CF. Wesley, 'The Principles of a Methodist Farther Explained,' *Works* (BE1), 9:176.

must flow from a holy heart (the heart of the new birth).[31] This is the mark of proper virtue.

The Ethics of an Impenitent Sinner

In summary, the ethics of an impenitent sinner works as follows. By means of prevenient grace, this person has a conscience, some degree of knowledge of what is good and bad, and is blessed with a small desire to do good, at least until the person stifles it. By grace, such a person is also endued with a power of free will, a power of choosing between doing evil and doing good. From this deposit of gifts, an impenitent sinner may respond to God's prevenient grace with the performance of action that is in some sense good. As shown in chapter 5, such action, even at this stage, requires the assistance of the Spirit. Indeed, the performance of action that is in a limited sense good is even possible for one who does not believe in God. However, given the sinful nature of the impenitent sinner's heart and the unwillingness to obey many of God's commandments, the performance of sinful action far exceeds any action that is in a limited sense good.

For Wesley, of course, an impenitent sinner does not possess all of the same blessings of a servant of God or a child of God. As will be shown, the impenitent sinner is different from a servant of God because the former does not both fear God and work righteousness. According to Wesley, a common problem for an impenitent sinner is that a lack of co-operation with God's prevenient grace leads to the "quenching" of the little prevenient grace that is received.[32] If not intentional about having a single eye for obeying God, an impenitent sinner can fall into a deep spiritual sleep, making it difficult to escape.

And yet, for Wesley, the condition of an impenitent sinner is not hopeless.[33] Unlike John Calvin, Wesley rejects that such a state is ever irresistible. In general, Wesley allows that the power of liberty (the power of free will) remains in the impenitent sinner. Therefore, such a person may choose to continue in evil or choose to do good in a limited sense. In his discussion of liberty, Wesley says, "through the grace of God assisting me," "I am free to choose whom I will serve, and if I choose the better part, to continue therein even unto death."[34] The moment that

---

[31] This point will be explored more below.
[32] Wesley, 'On Working Out Our Own Salvation,' *Works* (BE), 3:207
[33] See, for example, Wesley, 'A Call to Backsliders,' *Works* (BE), 3:211.

an impenitent sinner, by prevenient grace,[35] acknowledges his or her own sin and chooses to serve God by performing works of righteousness, the transition to becoming a servant of God has begun.

The Servant of God

Characteristics of a Servant of God

John Wesley recognizes a certain stage of living that he describes as a "servant of God." This view is inspired by Galatians 4:5-7, Romans 8:14-16, and the account of Cornelius in Acts 10.[36] One of the most common descriptions of a servant of God is that he or she "fears God and works righteousness."[37] This is what distinguishes a servant from an impenitent sinner. While the label "servant of God" can refer to an aspiring follower of Christ, it can also refer to a Jew, which is part of why Joe Gorman says, "Wesley recognized that God's presence gratuitously springs up throughout human cultures and even in religions other than Christianity."[38]

For Wesley, the meaning of the word "servant" is nuanced. As Rodes observes, Wesley sometimes uses the word "servant" to describe a child of God.[39] At other times, Wesley clearly distinguishes a servant from a "son" of God—also known as a "child" of God.[40] This distinction between servant and son is inspired by Romans 8 and Galatians 4:7. A child of God is one who has experienced the new birth, the entering of Christ into the heart, the love of God shed abroad in the heart, the witness of the Spirit that one is a child of God, Christian faith of a child of God, the Spirit of adoption, and freedom from the power of sin. On the other

---

[34] Wesley, 'What is Man?,' *Works* (BE), 4:24.

[35] It seems that all people, including impenitent sinners, will experience the passive aspect of repentance to some degree (Outler, editor, *Works* (BE), 3:203 and 1:265). What keeps impenitent sinners in their state is an unwillingness to respond to it. The impenitent sinner does not fear God and perform fruits meet for repentance.

[36] See the scripture for sermon 9 of Outler, editor, *Works* (BE), 1:249. See also Wesley's commentary on these passages in his *Explanatory Notes Upon the New Testament*, including his comments on Act 10:4 and 10:35 (*ENNT, 1788*).

[37] Outler, editor, *Works* (BE), 3:497 and 4:35.

[38] Joe Gorman, "John Wesley's Inclusive Theology of other Religions," *Wesleyan Theological Journal*, 48, (2013): 39.

[39] Rodes, 17.

[40] See, for example, Outler, editor, *Works* (BE), 3:497 and 4:35.

hand, a servant of God has not yet possessed these gifts. In this project, when the word "servant" is used, it is being used to refer to a servant who is not yet a child of God.

According to Wesley, a servant of God is also "accepted of God,"[41] and no longer has the wrath of God abiding.[42] The servant of God has faith "in its infant state,"[43] but such faith does not involve a consciousness of the forgiveness of sins and that Christ has died for oneself (it is not the faith of a child of God). Nevertheless, the faith of a servant of God is "properly saving."[44] In his diary, in reference to his state during the days right before his experience at Aldersgate on May 24, 1738, Wesley describes himself as having the faith of a servant rather than the faith of a son.[45]

A servant of God is one who has received repentance in addition to all of the gracious effects of prevenient grace offered to all people (conscience, a touching of one's desires, and a measure of free-will).[46] For Wesley, repentance involves a conviction of sin. This includes self-knowledge or awareness that one is corrupt in his or her inward nature, including total corruption in every faculty of the soul.[47] It includes an awareness of inward and outward sin, of utter guiltiness and helplessness, and of certain affections such as sorrow of heart, remorse and self-condemnation, and fear of wrath.[48]

Wesley's view of repentance involves both active and passive operations of the Spirit.[49] The passive operation of repentance is evident from his comment that the "Spirit of God does not 'wait for the call of man'" in regard to giving a feeling of the "burden of sin" and imposing "arrows of conviction."[50] The image of "arrows" underscores the pass-

---

[41] Wesley uses Acts 10:35 as the basis of the phrase "accepted of him" in reference to God's acceptance of a servant of God. See Wesley, 'On Faith,' *Works* (BE), 3:497.

[42] Wesley, 'On Faith,' *Works* (BE), 3:497.

[43] Wesley, 'On Faith,' *Works* (BE), 3:497.

[44] Wesley, 'On Faith,' *Works* (BE), 3:497.

[45] Wesley, *Works* (BE),18:235. See footnote a. These comments were added in 1775.

[46] Wesley makes it clear that a servant of God has already received the convincing of sin. See Wesley, 'On the Discoveries of Faith,' *Works* (BE), 4:34-35.

[47] Wesley, 'The Way to the Kingdom,' *Works* (BE), 1:225.

[48] Wesley, 'The Way to the Kingdom,' *Works* (BE), 1:225.

[49] See the discussion of passive operations of the Spirit in chapter 5.

[50] Wesley, 'The Spirit of Bondage and Adoption,' *Works* (BE), 1:265. Wesley

iveness of this aspect of repentance. Yet, in order to avoid losing the positive effects of such passive operation, it is often necessary for a person to respond with action.[51] This action includes "fruits meet for repentance."[52]

Although a servant of God is "accepted of God," Wesley seems to indicate that a servant of God is not capable of virtue or performing works that are good "strictly speaking."[53] This is because good action strictly speaking only flows from the heart of someone who has experienced the new birth, a state that has not yet arrived for a servant of God. And since virtue often involves a two-part process—good action flowing from a holy and transformed heart of love (as evident at the new birth)—, servants of God are not capable of virtue in a proper sense.

There is much evidence that suggests that Wesley believes that the performance of virtue and good works strictly speaking are necessarily conjoined with a state of the new birth. For example, in 1785, Wesley says that the Christian revelation affirms "the love of God to be the true foundation both of the love of our neighbor and all other virtues," and he says, "benevolence itself is no virtue at all, unless it spring from the love of God."[54] Also, when speaking of fruitful action, Wesley says in a clear manner on repeated occasions that fruitful actions before the new birth are not "good works, because they do not spring from faith and the love of God."[55]

Although a servant of God is not capable of good action properly speaking, he or she, like the impenitent sinner, is capable of performing action that is good in a limited sense. And yet, of course, the action of a servant of God has an improved effect in comparison to any fruitful action of an impenitent sinner. This is partly because the action of a servant of God flows from the fear and respect of God, something that the impenitent sinner chooses not to nurture. Also, presumably, the fruitful action of a servant of God usually far exceeds in abundance the fruitful action of an impenitent sinner because the servant of God is committed

---

also speaks of the arrows of repentance here: Wesley, 'The Principles of a Methodist Farther Explained,' *Works* (BE), 9:228.

[51] Wesley, 'The Spirit of Bondage and Adoption,' *Works* (BE), 1:265.

[52] These will be discussed more below.

[53] For the distinction between good works "strictly speaking" and works that are good in a limited sense, see comments from earlier in this chapter.

[54] Wesley, 'An Israelite Indeed,' *Works* (BE), 3:279-280.

[55] *Works* (Jackson), 8:428. CF. *Works* (Jackson), 8:47, 8:288 and 9:111.

to obeying all of God's commandments. Such action leads to a daily growing in grace, propelling the servant of God further along on the way of salvation.[56] For a servant of God, the performance of fruitful action is the same as working righteousness. Such action of an orthodox servant of God is similar in nature to the righteous work of a Pharisee (unorthodox in the Christian sense) and lacks the power of the good works of a child of God. Nonetheless, unlike for the case of the impenitent sinner, the fruitful action (works of righteousness) of a servant of God is "accepted" by God.

In order to protect against confusion, it is helpful here to consider a point regarding Wesley's view of the timing of justification. While it is clear that servants of God have not experienced the new birth (being born of God), one could raise the question of whether Wesley holds that a servant of God is justified in the Christian sense.[57] In other words, this question concerns whether or not Christian justification and the new birth are normally conjoined. While the evidence seems to suggest that the elderly Wesley does in fact hold that these events are normally conjoined,[58] the answer to this question seems *not* to have bearing on the discussion of this section. Both views (a servant of God is justified in the Christian sense or not) are compatible with what is being highlighted here. That is: Wesley teaches that before the new birth arrives, fruitful action that is good in a limited sense is necessary if there is time and opportunity.[59] Good works "strictly speaking" do not come until after the new birth. This is because, as mentioned above, Wesley seems to hold that along with virtue, the new birth and good works are normally conjoined.

---

[56] For an example of this kind of spiritual growth, see for example, Wesley, 'Scriptural Christianity,' *Works* (BE), 1:164.

[57] This question could be prompted by the point that a servant of God is both accepted by God and avoids the wrath of God (as shown above). One could ask: how can a servant of God have these and not be justified in a Christian sense? See also the discussion below concerning debates in secondary literature.

[58] Wesley, 'On God's Vineyard,' *Works* (BE), 3:506-507; Wesley, 'On Patience,' *Works* (BE), 3:174. Also, Wesley makes such statements published earlier in his life that he never retracts. Also, several years before his death, he claims that he has not contradicted himself between 1738 and 1788 (Wesley, *Letters*, 8:179).

[59] Wesley, 'The Principles of a Methodist Farther Explained,' *Works* (BE), 9:176. Cf. Wesley, 'The Scripture Way of Salvation,' (BE), 2:163.

On a number of occasions, Wesley stresses the importance of performing fruitful action (limitedly good action) before the new birth, if there is time and opportunity. This is evident by the following advice that Wesley gives to a servant of God:

> Exhort him to press on by all possible means, till he passes 'from faith to faith'; from the faith of a servant to the faith of a son...He will then have 'Christ revealed in his heart', enabling him to testify, 'The life that I now live in the flesh I live by faith in the Son of God, who loved me, and gave himself for me'—the proper voice of a child of God. He will then be 'born of God', inwardly changed by the might power of God from 'an earthly, sensual, devilish' mind to 'the mind which was in Christ Jesus.'[60]

Notice the phrase "by all possible means." This includes the performance of fruitful action in the form of practicing the means of grace. It includes performing the "first type" of fruitful action mentioned in chapter 5. Such "fruits meet for repentance" include: "forgiving our brother, ceasing from evil, doing good, using the ordinances of God, and, in general, obeying him according to the measure of grace which we have received."[61] If such action is neglected, then a person is at risk of not moving forward in the way of salvation or even losing the grace already received. As Wesley says, "God does undoubtedly command us both to repent and to bring forth fruit meet for repentance; which if we willingly neglect we cannot reasonably expect to be justified at all."[62] Wesley encourages people of all stages of the way of salvation to follow his guide for fruitful action which includes participating in Christian fellowship, following the *General Rules* of the Methodist Societies, and obeying the moral commandments of scripture.

For Wesley, the situation of a servant of God is comparable to the illustration of the flaming dart from chapter 2. For a servant of God, the faith of a child of God and the love of the new birth has not yet come, but it is certain that they will come at some unpredictable future time if one persists in seeking God and performing fruitful action.[63] According to Wesley, it is fine for a servant of God to expect (and hope for) such faith and love of the new birth to come *now*. This is because even in his oldest years, Wesley maintained that the new birth and justification are

---

[60] Wesley, 'On the Discoveries of Faith,' *Works* (BE), 4:35.
[61] Wesley, 'The Principles of a Methodist Farther Explained,' *Works* (BE), 9:176.
[62] Wesley, 'The Scripture Way of Salvation,' *Works* (BE), 2:162.
[63] Wesley, *Letters*, 6:287.

through faith alone.[64] The faith of a child of God is the only indispensable condition for the new birth. Such faith alone is sufficient for the new birth.[65] In support of this point, Wesley gives the illustration from Luke 23:40-43 of the thief on the cross who had no opportunity for any fruitful action except asking Jesus to remember him when Jesus comes in his kingdom.[66] Also, as Christine Johnson points out, in 1784, Wesley gives the report of criminals who heard Wesley's preaching soon before their execution.[67] From this report, it seems that the criminals who heard his preaching were blessed right away with the new birth and the faith of a child of God. Wesley says that in response to his preaching: "The power of the Lord was eminently present, and most of the prisoners were in tears."[68] It seems that in 1784, Wesley preached with the expectation that God could give the new birth this quickly.

In chapter 3, we explored Wesley's second meaning of the will, also known as "free will." This meaning of the will is equivalent to his understanding of liberty, a power of choosing. If by grace, a servant of God chooses to serve God[69] but does not have time to follow through with this resolution (by performing fruitful action) because of an unfortunate accident that ends his or her life early, this servant of God will nevertheless avoid God's wrath, and God will save him or her for all of eternity. If there was not time for this servant of God to receive the faith of a child of God and the new birth before death, then presumably God will give them after death.

Just as in the illustration of the flaming dart in chapter 2, it is acceptable for a servant of God to expect and hope for *now* the impact of the

---

[64] In 1738, in his sermon "Salvation by Faith," Wesley gives his commitment to "salvation or justification by faith only" (Wesley, 'Salvation By Faith,' *Works* (BE),1:125). He is not speaking here of final justification (see chapter 7). That is different. In 1790, Wesley says, "Only about fifty years ago, I had a clearer view than before of justification by faith: and in this from that very hour I never varied, no not an hair's breadth" (Wesley, *On the Wedding Garment*, 4:147). See also Wesley, 'Some Remarks on Mr. Hill's "Review,"' *Works* (BE), 13:473 - 474.

[65] Wesley, 'The Scripture Way of Salvation,' *Works* (BE), 2:163, paragraph III.3.

[66] Wesley, 'The Scripture Way of Salvation,' *Works* (BE), 2:163.

[67] Christine Johnson and Kenneth Collins, "From the Garden to the Gallows, The Significance of Free Grace in the Theology of John Wesley," *Wesleyan Theological Journal*, 48, (2013): 7; Wesley, 'Journal,' *Works* (BE), 23:340.

[68] Wesley, 'Journal,' *Works* (BE), 23:340.

[69] CF. the bottom of p. 24, Outler, editor, *Works* (BE), volume 4.

flaming dart (corresponding to the faith of a child and the love of the new birth). This is because of the point that the new birth comes alone through the faith of a child. It is best to hope that the flaming dart (the new birth) comes now, while also practicing fruitful action while there is opportunity. This is more preferable than other approaches such as: (a) doing fruitful action while assuming that the new birth must come later and (b) expecting the new birth to come now without doing any fruitful action. According to Wesley, in all stages of human living, it is important for fruitful action to be constantly performed, even if such fruitful actions are never in themselves sufficient for the new birth. If a servant of God persists in seeking God and performing fruitful action, then it is certain that God will at a future unknown time perform the new birth and give His love in the heart, just as God provides the impact of the flaming dart in the illustration.

The Ethics of the Servant of God

In summary, the ethics of the servant of God is as follows. Like the impenitent sinner, the servant of God possesses all of the gifts of prevenient grace. However, a number of factors crucially distinguish the ethics of a servant of God from the ethics of an impenitent sinner. The most crucial differences are that unlike impenitent sinners, servants of God are committed to a belief in and fear of God and are committed to obeying all of God's commandments. Also, for those committed to the Christian tradition, a servant of God intentionally seeks the greatest end of Christianity, which is to love God and neighbor. In pursuit of this end, a servant of God seeks Christian love and performs fruitful action, if there is time and opportunity. It is here that we observe the theme of gift that is evident in the pursuit.

According to Wesley, the pursuit by a servant of God of the greatest end of Christian living is an expression of God's gift and that the giftedness of this blessing is illuminated by a critical examination of the work of the Spirit with respect to the active and passive dimensions of a human being. It is through the work of the Spirit with respect to the active dimension of fruitful action (as explained in chapter 5) flowing from passive operation (the light of conscience, touches on the desires of the heart, and the feelings of the arrows of repentance) that a servant of God is able to performs works of righteousness and pursue the greatest end of Christian living, which is to love God and neighbor to one's full potential. A servant of God is not free from the power and bondage of sin and has not yet been given the gift of new birth. In other words, sinful desires and affections often dominate the consciousness of a servant of God. For this reason, the works of righteousness of a servant of God are typically not as abundant or as powerful as the good works of a child of God. Nonetheless, the works of righteousness (limitedly good actions) that are performed by a servant of God are made possible by the assistance of the Spirit and have some good effects. In this way, a servant of God's performance of fruitful actions and pursuit of Christian love is a reflection of God's gift, according to His mysterious and all-powerful plan of salvation for the world.

We showed that the situation of a servant of God is comparable to the illustration of the flaming dart from chapter 2. God can give *now* the gifts of the new birth. However, if God does not gives these now, as Wesley observes is often the case,[70] it is necessary for a servant of God to continue performing fruitful action as there is time and opportunity. According to Wesley, in all stages of human living, it is important for fruitful action to be constantly performed, even if such fruitful actions are never in themselves sufficient for the new birth.

The arrival of the first moment of the new birth (analogous to the impact of the flaming dart) involves events that are passive in a bare sense. However, as discussed in chapter 2 of this project, when viewed in a larger context, the arrival of the new birth is "not altogether" passive. This is because, if there is time and opportunity, graciously empowered fruitful actions before and after the first moment of the new birth have bearing on whether or not the new birth is received and maintained. Such fruitful actions themselves are a reflection of God's gift.

The Child of the New Birth

The Beginning of Sanctification

After the first moments of the new birth, a person has transitioned from being a servant of God to being a newborn child. Wesley uses the term "newborn" to refer to a child of God who has experienced the new birth but not yet perfect love.[71] (A newborn child is a spiritual condition, not a physical condition. A newborn here is often a physical adult). For

---

[70] Wesley, 'The Imperfection of Human Knowledge,' *Works* (BE), 2:584.
[71] See, for example, Outler, editor, *Works* (BE), 1:124, 2:105, 2:220.

Wesley, the new birth is the first moment of sanctification. Sanctification, or being made holy, is an important branch of salvation. It is distinct from justification. Nevertheless, Wesley says in October of 1787 that justification and sanctification first occur at the same time.[72] Justification is what "God *does for us*" and sanctification is what "God *works in us* by his Spirit."[73] Sanctification includes certain perceivable blessings that God performs on the heart and mind during the new birth and for the rest of the Christian journey. We will now consider Wesley's view of the spiritual blessings that first occur at the new birth. For each, we will show connections to scripture.

Faith of the Newborn Child, Witness of the Spirit, Justification

The moment that a person transitions from being a servant of God to being a newborn child (marking the occurrence of the new birth), a person possesses for the first time a collection of certain Spiritual gifts: the faith of a child of God, the witness of the Spirit that one is a child of God, the Spirit of adoption, the entering of Christ into the heart, and the love of God shed abroad in the heart.[74] Someone who is born of God also has power over sin.[75] The scriptures that Wesley sees as the basis of the new birth include but are not limited to: John 3, Romans 8:14-16, and Galatians 4:6.[76] When we speak here of the "new birth" (also known as the first moments of being "born of God"[77]), we are referring to the possession of these spiritual gifts that, generally, the Holy Spirit first gives to a person at the same time.[78]

[72] Wesley, 'On God's Vineyard,' *Works* (BE), 3:506. See also Wesley, 'The Scripture Way of Salvation,' *Works* (BE), 2:158

[73] Wesley, 'Justification by Faith,' *Works* (BE), 1:187.

[74] Wesley shows the conjoining of all six of these elements as early as 1738 (*Salvation by Faith*, paragraphs I.4 and II:7), in 1748 (*Marks of the New Birth*, paragraphs I.3, III.1, and IV.2), and at least as late as June 1788 (*On the Discoveries of Faith*, paragraphs 13 and 14).

[75] See, for example, Wesley, 'The Marks of the New Birth,' *Works* (BE), 1:419.

[76] See, for example, Outler, editor, *Works* (BE), 1:417, 2:187, 4:35-36, and 1:289.

[77] Wesley equates the "new birth" with the beginning phase of being "born of God." For evidence of this, see paragraph 1 of 'The Marks of the New Birth' and the remainder of the sermon (sermon 18 of Outler, editor, *Works* (BE)).

[78] Wesley shows the conjoining of all six of these elements as early as 1738 (*Salvation by Faith*, paragraphs I.5, II.4, and II:7), in 1748 (*Marks of the New Birth*,

In April of 1788, Wesley says "the faith of a child is properly and directly a divine conviction whereby every child of God is enabled to testify, 'The life that I now live, I live by faith in the Son of God, who loved me, and gave himself for me.' And whosoever hath this, 'the Spirit of God witnesseth with his spirit that he is a child of God.'"[79] These features are what distinguish the faith of a child of God from the faith of a servant of God. The faith of a child of God involves something that is passive in a bare sense, as clarified in chapter 2 of this project. This is not to deny that one's active power also plays a role in faith. If one chooses to reject faith, one always has the freedom and power to quench the Spirit and rid oneself of any faith he or she has.[80] Consistent with the above statements, Wesley also describes faith of a child as "not only an assent, an act of the understanding, but a disposition which God hath wrought in his heart; 'a sure trust and confidence in God that through the merits of Christ his sins are forgiven, and he reconciled to the favour of God.'"[81] The faith of a child of God is given at an unpredictable time and according to God's sovereign power. It is the gift of God's free grace.

Generally, there is overlap in Wesley's understanding of the faith of a child of God and his understanding of the witness of the Spirit. He bases his view of the witness of the Spirit in part on Romans 8:16 and perhaps also Galatians 2:20, Acts 3:19, and 2 Corinthians 5:20.[82] The account that Wesley gives of the witness of the Spirit is as follows: "the testimony of the Spirit is an inward impression of the soul, whereby the Spirit of God directly 'witnesses to my spirit that I am a child of God'; that Jesus Christ hath loved me, and given himself for me; that all my sins are blotted out, and I, even I, am reconciled to God."[83] As Joseph Cunningham points out, the witness of the Spirit is part of the Spirit's economic operation which helps to nurture and develop the relational participation of a human person in the divine life.[84] By Wesley's defini-

paragraphs I.3, III.1, and IV.2), and at least as late as June 1788 (*On the Discoveries of Faith*, paragraphs 13 and 14).

[79] Wesley, 'On Faith,' *Works* (BE), 3:498. See also from 1765, Wesley, 'The Scripture Way of Salvation,' *Works* (BE), 2:161; and from 1738, Wesley, 'Salvation by Faith,' *Works* (BE), I:5 and II:4.

[80] Cf., *Works* (Jackson), 1:426, 10:363.

[81] Wesley, 'The Marks of the New Birth,' *Works* (BE), 1:418.

[82] Wesley, 'The Witness of the Spirit I,' *Works* (BE), 1:274.

[83] Wesley, 'The Witness of the Spirit I,' *Works* (BE), 1:274.

[84] Cunningham, *John Wesley's Pneumatology, Perceptible Inspiration*, 136. See also the discussion of Cunningham's work in chapter 5.

tion of the witness of the Spirit that is stated above, we observe that much of what Wesley means by the faith of a child of God overlaps with his understanding of the direct witness of the Spirit. For Wesley, the witness of the Spirit is a "direct witness"[85] and involves an "impression of the soul."[86] This impression is something that by its nature, must be perceived by human consciousness. This feeling is something that is beyond full explanation and cannot be fully known except by one who experiences it. But for Wesley, it is an experience that is generally available for any person with normal psychological conditions who sincerely seeks it. It is evident from Wesley's reference to John 3 that the timing of the first experience of the witness of the Spirit is unpredictable and passive in a bare sense with respect to a person, as clarified in chapter 2 of this project. In regard to the witness of the Spirit, Wesley says in reference to John 3:8, "'The wind bloweth; and I hear the sound thereof'; but I cannot 'tell how it cometh, or whither it goeth.'"

In addition to the faith of a child of God and the witness of the Spirit, a newborn child also has a testimony of his or her own spirit (knowledge based on one's own reason and self-observations of being and conduct) that one is a child of God.[87] The testimony of one's spirit is grounded in a self-observation that one has received the fruits of the Spirit—love, joy, peace, long-suffering, goodness (the tempers discussed in chapter 4 of this project) — and also in observing one's own good works.[88] In summary, confirmation that one is a child of God generally involves testimony from two sources: the witness of the Spirit of God and the witness of one's own spirit or consciousness.[89]

With regard to justification,[90] Wesley makes a statement in 1790 concerning the consistency of his thought. He says that for the last fifty years, his view of justification has "never varied, no not an hair's breadth."[91] In a sermon published in 1787, Wesley reaffirms his com-

---

[85] Wesley, 'The Witness of the Spirit II,' *Works* (BE), 1:288.

[86] See above quote and Wesley, 'The Witness of the Spirit II,' *Works* (BE), 1:287.

[87] Wesley, 'The Witness of the Spirit I,' *Works* (BE), 1:270.

[88] Wesley, 'The Witness of the Spirit II,' *Works* (BE), 1:289.

[89] Wesley, 'The Witness of the Spirit II,' *Works* (BE), 1:289.

[90] For more information on Wesley's view of justification, see the above section on the servant of God.

[91] Wesley, 'On the Wedding Garment,' *Works* (BE), 4:147. See also 'Some Remarks on Mr. Hill's "Review,"' (BE), 13:473 - 474.

mitment to the doctrine of "justification by faith alone."[92] He defines justification as follows: "The plain scriptural notion of justification is pardon, the forgiveness of sins."[93] Justification makes one free from the guilt of sin. Scriptures that Wesley uses for his view of justification include Romans 4:5 and 3:25.[94] Justification is distinct from sanctification. The former is what God does for us; the latter is what God does in us.[95] Interpreters of Wesley agree that for Wesley, all children of the new birth have been justified. It is a gift of God's free grace.

The Love of God Shed Abroad in the Heart

Another important feature of the new birth is the love of God shed abroad in the heart. This of course is pertaining to the same idea in John 3 and also resembles the language of Romans 5:5. It is a defining mark of the beginning of sanctification. The first moment of the shedding of such love involves an instantaneous transformation of a person's heart. This involves a significant change of character.[96] As discussed in chapter 4, this is the event in which one's ruling inclination for love of the world is replaced by a ruling inclination for love of God and neighbor. Evil tempers are decreased and holy tempers are introduced by the Spirit. One now has power over sin and the "renewing of one's fallen nature."[97] It also involves an experience that is perceptible to one's consciousness. As discussed in chapter 2, such a transformation is passive in a bare sense but not altogether passive when viewed in a larger context. It is not altogether passive because, if there is time and opportunity, graciously-empowered fruitful action before and after the first moment of the new birth is necessary for receiving and maintaining the state of being born of God.

Instantaneous, Perceived, and Unpredictable Birth

For Wesley, the instantaneous nature of the first moment of the new birth (including the love of God shed abroad in the heart) is evident from the following comments:

[92] Paragraph I.4 and I.5, Wesley, 'On God's Vineyard,' *Works* (BE), 3:505.
[93] Wesley, 'Justification by Faith,' *Works* (BE), 1:189.
[94] Wesley, 'Justification by Faith,' *Works* (BE), 1:182 and 1:189.
[95] Wesley, 'Justification by Faith,' *Works* (BE), 1:187.
[96] Cf. Wesley's essay 'The Character of a Methodist.'
[97] Wesley, 'The New Birth,' *Works* (BE), 2:187.

> Whereas in that moment when we are justified freely by his grace, when we are accepted through the Beloved, we are born again, born from above, born of the Spirit... There is in that hour a general change from inward sinfulness to inward holiness. The love of the creature is changed into the love of the Creator, the love of the world into the love of God. Earthly desires, the desire of the flesh, the desires of the eyes, and the pride of life, are in that instant changed by the mighty power of God into heavenly desires.[98]

In this passage, Wesley is clearly indicating that sinful desires of the heart are changed into holy desires of the heart by "the mighty power of God." This transformation is performed in a moment. The transition from sinful desires to holy desires is not done in a week, month, or year but "in that instant." In 1787, Wesley compares the instantaneous nature of the new birth to a mother giving birth:

> And as in the natural birth a man is born at once, and then grows larger and stronger by degrees, so in the spiritual birth a man is born at once, and then gradually increases in spiritual stature and strength. The new birth, therefore, is the first point of sanctification, which may increase more and more unto the perfect day.[99]

Here, Wesley says that in regard to a spiritual birth, one is "born at once." This birth is only the first point of sanctification, which continues on after this first point in a manner that involves gradual growth.

In addition to being instantaneous, the first moment of the new birth is something that must be perceived and felt by the person experiencing it. First, a person perceives the impression of the direct witness of the Spirit mentioned above. In addition, such a person "feels the love of God shed abroad in his heart by the Holy Ghost which is given unto him."[100] The new birth involves a "consciousness of our having received, in and by the Spirit of adoption, the tempers mentioned in the Word of God as belonging to his adopted children; even a loving heart toward God and toward all mankind."[101] It involves a feeling of happiness: "As soon as the Father of spirits reveals his Son in our hearts, and the Son reveals his Father, the love of God is shed abroad in our hearts; then and not

---

[98] Wesley, 'On Patience,' *Works* (BE), 3:174. See also: Wesley, 'On the Death of George Whitefield,' *Works* (BE), 2:343.

[99] Wesley, 'On God's Vineyard,' *Works* (BE), 3:507. See also Wesley, 'The New Birth,' *Works* (BE), 2:198.

[100] Wesley, 'The New Birth,' *Works* (BE), 2:192.

[101] Wesley, 'The Witness of Our Spirit, I,' *Works* (BE), 1:273.

till then, we are happy. We are happy . . . in all the heavenly tempers he has wrought in us by his Holy Spirit."[102]

Although all perceive the new birth in some way, some people experience it in a way that feels vivacious, and others experience it in a way that feels more moderate. Wesley says:

> There is an irreconcilable variability in the operations of the Holy Spirit on the souls of men, more especially as to the manner of justification. Many find Him rushing upon them like a torrent, while they experience 'The o'erwhelming power of saving grace.' This has been the experience of many; perhaps of more in this late visitation than in any other age since the times of the Apostles. But in others He works in a very different way: 'He deigns His influence to infuse, Sweet, refreshing, as the silent dews.'[103]

It is clear that Wesley is indicating in these comments that there is an "irreconcilable variability" corresponding to the varying degrees of vivaciousness that may be perceived by a person during the reception of the new birth.

As mentioned before, Wesley's understanding of the timing of the new birth is comparable to the illustration of the flaming dart from chapter 2. This is because, like the impact of the flaming dart, the timing of the first moments of the new birth is unpredictable. In 1784, Wesley says:

> It is doubtless the peculiar prerogative of God to reserve the 'times and seasons in his own power'. And we cannot give any reason why of two persons equally athirst for salvation, one is presently taken into the favour of God and the other left to mourn for months or years. One, as soon as he calls upon God, is answered, and filled with peace and joy in believing. Another seeks after him—and it seems with the same degree of sincerity and earnestness—and yet cannot find him, or any consciousness of his favour, for weeks, or months, or years. We know well this cannot possibly be owing to any absolute degrees, consigning one before he was born to everlasting glory, and the other to everlasting fire. But we do not know what is the reason for it; it is enough that God knoweth.[104]

Wesley also references John 8:3 in regard to how the Spirit works in the new birth: "the wind bloweth where it listeth" of John 8:3 that it is

---

[102] Wesley, 'The Unity of the Divine Being,' *Works* (BE), 4:67.
[103] Wesley, *Letters*, 7:298.
[104] Wesley, 'The Imperfection of Human Knowledge,' *Works* (BE), 2:584.

"not by thy [human] power or wisdom."[105] The unpredictability of when the first moments of the new birth occur underscores the passiveness (in a bare sense) of the new birth. In this way, for Wesley, the new birth is the work of God alone and is the effect of the free grace of God.[106]

In this chapter, we explored Wesley's understanding of the path to the new birth and we have begun to consider Wesley's view of the new birth itself. However, we have not yet fully considered his understanding of the ethics of the newborn child. In the next chapter, we will carry on this task and other tasks as we continue to follow along Wesley's "way of salvation" and the corresponding stages.

[105] Wesley, 'The New Birth,' *Works* (BE), 2:191.
[106] Collins, *The Theology of John Wesley*, 160-165.

Chapter 7

From New Birth to Perfect Love and the Rewards of Heaven

In this chapter, we will continue the task of exploring John Wesley's view of ethics for each stage along the way of salvation. We finished the last chapter by beginning a discussion of Wesley's view of the new birth. The new birth is a spiritual transformation that, in its first moments, involves having the faith of a child of God, the witness of the Spirit, the Spirit of adoption, the entering of Christ into the heart, and the love of God shed abroad in the heart. Also, all children of the new birth have received justification and power over sin. For this chapter, we will first consider more of Wesley's view of the newborn child. After this, we will consider his view of the child of perfect love and the inhabitant of heaven. Last, in this chapter, we will consider some debates in secondary literature relevant to the later stages of the way of salvation. Over the course of this chapter, it will be argued that regardless of the stage, according to the view of John Wesley, a person's pursuit of the greatest end of ethics is an expression of God's gift and that the giftedness of this blessing is illuminated by a critical examination of the work of the Spirit with respect to the active and passive dimensions of a human being.

The Child of the New Birth

The Repentance of Believers

For Wesley, a newborn child is in need of repentance. The kind of repentance for the newborn (often a physical adult) is different from the kind that occurs before the new birth. This type of repentance is called the repentance of a believer.[1] In contrast to the repentance before the new birth, the second kind does not include a conviction of sin properly speaking. According to Wesley, "'Sin, properly speaking' is neither more nor less than a "voluntary transgression of a known law of God."[2] It seems that all children of the new birth do not commit sin "properly speaking."[3] Therefore, this type of repentance does not apply for such people at this stage. But there is a second type of repentance. This is the "knowing ourselves sinners, yea, guilty, helpless sinners, even though we know we are children of God."[4]

The sin of believers is not sin "properly speaking" but rather it is sin of a different type. As mentioned in chapter 4, the ruling inclination of a child of God is Christian love, not love of the world. However, even for newborn children, the love of the world and the associated evil tempers remain at some smaller level. Such children are still able to "feel"[5] such evil tempers remaining in the heart, even though such people do not commit voluntary transgressions of known laws of God. These feelings are passive in a bare sense, as described in chapter 2. They are a "heart 'bent towards backsliding.'"[6] Although these feelings are not sin properly speaking, they are called "inbred sin,"[7] also known as the "being" of sin.[8] For newborn children, sin "does not *reign*, but it does *remain*"[9], partly in the form of this inbred sin. Conviction of such inbred sin is one branch of the repentance of believers.

---

[1] See, for example, Wesley's sermon 'The Repentance of Believers,' sermon 14, Outler, *Works* (BE).

[2] Wesley, 'Letters to a Young Disciple,' *Works* (Jackson),12:448. See also: Wesley, 'A Letter to Mr. Hosmer,' *Works* (Jackson), 12:239; Wesley, 'A Letter to Mrs. Elizabeth Bennis,' *Works* (Jackson), 12:394.

[3] For evidence that Wesley believes that children of the new birth do not commit voluntary sin, i.e. sin properly called, see: Wesley, 'Marks of the New Birth,' *Works* (BE), 1:420; Wesley, 'The Great Privileges of Those who are born of God,' *Works* (BE), 1:436; Wesley, 'On Sin in Believers,' *Works* (BE), 1:320, 332.

[4] Wesley, 'The Repentance of Believers,' *Works* (BE), 1:336.

[5] Wesley, 'The Repentance of Believers,' *Works* (BE), 1:337.

[6] Wesley, 'The Repentance of Believers,' *Works* (BE), 1:341.

[7] See, for example, Wesley, 'On Patience,' *Works* (BE), 3:175 and Wesley, 'The Repentance of Believers,' *Works* (BE), 1:346.

[8] Wesley, 'On Sin in Believers,' *Works* (BE), 1:328.

[9] Wesley, 'The Repentance of Believers,' *Works* (BE), 1:337.

Besides a conviction of inbred sin, the repentance of believers also involves a conviction of outward sin. This outward sin is active in nature but it is different from sin properly speaking. The difference is that the outward sin of newborn children is involuntary, while sin "properly speaking" is voluntary. For a newborn child, like those before the new birth, outward sin flows from evil inward affections. Such outward sin includes uncharitable conversation, unprofitable conversation, and sins of omission.[10] However, for a newborn child, unlike an impenitent sinner or servant of God, it seems that it is not evident at the time of acting that such actions are transgressions, and in this way, they are involuntary. Yet, such transgressions may become evident to the agent sometime after they occur. Such conviction is another branch of the repentance of believers. Also, for newborn children, inbred sin "cleaves to all our words and actions" in a way that cannot be avoided.[11] In summary, the repentance of believers (the repentance of newborn children) involves conviction of both inbred and outward sin. This is a conviction of "guiltiness," still worthy of death.[12]

The repentance of believers also involves conviction of one's "utter helplessness . . . to think one good work, or do one good work, than before they were justified, that they have still no kind or degree of strength of their own, no power either to do good or resist evil; no ability to conquer or even withstand the world . . . by their own strength." But they know they "have power to overcome all these enemies" because of "'the mere gift of God.'"[13] This point underscores the thesis of this project once again. Even the good works properly speaking that come after the new birth are an expression of God's gift. The pursuit of the greatest end of ethics, as it involves a resolution and a performance of such good works, is an expression of God's gift.

Virtuous Action

For Wesley, virtue is possible only after possessing God's love in the heart.[14] It seems that in some cases, virtue has at least a passive aspect,

---

[10] Wesley, 'The Repentance of Believers,' *Works* (BE), 1:345.

[11] Wesley, 'The Repentance of Believers,' *Works* (BE), 1:345.

[12] Wesley, 'The Repentance of Believers,' *Works* (BE), 1:344.

[13] Wesley, 'The Repentance of Believers,' *Works* (BE), 1:345. See also Wesley, 'The Scripture Way of Salvation,' *Works* (BE), 2:166.

[14] Wesley, 'An Earnest Appeal to Men of Reason and Religion,' *Works* (BE), 11:45; Wesley, 'An Israelite Indeed,' *Works* (BE), 3:279-280; See also the discussion of virtue in

such as when Wesley associates the virtues with humility, faith, hope, and charity.[15] In other cases, virtue refers to a holistic scheme that clearly involves both a passive aspect and an active aspect. Such is the case for what leads to a virtuous action. For example, a virtuous action is a fruitful action that flows from a passive inclination of a holy heart of love.[16] While before the new birth, no fruitful action is virtuous, after the new birth, all fruitful action is virtuous. While the impenitent sinner and servant of God are not capable of performing virtuous action properly speaking, such virtuous action is characteristic of a newborn child.

Virtuous action refers to the performance of any morally preferable action by a child of God (including newborn children). It includes following any part of Wesley's guide for fruitful action. This includes the performances of good works properly speaking such as works of piety (prayer, taking the Lord's Supper, studying the scriptures, and fasting) and works of mercy (feeding the hungry, clothing the naked, entertaining the stranger, visiting those in prison, instructing the ignorant and more).[17] It includes participating in forms of Christian fellowship such as attending church services, watch night-services, preaching services, classes, bands, and love feasts. It includes practicing the means of grace, following the *General Rules* of the Methodist societies, and obeying the moral commandments of scripture.

Ultimately, for Wesley, virtue cannot last without free will, one's power of liberty. As discussed in chapters 1 and 2, for Wesley, a system of necessity and absolute predestination, as he believed was exemplified in the thought of Jonathan Edwards, makes void the possibility of virtue and vice and ethics altogether. This is because, according to Wesley, if fruitful action is only the result of necessity, then humans are no different from clocks and therefore, they cannot be virtuous or held accountable. If a child of the new birth does not use his or her liberty to perform virtuous action on a regular basis, then the effects of grace that have been received on prior occasions will be lost.

Indeed, in order to keep the status of being a child of the new birth and maintain the love of God shed abroad in the heart, it is necessary

---

chapter 1.

[15] Wesley, 'Circumcision of the Heart,' *Works* (BE), 1:403.

[16] Outler, *Works* (BE), 3:279-280; See also the discussion of virtue in chapter 1.

[17] Wesley, 'The Scripture Way of Salvation,' *Works* (BE), 2:166.

for one to perform virtuous action. In order to illustrate this point, Wesley uses the parable of the talents from Matthew 25:14-30. Wesley says,

> whoever improves the grace he has already received, whoever increases in the love of God, will surely retain it. God will continue, yea, will give it more abundantly; whereas whoever does not improve this talent cannot possibly retain it. Notwithstanding all he can do, it will infallibly be taken away from him.[18]

Wesley indicates that if a newborn child chooses to perform virtuous action, then more grace is received. If such a newborn does not preform virtuous action, then he or she will lose the grace that has already been given. That is, such a person will lose the effects of the new birth. Such a person will grow "dead and cold" and "destroy all the life of God out of their souls."[19]

The Ethics of the Newborn Child

For a newborn child, the various features of the soul have been transformed by the Holy Spirit. This transformation involves an array of passive experiences. At the first moment of the new birth, the love of God is shed abroad in the heart. This involves receiving the Spirit of adoption and the Spirit of the Son entering the heart. It involves the transformation of one's tempers and a replacement of one's ruling inclination of the heart. Such a newborn also has the faith of a child of God, the witness of the Spirit, and the witness of one's own spirit that one is a child of God. The newborn child also feels a second type of repentance. This repentance is a conviction that although sin does not reign, it remains. It involves a conviction of inbred sin and sin improperly speaking. Inbred sin involves the lingering influence of evil inward tempers, and sin improperly speaking involves involuntary transgressions of God's law.

The ethics of a newborn stresses the importance of virtuous action. For a newborn child, a holy heart makes the doing of right action come easily. The "springs" of the heart facilitate the doing of such good action. Wesley speaks of the love of the new birth as making one "constrained to love all men as yourselves; with a love not only ever burning in your

---

[18] Wesley, 'An Israelite Indeed,' *Works* (BE), 3:284.
[19] Wesley, *Letters*, 7:109.

heart, but flaming out in all your actions and conversations."[20] Such flaming actions are fruitful actions, and all fruitful actions after the new birth are virtuous actions. Virtuous action must be performed or else one will lose all of the spiritual effects of the new birth.

For Wesley, a newborn child is subject to two types of spiritual growth. One is gradual. The other type involves an instantaneous transformation. In chapter 2 of this project, we explored analogies corresponding to each type of spiritual growth. The gradual process of growth is comparable to the illustration of the fit woman, and the other type is comparable to the illustration of the flaming dart. For the case of the newborn child, we will introduce the flaming dart as a *second* flaming dart.

For Wesley, gradual growth typically occurs in sanctification between the two major foci of sanctification, which are the first moment of the new birth and the first moment of Christian perfection.[21] In the illustration of the fit woman, the act of exercising leads to a nurturing of one's inclination for exercise. Similarly, in the life of a newborn child, the practice of good works leads to the nurturing of one's tempers of the heart. As discussed in chapter 5, these good works are only possible by grace and are themselves co-operating action. The Spirit is the doer. The performance of such good works leads to reflexive Christian growth that occurs gradually.[22] Such reflexive growth is only possible by grace.

For the newborn child, as for all other stages of the Christian life, the highest goal of Christian living is to love God and neighbor to one's full potential. The newborn already possesses Christian love and so in a sense has already partly reached the highest goal. Yet, for a newborn, there remains room for growth. Wesley has a notion of perfect love, i.e. Christian perfection, a state of being that is above being a newborn child. The first moment of Christian perfection marks a spike in spiritual growth. It represents a distinctively higher capacity to love God and other people. As a newborn child seeks the greatest end of Christian living, such a newborn is seeking perfect love, as this largely represents the fulfilment of this greatest end of Christian living.

---

[20] Wesley, 'The Marks of the New Birth,' *Works* (BE), 1:428.

[21] Wesley, *Letters*, 3:213; Wesley, *Letters*, 5:39; Wesley, 'The Wilderness State,' *Works* (BE), 2:220; Wesley, 'The New Birth,' *Works* (BE), 2:198.

[22] For discussions of Wesley's view of gradual growth, please see, for example, Outler, editor, *Works* (BE), 1:164, 1:520, 2:19, 2:43, 2:60, and 2:235.

The pursuit of perfect love is comparable to the illustration of the flaming dart from chapter 2, except now the illustration involves a *second* flaming dart. We considered the situation of the first flaming dart in the discussion in chapter 6 concerning the servant of God. The impact of the first flaming dart is analogous to a person's experience of the first moment of the new birth, the point of time when a servant of God transitions to becoming a newborn child. In this chapter, the focus is on a second flaming dart, analogous to the first moment of perfect love, the point in time when a newborn child transitions to being a child of perfect love. For a newborn child, the situation is parallel to the situation of the servant of God. Like before, faith is the only indispensable condition for the spiritual change. Fruitful action is necessary for perfect love, only if there is time and opportunity.

Since the faith alone regarding perfection is sufficient for perfect love and is the only indispensable condition, it is fine for a newborn to hope for perfect love to come *now*. This is like in an illustration of a second flaming dart in which one hopes for the second dart to come *now*. Wesley makes the following remark in reference to perfect love:

> If by works, you want something to be done *first, before* you are sanctified. You think, 'I must first *be* or *do* thus or thus.' Then you are seeking it by works unto this day. If you seek it by faith, you may expect it as you are: and if as you are, then expect it *now*.[23]

It is best to hope that perfect love (the second flaming dart) comes now, while also practising fruitful action as there is opportunity. This is more preferable than other approaches such as: (a) doing fruitful action while assuming that perfect love must come later and (b) expecting perfect love to come now without doing any fruitful action.[24] According to Wesley, in all stages of human living, it is important for fruitful action to be constantly performed, even if such fruitful actions are never in themselves sufficient for gifts such as the new birth and Christian per-

---

[23] Wesley, 'The Scripture Way of Salvation,' *Works* (BE), 2:169. He repeats his message to expect perfection "now" in his 1784 sermon, *On Patience*. See Wesley, 'On Patience,' *Works* (BE), 3:179.

[24] In response to approach b, consider Wesley's comment, "God can give the end without any means at all; but you have no reason to think he will. Therefore constantly and carefully use all these means which he has appointed to be the ordinary channels of his grace" (Wesley, 'The Nature of Enthusiam,' *Works* (BE), 2:59).

fection. Anything less than a constant performance of fruitful action is bound to lead to spiritual laziness and backsliding.

The arrival of the first moment of perfect love (analogous to the impact of the second flaming dart) involves events that are passive in a bare sense. However, as discussed in chapter 2 of this project, when viewed in a larger context, the arrival of perfect love is "not altogether" passive. This is because, if there is time and opportunity, graciously-empowered fruitful action before and after the first moments of perfect love have bearing on whether or not perfect love is received and maintained.

Wesley never backs down from the importance that he gives in pursuing perfect love. He continues to encourage this pursuit in the 1760s until the end of his life.[25] In 1779 he says, "exhort all the believers strongly and explicitly to go on to perfection," and in 1791, the year of his death, he says: "Whenever you have opportunity of speaking to believers, urge them to go on to perfection."[26] His confidence arises in part from the multitude of cases he has observed in the Methodist revival in addition to what he considered to be an obvious teaching in the scriptures. As in the illustration of the second flaming dart, the timing of the arrival of perfect love is unpredictable. Nevertheless, if one maintains a constant pursuit of such perfect love, it will certainly come at an unknown future time. The pursuit itself of perfect love involves the performance of fruitful action.

For a newborn child, fruitful action is always virtuous action (and also a good work properly speaking), and it is the expression of God's gift. This is because, in every instance of its occurrence, virtuous action must spring from a holy heart of love. Such a holy heart of love involves a passive inclination and is the effect of the work of God alone. God's role does not cease after the transformation of the heart but is "flaming out"[27] in all virtuous action. As always, the active nature of fruitful action is co-operating. The person is never acting alone but always in partnership with the Holy Spirit. Such co-operation is in response to the prior passive operations of the Spirit on the heart and soul (the love of God shed abroad in the heart, the faith of a child of God, the witness of the Spirit). In this way, we observe how once again for Wesley, the pursuit

---

[25] For example, see: Wesley, *Letters*, 4:242, 5:346, 6:343, 7:170, 8:258. The latest letter of this list was written in 1791.

[26] Wesley, *Letters*, 6:343, 8:258.

[27] Wesley, 'The Marks of the New Birth,' *Works* (BE), 1:428.

of Christian love and the performance of fruitful action are the expressions of God's gift.

The Child of Perfect Love

Throughout his life, Wesley maintained a scriptural doctrine of Christian perfection. As Henry Rack points out, holding this doctrine did not come without some controversy and disagreement.[28] Nevertheless, Wesley supported this doctrine by insisting that it emerges from a careful reading of scripture, from how he observed the Holy Spirit to be working throughout the revival of his time, and from his experiences in dealing with the Methodist communities. In response to his critics, Wesley writes in regard to Christian perfection: "This perfection cannot be a delusion, unless the Bible be a delusion too; I mean, 'loving God with all our heart and our neighbor as ourselves.' I pin down all its opposers to this definition of it."[29] This is to say that Wesley finds confidence in this doctrine because he believes that it is simply obedience to the greatest commandment of scripture: Deuteronomy 6:5, Matthew 22:37-39, etc.[30] This is the greatest commandment of the Bible, as given in the Old Testament and from the mouth of Jesus himself.

Wesley also quotes Matthew 5:48: "Ye shall therefore be perfect, as your Father who is in heaven is perfect."[31] He also frequently cites many other scriptures in support of the doctrine of perfection.[32] In addition

---

[28] Henry Rack. *Reasonable Enthusiast, John Wesley and the Rise of Methodism* (Nashville, TN: Abingdon Press, 1993), 334.

[29] Wesley, *Letters*, 5:102

[30] In support of his doctrine of perfection Wesley cites Matthew 5:48, Matthew 22:37 (Wesley, 'A Plain Account of Christian Perfection,' *Works* (BE), 13:162) and Deuteronomy 6:5 (Wesley, 'A Plain Account of Christian Perfection,' *Works* (BE), 13:159).

[31] Wesley, 'A Plain Account of Christian Perfection,' *Works* (BE), 13:189. Here he cites the Greek word for perfect, τέλειοι. For more discussion of this Greek term, see Wesley's discussion of James 1:4 in his sermon *On Patience* (Wesley, 'On Patience,' *Works* (BE), 3:179)

[32] These includes, for example, James 1:4 (Wesley, 'On Patience,' *Works* (BE), 3:170), Hebrews 6:1 (Wesley, 'On Perfection,' *Works* (BE), 3:71), Phillipians 3:12 (Wesley, 'Christian Perfection,' *Works* (BE), 2:99), Deuteronomy 30:6 (Wesley, 'The Imperfection of Human Knowledge,' *Works* (BE), 2:584), and those from *A Plain Account of Christian Perfection* found in the *Works* (Jackson): include: Phillipians 3:15 and 1 John 4:18 (11:442), Hebrews 10:14 (11:418), Romans 13:9-10(11:416), 1 Corinthians 13 (11:390), John 17:20-23 (11:390), and 2

to using scripture as a foundation for this doctrine of Christian perfection, Wesley shows that it fits what is observed in the real world. It fits the accounts of how numerous people in the real world have experienced the work of the Holy Spirit. He says, "That perfection which I believe, I can boldly preach, because I think I see five hundred witnesses of it."[33]

As mentioned above, Wesley defines his scriptural doctrine of Christian perfection as loving God with all one's heart, soul, mind, and strength and loving one's neighbor. Harald Lindström describes love to God as the highest end in Wesley's teleology.[34] This is "perfect love."[35] He also describes it as "the mind which was in Christ," "the renewal of the heart in the whole image of God," and a full "circumcision of the heart."[36] "Perfect" is the English translation of the Greek word from the Bible τέλειος.[37] Some offer that "perfect" (or "perfection") is a misleading translation and that one could also translate this Biblical term as "reaching an ideal" or "being made complete."

We will use the phrase "perfected child" to refer to someone for whom God has given perfect love. At the moment that a person first experiences perfect love, this person shifts from being a newborn child to being a child of perfect love. A child of perfect love is still a "child" of God (not a newborn), but such a perfected child possesses some spiritual gifts that a newborn has not yet received. At the first moment of experiencing perfect love, a person possesses for the first time the faith of a perfected child, a pure heart, the freedom from evil thoughts, and the witness of a perfected child. As Geordan Hammond observes, for Wesley, Christian perfection also involves imitating Christ.[38] We will now consider in more depth the spiritual blessings that first occur when a person becomes a child of perfect love.

Corinthians 7:1 and Deuteronomy 30:6 (11:389).

[33] Wesley, *Letters*, 5:20.

[34] Harald Lindström, *Wesley and Sanctification* (London: The Epworth Press, 1946), 189.

[35] Wesley, 'A Plain Account of Christian Perfection,' *Works* (BE), 13:187.

[36] Wesley, 'A Plain Account of Christian Perfection,' *Works* (BE), 13:189.

[37] For Wesley's discussion of this term, see Wesley, 'A Plain Account of Christian Perfection,' *Works* (BE), 13:189 and Wesley, 'On Patience,' *Works* (BE), 3:179. The plural form is used here because this is what Wesley uses when he quotes the scripture.

[38] Geordan Hammond, "John Wesley and 'Imitating' Christ," *Wesleyan Theological Journal*, 45, (2010): 212.

Faith of the Perfected Child, Pure Heart, and the Witness of the Perfected Child

The first moment of being a child of perfect love immediately accompanies the first moment of having the faith of a perfected child. Wesley believes that perfect love is the free gift of God, the effect of free grace, and is "is to be received by plain, simple faith."[39] This faith involves a belief that God has promised to save one from all sin and to fill one with all holiness; that God is able to save one to the uttermost—including giving perfect love—; that He is willing to do this; and that He is willing to do this now.[40] God gives this faith so as to "enable you to believe, it [Christian perfection] is done."[41] There seems to be a passive aspect of this faith of a perfected child.

The first moment of experiencing perfect love also includes God's creation of a pure heart. Although when a person becomes a newborn child, there is a partial transformation of the heart, a full transformation of the heart does not occur until experiencing perfect love. The hearts of newborns are "truly, yet not entirely, renewed."[42] "Sin is then overcome, but it is not rooted out; it is conquered, but not destroyed."[43] While the newborn child continues to have passive feelings of inbred sin (including sinful affections and lusts[44]), the child of perfect love has all inbred sin taken away.[45] For a perfected child, "no wrong temper"... "remains in the soul,"[46] "there is no mixture of any contrary affections,"[47] and there is no interruption of love.[48] In other words "inbred sin," also known as the "being of sin," is removed.[49] Love is already the ruling inclination before perfect love. Yet, perfect love also implies the implanting of more good dispositions.[50] All of this is why a perfected child has a

---

[39] 'On Patience,' *Works* (BE), 3:179.
[40] 'On Patience,' *Works* (BE), 3:179.
[41] 'On Patience,' *Works* (BE), 3:179.
[42] Wesley, 'On Sin in Believers,' *Works* (BE), 1:326.
[43] Wesley, 'The Deceitfulness of the Human Heart,' *Works* (BE), 4:157.
[44] Wesley, 'On Sin in Believers,' *Works* (BE), 1:329.
[45] Wesley, 'A Plain Account of Christian Perfection,' *Works* (BE), 13:159.
[46] Wesley, 'A Plain Account of Christian Perfection,' *Works* (BE), 13:167.
[47] Wesley, 'On Patience,' *Works* (BE), 3:176.
[48] Wesley, 'On Patience,' *Works* (BE), 3:176.
[49] For citations concerning "inward sin," "inbred sin," and the "being" of sin, see above.
[50] Wesley, 'On the Discoveries of Faith,' *Works* (BE), 4:37.

"pure heart." The heart is now completely full of love, not partly full of love. Unlike a newborn child, a child of perfect love is also rid of all evil thoughts.[51]

At the initial moment of experiencing perfect love, it is common for a person also to experience a witness that one is a child of perfect love. The witness of the perfected child does not exclude the type of witness that is found in a newborn child. A perfected child has all the witnesses of the newborn child (the witness of the Spirit that Christ died for me and that my sins are forgiven and the witness of my own spirit of this forgiveness that comes from observing in myself the love of God and fruits of the Spirit), plus an additional witness. The witness that is held only by a perfected child and not by a newborn child is what is being described here as a "witness of a perfected child." In a sense, the latter is parallel in form to the former. In regard to form: like for the witness of a newborn, the witness of a perfected child involves a certain testimony from two sources: (1) the witness of the Spirit of God and (2) the witness of one's own human spirit.[52]

Unlike the witness of a newborn child, the witness of a perfected child is "'an inward witness, that I am fully renewed, as that I am justified.'"[53] The Spirit gives this witness of perfect love directly by means of performing an impression upon the soul. By contrast, the witness of one's own spirit is an inference that one can make about oneself in regard to reaching perfect love. This inference is made by observing within oneself the perceivable effects of perfect love, such as a fullness of love, the absence of the passive feelings of sinful tempers, and a stronger presence of the fruits of the Spirit. The witness of the Spirit is passive in a bare sense. In regard to the feeling of a fullness of love and the absence of evil tempers, the witness of one's own spirit is also passive in a bare sense. The first occurrences of these witnesses are unpredictable and not fully subject to one's active regulation.

[51] Wesley, 'Remarks on Mr .Hill's "Review,"' *Works* (BE), 13:465.

[52] For a discussion of the witness that one is perfected child, see Wesley, 'A Plain Account of Christian Perfection,' *Works* (Jackson), 11:420-421, 11:426. For a discussion of the witness that one is a child of God, see, for example, Wesley, 'The Witness of the Spirit, II,' *Works* (BE), 1:289.

[53] Wesley, 'A Plain Account of Christian Perfection,' *Works* (Jackson), 11:398-399, 11:402, 11:426. Wesley also says, "In the *Thoughts on Perfection* it is observed that, before any can be assured they are saved from sin, they must not only feel no sin but 'have a direct witness' of that salvation." Wesley, *Letters*, 4:269.

In addition to the witness that one is a child of God and the witness that one is a perfected child, there are other forms of spiritual testimony in Wesley's thought. For some, this may make Wesley's view of spiritual testimony seem rather complicated. Wesley teaches that there is something called the "full assurance of faith" and the "full assurance of hope." The full assurance of faith is possessed by someone who is at a spiritual stage no lower than a "young" person in Christ.[54] Possessing this is what distinguishes a young person (spiritually speaking) from a newborn child. A perfected child, like a young person, will often have this type of assurance. The full assurance of faith is an abiding witness of the Spirit that one is a child of God, and it tends to exclude doubts and tormenting fear.[55] This is a stronger and more continuous witness of the Spirit than what is given to a newborn child. Wesley says that the newborn child will have a less abiding witness and suffer more doubts and more tormenting fears.[56]

The full assurance of hope is different from the full assurance of faith. Only those who are no lower than a perfected child may receive the "full assurance of hope," and this is not a gift possessed by all perfected children.[57] The full assurance of hope is a confidence that one is not only saved but also sure that one will remain saved and reign with Christ in glory.[58]

Instantaneous, Perceived, and Unpredictable Beginning of Perfection

Wesley's view of the instantaneous nature of the first moment of experiencing perfect love is evident from the following comments concerning perfect love: "the gift itself is always given instantaneously. I never knew or heard of any exception; and I believe there never was one."[59] He repeats this view in various comments after 1758.[60] In 1789 (two years

---

[54] Wesley, 'On the Discoveries of Faith,' *Works* (BE), 4:36.
[55] Wesley, 'On the Discoveries of Faith,' *Works* (BE), 4:36.
[56] Wesley, 'On the Discoveries of Faith,' *Works* (BE), 4:36.
[57] Wesley, 'On the Discoveries of Faith,' *Works* (BE), 4:37.
[58] Wesley, 'On the Discoveries of Faith,' *Works* (BE), 4:37.
[59] Wesley, *Letters*, 3:213.
[60] See, for example, Wesley, *Letters*, 5:39; Wesley, 'On Patience,' *Works* (BE), 3:178; and Wesley, 'A Plain Account of Christian Perfection,' *Works* (BE), 3:178. In the latter case, Wesley argues that perfection is instantaneous in some cases where the change in this instant is not perceived right way.

before his death), he repeats this claim again: "full deliverance from sin, I believe, is always instantaneous — at least, I never yet knew an exception."[61]

For Wesley, the possession of perfect love is something that a perfected person perceives. The first moment of such perfect love is usually perceived. This point is clear from Wesley's view of the witness of a perfected child discussed above. This may not be true for all people,[62] but all people should at some point perceive the effects of having gained perfect love, if not at the first moment. The perceivable aspect of perfect love is also evident from how at the first moment of perfect love, the heart is transformed in a perceivable way. After experiencing perfect love, one then no longer feels the passive feelings of evil tempers. One now feels instead a fuller sense of the passive feelings of God's love and other associated holy tempers. In the child of perfect love, there is "an experimental verity and a plenitude of the presence of the ever-blessed Trinity."[63] Another perceivable aspect of perfect love is happiness. Wesley says "according to the degree of our love is the degree of our happiness,"[64] and he says when we are "'complete in him' . . . then we are completely happy."[65]

The first moment of experiencing perfect love is unpredictable. This is evident from many observations in the context of doing ministry. Wesley says,

> There is likewise a great variety in the manner and time of God's bestowing his *sanctifying grace*, whereby he enables his children to give him their whole heart, which we can in no wise account for. We know not why he bestows this on some even before they ask for it (some unquestionable instances of which we have seen); on some after they have sought it but a few days; and yet permits other believers to wait for it perhaps twenty, thirty, or forty years; nay, and others till a few hours or even minutes before their spirits return to him. For the various circumstances also which attend the fulfilling of that great promise, 'I will circumcise thy heart, to love the Lord thy God with all thy heart and with all they soul,' God undoubtedly has reasons; but those reasons are generally hid from the children of men.[66]

[61] Wesley, *Letters*, 8:190.
[62] Wesley, 'A Plain Account of Christian Perfection,' *Works* (BE), 13:188.
[63] Wesley, 'On the Discoveries of Faith,' *Works* (BE), 4:37.
[64] Wesley, 'An Israelite Indeed,' *Works* (BE), 3:283.
[65] Wesley, 'Spiritual Worship,' *Works* (BE), 3:96-97.
[66] Wesley, 'The Imperfection of Human Knowledge,' *Works* (BE), 2:584.

Some receive perfection before they ask for it. Others, who work equally hard in seeking it, receive it at different times. Some wait a few minutes, some wait a few hours, and some wait many years. The reasons for variation in timing are unknown to a person. The lack of predictability concerning the instantaneous arrival of perfection is a point that Wesley makes on multiple occasions throughout the 1760s and 1780s.[67] Such a lack of predictability underscores the passivity of the first moment of perfection. In this way, the first moment of perfection is comparable to the illustration of a second flaming dart that is discussed above.

Not Absolute Perfection

A perfected child is perfect in the sense that such a person does not commit sin properly speaking (a voluntary transgression of a known law of God), does not have "inbred sin" (the passive feeling of evil tempers), and has gained a fullness of love and associated holy tempers. However, Wesley teaches that there is not "absolute perfection" on earth.[68] Even perfected children suffer from the following conditions that prevent them from reaching absolute perfection: ignorance, errors, infirmities and involuntary transgressions (sin improperly speaking).[69]

"Infirmities" include involuntary failings such as inadvertently saying something is true when it is false and hurting a neighbor without knowing it.[70] They also include inward and outward imperfections such as slowness of understanding, dullness of apprehension, irregular quickness or heaviness of imagination, and slowness of speech.[71] They include what are called "bodily infirmities," and a thousand other defects of conversation or behaviour.[72] Wesley indicates that an infirmity can lead to a wrong judgment or wrong affection which leads to wrong words and actions.[73] In this way, although perfected children do not have

---

[67] Wesley, *Letters*, 5:39 and 4:321; Wesley, 'A Plain Account of Christian Perfection,' *Works* (Jackson), 11:423.

[68] Wesley, 'Christian Perfection,' *Works* (BE), 2:104; Wesley, 'A Plain Account of Christian Perfection,' *Works* (BE), 13:187.

[69] Wesley, 'On Perfection,' *Works* (BE) 3:73; Wesley, 'A Plain Account of Christian Perfection,' *Works* (BE), 13:169.

[70] Wesley, 'The First-Fruits of the Spirit,' *Works* (BE), 1:241.

[71] Wesley, 'Christian Perfection,' *Works* (BE), 2:103.

[72] Wesley, 'Christian Perfection,' *Works* (BE), 2:103.

[73] Wesley, 'On Perfection,' *Works* (BE), 3:73.

inbred sin, their infirmities can lead them to commit involuntary transgressions.[74]

In addition to being subject to infirmities and involuntary transgressions, a perfected child is also subject to temptations.[75] Some infirmities in fact lead to temptations. Here is where one may raise the question: if a perfected child does not possess inbred sin (the feeling of evil tempers or inclinations), how can such a person be tempted? On Wesley's behalf, there are two possible ways to answer this question. One way is to offer yet again that a temper is different from a fleeting affection.[76] An infirmity can lead to a temptation that is a clearly felt affection, but this is fleeting and short-lasting. All inbred sin—understood as tempers, which are more lasting inclinations and feelings—remains fully cleansed. Another way to answer this question is to say that when a perfected child suffers a "grievously"[77] troublesome temptation, this is more descriptive of an external force than an evil feeling. Consider Wesley's analogy of a man striking another man in the face.[78] If the strike is somewhat hard, it is grievously troublesome. However, as the illustration goes, the reaction is for the recipient of the strike to feel nothing but a "heart that overflows with love."[79] The reaction does not involve a flare up of an evil feeling, which in this case would be anger. In this way, the temptation refers more to an external force and less to an evil feeling.

For Wesley, repentance is possible even for perfected children.[80] It is clear that he believes that perfected children should be aware of ways that they fail to reach absolute perfection. Perfected children may have convictions of their involuntary outward transgressions of the moral law. Also, perfected children must continue to recognize that all good that is in them and done by them is only possible through the free grace of God that precedes, empowers, and accompanies for every good work.

---

[74] Wesley, 'A Plain Account of Christian Perfection,' *Works* (BE), 13:170, 'On Temptation,' *Works* (BE), 3:162.

[75] Outler, editor, *Works* (BE), 2:105 and 3:162;*Works* (BE), 9:54.

[76] See the related discussion in chapter 4.

[77] See Wesley, 'A Plain Account of Christian Perfection,' *Works* (BE), 13:151. He uses the word "grievously" in regard to temptation.

[78] Wesley, 'A Plain Account of Christian Perfection,' *Works* (Jackson), 11:419. On some occasions, it is useful to cite the Jackson edition of this treatise since, unlike the bicentennial edition, the former edition quotes the whole text.

[79] Wesley, 'A Plain Account of Christian Perfection,' *Works* (Jackson), 11:419.

[80] See, for example, Wesley, *Letters*, 4:189-190.

In this way, perfected children are aware that their fruitful action is nothing more than an expression of God's gift.

The Ethics of the Perfected Child

The child of perfect love has all of the spiritual gifts of the newborn child, except that for a child of perfect love, the repentance of inbred sin is no longer necessary (see diagram 7.1). The perfected child has received some spiritual gifts that the newborn does not yet have. This includes having the faith of a perfected child, a pure heart,[81] the full assurance of faith, and the witness (from God and oneself) that one is perfect in love. Perfected children sometimes also have a full assurance of hope. All of these gifts involve some degree of passive experience and the work of God alone. Having a pure heart means that a perfected child has a higher capacity for loving God and neighbor. A perfected child is now able to love God with all of his or her heart, soul, mind, and strength. This means that a perfected child has basically reached the *telos*, the greatest end of Christian living. However, one has only "basically" reached this greatest end because Wesley teaches that even a perfected child has room for further spiritual growth.

For Wesley, a perfected child must continue to perform fruitful action (also known in this case as good works and virtuous action) or else this person will lose the grace that enables this person to be a perfected child. In regard to Christian perfection, Wesley says, "I do not include an impossibility of falling from it, either in part or in whole."[82] By following Wesley's guide for fruitful action, which includes imitating Christ, practicing the means of grace, following the *General Rules* of the Methodist societies, and obeying the moral commandments of scripture, one removes any possibility of falling from perfect love. Such action also assists the gradual growth that takes place after Christian perfection.[83] In regard to such growth of a perfected child Wesley says, "Yet he still grows in grace, in the knowledge of Christ, in the love and image of God; and will do so, not only till death, but to all eternity."[84]

---

[81] Welsey, 'A Plain Account of Christian Perfection,' *Works* (BE), 13:155.

[82] Wesley, *Letters*, 5:38.

[83] For Wesley's discussion of the gradual growth that takes place after perfection, see, for example: *Works* (BE), 11:126 and 13:175; Wesley, *Letters*, 5:39.

[84] Wesley, 'A Plain Account of Christian Perfection,' *Works* (BE), 13:175.

The kind gradual growth that takes place here in some way resembles the illustration of the fit woman in chapter 2. This is the same type of gradual growth that we observed for a newborn child that takes place between the first moment of the new birth and the first moment of Christian perfection. Yet, here, gradual growth is taking place for one who is at a higher spiritual state. In the illustration of the fit woman, the act of exercising leads to a nurturing of one's inclination for exercise. Likewise, in the life of a child of perfect love, the practice of good works leads to the nurturing of one's pure tempers of the heart. As discussed in chapter 5, these good works are only possible by grace and are themselves co-operating action. The Spirit is the doer. The performance of such good works leads to reflexive Christian growth that occurs gradually.[85] Such reflexive growth is only possible by grace.

One may ask the question: if one already has a pure heart, how is there room for gradual growth? Wesley makes it clear in the above statement that one is growing in the knowledge and love of God. Thus, as a perfected child grows spiritually, this person becomes more knowledgeable and the magnitude of his or her inclination of love increases. Thus, as a perfected child grows in love, this person possesses even a stronger desire, a stronger "fire" so to speak, to love and serve God and neighbor.

Another factor to consider for the ethics of a perfected child is a consideration of the rewards that one will receive in heaven in proportion to the good works that one performs on earth.[86] Indeed, in agreement with his close associate John Fletcher, Wesley holds the doctrine of final justification by works.[87] Here, there is not as much concern for whether there is time and opportunity. If there is not time and opportunity during normal life on earth, there will be time on the day of judgment, at which time a person will have the time do what needs to be done and say what needs to be said.[88]

---

[85] For discussions of Wesley's view of gradual growth, please see, for example, Outler, editor, *Works* (BE), 1:164, 1:520, 2:19, 2:43, 2:60, and 2:235.

[86] Wesley, 'Of Hell,' *Works* (BE) 3:37. This point will be discussed more later in this chapter. See the section "Final Justification and the Rewards of Heaven."

[87] Wesley, 'The Great Assize,' *Works* (BE), 1:363. This point will be discussed more later in this chapter. See the section "Final Justification and the Rewards of Heaven."

[88] Wesley, 'The Great Assize,' *Works* (BE), 1:363-364.

However, usually, there will be time and opportunity for doing good works during normal life on earth, either as a newborn or as a perfected child. Wesley teaches that the rewards that a person will receive in heaven are in proportion to such good works.[89] This is further reason for a perfected child to perform fruitful action. Nevertheless, the primary reason that a perfected person performs fruitful action is because this person's heart is completely full of love and because he or she cares about God and neighbors. This loves strongly motivates the perfected child to love God and neighbor, making such a way of living come easy. There does not need to be any promise of reward for this to happen. However, at the Day of Judgment people are rewarded according to their works, and so this is further reason for a perfected child to do good works all the more.

In summary of the ethics of the perfected person, the fruitful actions of a perfected child are not possible because of anything inherent in the human doer. For this child of perfect love, the pursuit of higher levels of love and the virtuous actions that help constitute this pursuit are the expression of God's gift. This is because, in every instance of its occurrence, virtuous action must spring from a pure heart of love. Such a pure heart of love involves a passive inclination and is the effect of the work of God alone. God's role does not cease after giving the gift of perfect love but is "flaming out"[90] with flames of perfect love in all virtuous action. As always, the active nature of fruitful action is co-operating. The person is never acting alone but always in partnership with the Holy Spirit in response to the prior passive operations of the Spirit on the heart and soul (a heart of perfect love, the faith of a perfected child, the full assurance of faith, the witness of the Spirit that one is perfected, etc.). In this way, we observe how once again for Wesley, the pursuit of Christian love and the performance of fruitful action are the expressions of God's gift.

The Inhabitant of Heaven

For Wesley, when a saved person dies, he or she will end up in heaven for all eternity. Wesley refers to a person who makes it to heaven as an

---

[89] The evidence in support of this point will be explored later in this chapter.

[90] Wesley, 'The Marks of the New Birth,' *Works* (BE), 1:428.

"inhabitant of heaven."[91] For this section, we will explore Wesley's view of such an inhabitant and then consider the ethics of such a person.

From Death to the Great Judgment

Wesley teaches that when a person dies, this person's soul is immediately separated from the body,[92] and the soul is sent to Hades.[93] Even though the great judgment, also known as the "great assize," does not occur until later, the person will usually know right away at death whether he or she is going to heaven or hell.[94] Note that for Wesley, Hades is distinct from heaven and hell.[95] Hades is where all souls of those who are dead go before the judgment, and heaven and hell are places where all people go after the judgment.[96] In Hades, there is a great gulf separating the holy and unholy souls.[97] All souls will remain in Hades until the great judgment.[98] The great judgment occurs at the end of the world—the end of regular life on earth for all humankind—, when the throne comes down from heaven and Jesus the Son of Man comes with clouds to judge the living and the dead.[99] Although most souls are aware in Hades of whether they are going to heaven or hell, there is only one judgment and this occurs when Jesus comes in the scenario just described.[100] At the judgment, all the souls from Hades are reunited with

[91] Wesley, 'On Eternity,' *Works* (BE), 2:365, bottom of page.
[92] Wesley, 'The Good Steward,' *Works* (BE), 2:292. This sermon was first published in 1768, with later publications as a single sermon in 1782, 1784, and 1788.
[93] Wesley, 'On Faith,' *Works* (BE), 4:189
[94] Wesley, 'The Good Steward,' *Works* (BE), 2:292. This sermon was first published in 1768, with later publications as a single sermon in 1782, 1784, and 1788.
[95] Wesley, 'On Faith,' *Works* (BE), 4:190-191.
[96] Wesley, 'On Faith,' *Works* (BE), 4:189-191.
[97] Wesley, 'On Faith,' *Works* (BE), 4:190.
[98] Wesley, 'On Faith,' *Works* (BE), 4:190.
[99] Wesley, 'The Good Steward,' *Works* (BE), 2:293. The sermon was first published in 1768 and published later as a single sermon in 1782, 1784, 1788]. Wesley, 'The Great Assize,' *Works* (BE), 1:358. This sermon was first published in 1758, with later publications of this single sermon in 1782, 1783, 1784, 1785, and 1787.
[100] Wesley, 'The Good Steward,' *Works* (BE), 2:292. This sermon was first published in 1768, with later publications as a single sermon in 1782, 1784, and 1788.

their bodies[101] and judged and rewarded "according to their works."[102] The holy people are given final justification and sent to heaven and the unholy people are sent to Hell.[103]

Final Justification and the Rewards of Heaven

There has been some discussion and debate over whether or not Wesley's eschatology (view of the end times) is best described as premillennialist, postmillennialist, or amillenialist.[104] Regardless of any possible room for debate, some aspects of his view of the end times remain clear. It is clear that Wesley believes the following concerning the end times: (1) God leads a judgment of all people after regular human life on earth has finished, (2) the gift of final justification will be given to certain people on this day of judgment, and (3) people will be rewarded or punished in proportion to their works during their previous life on earth. It is apparent that God gives the gifts of final justification and other heavenly rewards in a manner that is first passive with respect to the person. These are the works of God alone. However, fruitful action during life on earth has a relation to whether or not the Spirit will later give these gifts and the level at which heavenly rewards will be given. This is because the way God gives these gifts (or whether he gives them) is done "according to"[105] what a person does during normal life on earth.

Consider Wesley's view of final justification.[106] This kind of justification means "acquittal at the last day."[107] The fact that Wesley believes

---

[101] Wesley, 'The Great Assize,' *Works* (BE), 1:358. This sermon was first published in 1758, with later publications of this single sermon in 1782, 1783, 1784, 1785, and 1787.

[102] This idea of being rewarded according to one's works will be discussed more below.

[103] Wesley, 'On Faith,' *Works* (BE), 4:190-191.

[104] Maddox, *Responsible Grace*, 236.

[105] Wesley, 'The Great Assize,' *Works* (BE), 1:359 (This sermon was first published in 1758, with later publications of this single sermon in 1782, 1783, 1784, 1785, and 1787). It should also be remembered that the basis of judgment is not necessarily quantity of works. Consider Wesley's point about the poor widow and how Jesus did less works than some of the disciples (Wesley, 'A Plain Account of Christian Perfection,' *Works* (BE), 13:173).

[106] John Fletcher, Wesley's close partner and ally in religious discourse, has much to say on this subject. Wesley cautions his critics by saying that Wesley's view could be different from Fletcher's view on some matters (Wesley, 'Some Remarks on Mr. Hill's "Review,"' *Works* (BE), 13:476). Yet, in Fletcher's "checks"

there is a final justification in the first place is evident by his comment, "I do not deny that there is another justification (of which our Lord speaks) at the last day. I do not therefore condemn the distinction of a two-fold justification."[108] Yet, Wesley goes further than simply holding a doctrine of final justification: he adds that this final justification is by works.[109] Final justification is not to be confused with first justification—something that Wesley believes the scriptures teach is by faith alone. Wesley claims that these two doctrines are not in conflict with each other and are faithful to what the Bible teaches in the writings of Paul, James, and the gospels.[110] Justification by faith alone is evident from Paul's teachings in Romans 4:5 and Romans 3:28.[111] One could argue that final justification by works is apparent from Paul's teachings in Romans 2:13:

---

to Antinomianism, Fletcher sees himself as defending Wesley's view, particularly with respect to claims concerning human action made in the 1770 Minutes. Fletcher discusses the doctrine of final justification in many places in his writings. See, for example, John Fletcher, *Logica Genevensis or a fourth Check to Antinomianism* (Bristol: W. Pine, 1772), 58.

[107] Wesley, 'Letter to Reverend Dr. Horne,' *Works* (Jackson), 9:110.

[108] Wesley, 'Some Remarks on Mr. Hill's Farrago Double-Distilled,' *Works* (BE), 13:507.

[109] Wesley, 'The Great Assize,' *Works* (BE), 1:363; Wesley, 'Remarks on Mr. Hill's Farrago Double-Distilled,' *Works* (BE), 13:509. Notice that, in his sermon 'The Great Assize,' Wesley adds here the words "as well as works." This comment underscores the view that final justification is by works. The comment "as well as works" was included in every published edition of this sermon, including versions in 1758, 1784, 1785, and 1787. See also Fletcher's affirmation that Wesley holds final justification by works (John Fletcher, *A Second Check to Antinomianism* (London, 1771), 2). In the following pages of the same work, Fletcher goes on to make a further defense of the view of final justification by works.

[110] See, for example, Wesley, 'Letter to Reverend Dr. Horne,' *Works* (Jackson), 9:110 and 9:116; and Wesley, 'Some Remarks on Mr. Hill's Farrago Double-Distilled,' *Works* (BE), 13:507. Note that in Wesley's comments to the Rev. Dr. Horne concerning Abraham, it is difficult to see whether Wesley intends a third sense of justification (one after first justification but before final justification), one that is in addition to the two mentioned in this project. Cf. Wesley's comments on James 2:24 in the *Explanatory Notes Upon the New Testament*. One way or another, it is clear that Wesley does not see James, Paul, and the gospels in conflict with each other concerning first and final justification.

[111] For Wesley's discussion of a first justification grounded in the teaching of Paul, see, for example, Wesley, 'Some Remarks on Mr. Hill's Farrago Double-Distilled,' *Works* (BE), 13:507.

"For not the hearers of the law are just with God, but the doers of the law shall be justified."[112] Wesley argues that the doctrine of a final justification by works is evident from Matthew 12:36-37 and Matthew 25.[113]

Besides the gift of final justification, on the Day of Judgment, God also makes available the gifts of other kinds of heavenly rewards. Not all people will be rewarded the same and not all people will be punished the same. In other words, among those who receive final justification, not all will receive the same heavenly rewards, and among those who are sentenced to hell, not all of these will receive the same degree of punishment. The scriptures[114] that Wesley uses as the basis of this view include the following: Matthew 16:27, "For the Son of man shall come in the glory of his Father, with his angels; and then shall her render to every man according to his work";[115] Luke 16:2, "Give an account of thy stewardship, for thou canst be no longer stewards";[116] 1 Corinthians 3:8, "every one shall receive his own reward, according to his own labour";[117] and Revelation 20:12 "the dead were judged out of the things that were written in the books, according to their works."[118] All of these scriptures reflect the principle that there will be rewards in heaven and hell in proportion to works performed during one's previous life on earth. Influenced by these scriptures, Wesley speaks of "that reward in heaven which will be in proportion to our holiness on earth."[119]

---

[112] Wesley appears not to make much discussion of Romans 2.13. However, Wesley is supportive of his *Explanatory Notes Upon the New Testament* that does comment on it some. See the commentary on Romans 2:13 in Wesley, *Explanatory Notes Upon the New Testament* (Fifth Edition, London: 1788), 464.

[113] In support of a doctrine of justification by works, Wesley makes explicit reference to Matthew 12:36-37 in his sermon Wesley, *The Great Assize*, 1:363; and he makes explicit reference to Matthew 25 in this way in Wesley, 'Some Remarks on Mr. Hill's Farrago Double-Distilled,' *Works* (BE), 13:509.

[114] Compare those mentioned below with: Luke 6:38, Proverbs 24:12, Psalms 62:12.

[115] Wesley's reference to this scripture is found here: Wesley, 'Of Hell,' *Works* (BE) 3:37; Wesley, 'God's Love to Fallen Man,' *Works* (BE), 2:432.

[116] Wesley's reference to this scripture is found here: Wesley, 'The Great Assize,' *Works* (BE), 1:358.

[117] Wesley's reference to this scripture is found here: Wesley, 'Of Hell,' *Works* (BE), 3:37; Wesley, 'God's Love to Fallen Man,' *Works* (BE), 2:432.

[118] Wesley's reference is found in his own footnote—footnote o— of the *The Great Assize*. This sermon was first published in 1758 and later published as a single sermon in 1782, 1783, 1784, 1785, and 1787. Wesley, 'The Great Assize,' *Works* (BE), 1:359.

Wesley discusses this point in his sermon, "The More Excellent Way." In reference to those Christians who are not as strict in doing good, he says: "Let it be well remembered, I do not affirm that all who do not walk in this way are in the high road to hell. But thus much I must affirm: they will not have so high a place in heaven as they would have had if they had chosen the better part."[120] He says that the variety of rewards and punishments will

> arise partly from the just judgment of God 'rewarding every man according to his works'. For we cannot doubt but this rule will take place no less in hell than in heaven. As in heaven, 'every man will receive 'his own reward', incommunicably his own, according to 'his own labours', incommunicably his, that is, the whole tenor of his tempers, thoughts, words, and actions; so undoubtedly every man in fact will receive his own bad reward, according to his own bad labour.[121]

It is explicit from these comments and from others that Wesley takes from scripture the view that God will give rewards at the judgment in proportion to what a person does during normal life on earth. But it is wrong to think of a person as owner of such works. Wesley says, "Neither is salvation of the works we do when we believe. For 'it is' then 'God that worketh in us'. And therefore, that he giveth us a reward for what he himself worketh only commendeth the riches of his mercy, but leaveth us nothing whereof to glory."[122] So when a person is justified by works and given rewards in heaven according to such works, God is not rewarding a person for what the person had done alone but rather rewarding the person for the work that God did in the person. This point further underscores the co-operating nature of fruitful action as good works. It is because of the work of the Spirit in the active life of a person on earth that this person will later receive rewards in heaven.

The Ethics of the Inhabitant of Heaven

It is difficult to give an account of the life of an inhabitant of heaven because there is little Wesley can know about heaven. It is known that the inhabitant of heaven enjoys having been given final justification and

---

[119] Wesley, 'Heaviness Through Manifold Temptation,' *Works* (BE), 2:234.
[120] Wesley, 'The More Excellent Way,' *Works* (BE), 3:266.
[121] Wesley, 'Of Hell,' *Works* (BE), 3:37.
[122] Wesley, 'Salvation by Faith,' *Works* (BE), 1:126.

the rewards of heaven. The nature of these rewards is not fully clear. Such rewards could in fact be higher expectations to do good works in heaven. See diagram 7.1 for an overview of Wesley's view of the stages of the way of salvation.

Wesley indicates that an inhabitant of heaven "grows in grace, in the knowledge of Christ, in the love and image of God."[123] Thus, it seems that love remains a key feature of the life of an inhabitant of heaven. As discussed in chapter 5, for Wesley, such a love is in various ways a manifestation of the Trinity. This love has both a passive and an active aspect. The active aspect is fruitful action, also known in this case as good works and virtuous action. Since it appears that there is love in heaven, it seems likely that there will also be good works. In the above quotation, Wesley indicates that an inhabitant of heaven continues to grow in the image of God. If Wesley is correct in his portrait of the image of God (the natural image as understanding, will, and liberty; the moral image as the possession of righteousness and holiness; and the political image as governance over lower beings), then it is possible—if not probable— that human beings will in some way maintain these features in heaven as well.

In such an eternity of love, virtuous action (active force) flows forth from a person who is pure in heart and has had a number of passive spiritual experiences (purity of heart, faith of the highest degree, the witness of the Spirit, final justification, the rewards of heaven, etc.). In this way, such virtuous action is part of the complete fulfilment of eschatology and the reigning of God's kingdom. Such love and good works are the highest fulfilment of the greatest end of Christian living. They are the expression of God's gift, one that lasts for all of eternity.

We have now considered the final stages of Wesley's view of the way of salvation. We will now turn to some relevant debates in secondary literature.

Responding to Secondary Literature: Maddox, Collins, and Colón-Emeric

In his book *Wesley, Aquinas & Christian Perfection*, Edgardo Colón-Emeric includes a chapter entitled "Wesley on the Way to Christian Perfection."

---

[123] Wesley, *A Plain Account of Christian Perfection* (Wesley), 11:402.

In this chapter, he recites much of the standard and widely-accepted view of Wesley's view of this phase of the Christian journey. Colón-Emeric is correct in stating:

> Wesley introduces an important caveat at this point—that we must seek and strive for perfection. God is not irrational or arbitrary in the dispensing of his gifts. "God does not, will not, give that [perfect] faith, unless we seek it with all diligence, in the way which he hath ordained." The way that leads to perfection consists of absolute obedience, zealous observance of the commandments, and self-denial.[124]

It is clear from this statement that for Wesley, seeking perfection, the greatest end of Christian living, requires some effort. As argued above, this effort and these actions, while active with respect to a person, are in fact the expression of God's gift. No one in Wesleyan studies would deny that for Wesley, such fruitful actions are important and necessary for seeking perfection if there is time and opportunity for them.

However, in this same chapter, Colón-Emeric makes another claim that is more open to debate. He makes the following claim in regard to Wesley's view of grace along the way of salvation:

> These various senses of grace do not represent actually different kinds or "flavors" of grace. Rather, they describe different effects of grace, effects that are suited to meet the needs of the person at the state of the journey in which they find themselves. As Luby avers, "grace in all is one; but the situation of the individual changes the specific way in which grace affects us."[125]

This statement appears to be in direct conflict with a statement by Kenneth Collins from a previous year. While Colón-Emeric says there are not different "kinds or 'flavors' of grace," Collins argues there are "qualitatively distinct graces" in Wesley's thought.[126] Collins speaks of "two major *qualitative* transformations of the Christian life," which are justification and regeneration (those events pertaining to the new birth) on the one hand and entire sanctification (the events pertaining to

---

[124] Edgardo Colón-Emeric, *Wesley, Aquinas & Christian Perfection, An Ecumenical Dialogue* (Waco: Baylor University Press, 2009), 49.

[125] Colón-Emeric, *Wesley, Aquinas & Christian Perfection*, 43. See also Daniel Luby, "The perceptibility of Grace in the Theology of John Wesley. A Roman Catholic Consideration" (PhD diss., Pontifical University of St. Thomas, 1994), 81.

[126] Collins, *The Theology of John Wesley*, 15 and 295.

Christian perfection) on the other hand.¹²⁷ Both transformations are the effects of free grace, a grace that is qualitatively distinct from responsible grace, something which pertains to gradual growth. For Collins, "monergism" pertains to the work of free grace, while "synergism" pertains to responsible grace.¹²⁸

For Colón-Emeric and Daniel Luby, Wesley's view of grace is uniform and simply affects a person in different ways depending on the situation.¹²⁹ For Collins' interpretation of Wesley, grace is not uniform in all cases but has "qualitatively distinct" types. Collins' reason for claiming that there are qualitatively distinct types of grace is rooted at least partly in his concern to argue that for Wesley, there is more emphasis on what the Spirit does at the start of the two foci of salvation (the new birth and Christian perfection) than what some interpreters acknowledge. Interpreters such as Colón-Emeric, Luby, and Maddox acknowledge the variation in how the Spirit acts in salvation, but they are not as concerned with highlighting that the older Wesley emphasizes a larger and unpredictable impact of spiritual growth at the start of the two foci of salvation.

As Colón-Emeric notes, Randy Maddox interprets the older Wesley as placing more emphasis on responsible grace and gradual growth and holding that such responsible grace is "most characteristic" of Wesley.¹³⁰ In perhaps a different manner, Collins argues that in addition to responsible grace, Wesley also emphasizes the work of monergism and free grace at the start of the new birth and Christian perfection, the two foci of salvation.¹³¹ For Collins, this emphasis on free grace pertains to a kind of spiritual growth that is different from the gradual type of spiritual growth that occurs at other periods in the Christian journey. Collins believes that there is not enough evidence in the late Wesley to conclude that Wesley retracts this emphasis during the latest years of his life.¹³²

---

¹²⁷ Collins, *The Theology of John Wesley*, 125.

¹²⁸ For more of a discussion of monergism and synergism, see my dissertation, *Pursuing Christian Love According to the Theology of John Wesley*, completed at the University of Manchester.

¹²⁹ Luby, "The perceptibility of Grace in the Theology of John Wesley. A Roman Catholic Consideration," 81.

¹³⁰ Colón-Emeric, *Wesley, Aquinas & Christian Perfection*, 162.

¹³¹ This point was discussed in chapter 1.

¹³² For Collins' discussion of free grace and perfection (entire sanctification), see: Collins, *The Theology of John Wesley*, 162 and 293 – 296.

Some earlier interpreters seem unaware of the underlying concerns of Collins regarding a distinction between types of spiritual growth in Wesley's thought. For example, in his essay, "John Wesley as a Theologian of Grace," Robert Rakestraw says "there is a remarkable consistency in his synergistic view of both justification and sanctification."[133] Rakestraw supports the interpretation of Cannon regarding the need to emphasize a person's role in salvation and holding that a person has the "final say."[134] Rakestraw does not highlight the unpredictable nature of the first moment of Christian perfection. He does not clarify the passive aspect of Christian perfection or the way in which it is the work of God alone. Yet, many of these are points of focus for Collins.

Unlike Rakestraw, Collins underscores how synergism pertains only to gradual growth and responsible grace and not to the first moment of Christian perfection (entire sanctification). Collins says:

> If, however, one fails to distinguish between the process of sanctification, that is, growing more holy in increasing *degrees*, and entire sanctification itself, being *now* pure in heart, a change in *quality*, and if one also operates almost exclusively out of a catholic synergistic paradigm, then one will likely (and mistakenly) conclude that entire sanctification is a process.
>
> If entire sanctification occurs, if it is actualized, there will be a moment of its instantiation (whether that moment is recognized or not), for it marks a change not in degree but in quality; it is, for want of better terminology, a "threshold transformation."[135]

For Collins' view of Wesley, the first moment of Christian perfection is not a change in degree according to the same rate of incremental growth observed earlier in the way of salvation (after the new birth and before perfection). Rather the first moment of perfection involves a vast change or change in quality, what he calls a "threshold transformation." This is not the effect of responsible grace, a grace that Collins argues is in effect for gradual growth at other periods. It is the effect of monergism, what Collins calls "free grace," a grace that is qualitatively distinct from responsible grace, the grace that pertains to synergy.

As mentioned above, the view of Edgardo Colón-Emeric and Luby that in regard to Wesley's thought, there are not different kinds of graces

---

[133] Robert Rakestraw, "John Wesley as a Theologian of Grace." *Journal of the Evangelical Theological Society.* 27, 2, (1984): 200.

[134] Rakestraw, "John Wesley as a Theologian of Grace," 199.

[135] Collins, *The Theology of John Wesley*, 294 - 295.

is in conflict with Collins' view that there are "qualitatively distinct" graces. We will not need to evaluate this debate here. This project will not try to consider whether Maddox, Collins, or Colón-Emeric makes the best argument. Determining the best argument concerning Wesley's ontology of grace is not required for the present purpose of this study. Rather than focus on the *ontology* of grace, we will consider here the *experience* of grace by the recipient of salvation.

The crucial point here is the need to analyze and clarify the *experience* of a kind of spiritual growth (i.e. the kind that pertains to the first moments of the new birth and first moments of perfection) that previously had not been given adequate attention. In other words, from the perspective of a recipient's experience, there is something distinct and important about the first moments of the new birth and first moments of perfection that previous discussions in secondary literature may not have clarified in a satisfactory way.

What is being argued here is that a helpful way to capture and illuminate the important and neglected aspects of the new birth and Christian perfection is by considering the concepts of active and passive, including how they relate to one of the two kinds of spiritual growth mentioned in chapter 2. As mentioned in chapter 2, on the one hand, there is the kind of growth that is gradual and mostly reflexive. This is comparable to the illustration of the fit woman, who nurtures an inclination for exercise in direct proportion to how much she chooses to exercise. This type of spiritual growth is the gradual growth of heart that occurs when a person, by grace, performs fruitful action. Since this kind of growth is mostly reflexive, it requires the use of the active power and the simultaneous nurturing of a passive inclination. Its occurrence is predictable for the doer.

On the other hand, there is the kind of growth that is comparable to the illustration of the flaming dart mentioned above. This involves a change of the tempers and affections of the heart that occurs at an unpredictable time. The change in heart that occurs is passive in a bare sense and involves a lesser amount of reflexivity. As mentioned above, this is the kind of spiritual growth that pertains to the first moments of the new birth and first moments of Christian perfection. In both cases, it involves often a detectable change in one's heart and feelings, along with the direct witness of the Spirit.[136] The experience of this kind of

---

[136] As observed above, Wesley says that the first moment of Christian per-

spiritual growth is not "altogether passive" because there are actions a person can take to block or quench the effects of the Spirit. Clarifying these aspects of spiritual growth is what has been deficient in secondary literature in the past.

Distinguishing these important kinds of spiritual growth is not meant to be an esoteric theological discussion but pertains to what people can expect normally to experience in the Christian journey. Although, for Wesley, there are a variety of ways people experience the new birth and perfection, the point is that, in most cases, each person does experience *something* rather than nothing and there is typically a degree of commonality in what is experienced. Distinguishing different kinds of spiritual growth in a way that relates to common experience and showing how they relate to the roadmap for the Christian life are core practical concerns for Wesley.

In this chapter, we explored Wesley's understanding of the path from the new birth to Christian perfection and from Christian perfection to the rewards of heaven. We showed that there is even room for growth for an inhabitant of heaven. For each stage of Wesley's "way of salvation," his roadmap for the Christian life, we showed how a person's pursuit of Christian love is an expression of God's gift and that the giftedness of this blessing is illuminated by a critical examination of the work of the Spirit with respect to the active and passive dimensions of a human being.

We will now consider a more detailed account of Wesley's understanding of the range of actions that makes up what it means to pursue Christian love.

---

fection is sometimes not detected but in such cases, the effects are typically detected later.

Chapter 8

A Method for Fruitful Action

In this project, we have been exploring John Wesley's view of ethics. In the earlier chapters, we examined Wesley's view of the features of the human soul. After this, we considered God's main role in ethics. We looked at how the Spirit operates in a manner that empowers a person to carry out fruitful actions and pursue Christian love. We then explored this occurrence for each stage of Wesley's "way of salvation," his roadmap for the Christian life that he finds in scripture. We looked at the ethics of the servant of God, the newborn child, the perfected child, and the inhabitant of heaven. In this chapter, we will consider in more depth the specific kinds of actions that Wesley prescribes for pursuing Christian love. These are fruitful actions, actions that are only possible by the Spirit of God preventing, accompanying, doing, and following at every moment.

In chapter 2, we clarified what is meant by action. It was argued in chapter 2 and chapter 3 that Wesley's meaning of liberty, understood as a power of choosing and also the same as Wesley's second meaning of the will, is equivalent to the human active power. Every choice to do a fruitful action—whether the choice is to attend a class meeting, to pray in the morning and evenings, to give food to the hungry and clothes to the naked or any other fruitful deed—is an exercise of one's liberty. Consistent with this point, Wesley says in a passage concerning liberty: "And although I have not an absolute power over my own mind, because of the corruption of my nature, yet through the grace of God assisting me I have a power to choose and do good as well as evil. I am free to choose whom I will serve, and if I choose the better part, to continue therein even unto death."[1]

---

[1] Wesley, 'What is Man?,' *Works* (BE), 4:24.

In Wesley's view, emphasizing the need to perform fruitful action is a core priority for Methodism, the revival movement that he led. This is because he saw fruitful action as important for opposing "antinomianism." Antinomianism is a certain way of living. It is something Wesley viewed as one of the most troubling problems of his time. Wesley describes "practical antinomianism" as "making void the law through faith."[2] It exhibits the problem discussed in the book of James that faith without works is dead. The main idea of antinomianism is that a person is not putting forth much effort to perform fruitful actions. With respect to his theological discussions, Wesley fought against practical antinomianism in various ways throughout his life, including in his debates with the mystics, Moravians, his correspondence with James Hervey, and in his debates with various Calvinists in defense of the conference Minutes of 1770.[3]

Wesley's ideal solution for correcting the problem of a lack of effort for performing fruitful action was *not* in fact to prescribe the ethics of a Pharisee, doing righteous action without a transformed heart. But his solution does require that as there is time and opportunity, a sincere follower of Christ must put forth diligent and constant effort to perform fruitful actions *regardless* of where he or she is along the way of salvation. If the person has not received the new birth, then Wesley's recommendation is to perform fruitful action (the kind that is not yet good works). If the person has already received the new birth or Christian perfection, then the recommendation is to perform fruitful action, which is now good works properly speaking. Furthermore, in most cases, the specific kinds of practices that exemplify fruitful actions; such as serving the

---

[2] Wesley, 'The Law Established Through Faith, I,' *Works* (BE), 2:30.

[3] For a helpful overview of Wesley's disputes with the mystics and Moravians concerning Antinomianism, see Thompson, "John Wesley and the Means of Grace" (PhD Dissertation, Duke University, 2012), chapter 3. See also Wesley, 'A Dialogue Between an Antinomian and His Friend,' *Works* (Jackson), volume 10; Wesley, 'A Second Dialogue Between An Antinomian and His Friend,' *Works* (Jackson), volume 10; and Wesley, 'A Blow at the Root: or Christ Stabbed in the House of His Friends,' *Works* (Jackson), volume 10. For an account of Wesley's dispute with Hervey and the former's concern of Antinomianism, see for example Herbert McGonigle, *Sufficient Saving Grace* (Carlisle, Cumbria: Paternoster Press, 2001), chapter 9, especially page 226. For Wesley's debates with the Calvinists concerning Antinomianism, see for example: Jackson, editor, *The Works of John Wesley*, 10:374, 10:415, and 10:446. See also John Fletcher's publications on the checks to Antinomianism.

poor, attending the Lord's Supper, etc.; are possible for all people, regardless of their spiritual stage. For example, Wesley would recommend the Lord's Supper, prayer, searching the scriptures, helping the needy, etc. just as much for servants of God as for newborn children or perfected children.

Wesley's approach is by grace to be as prudent as possible in selecting and prioritizing a set of actions in pursuit of the highest end of ethics. Scripture is his most authoritative source for creating such a plan of action. This plan of action can be thought of as a method. In this case, "method" means a way of ordering, as it pertains to practices.

The methods for doing fruitful action used by Wesley and his followers could have been part of what led to Wesley's group being called Methodists.[4] Regardless of how this may or may not be true, the *concept* of method applies to John Wesley's approach to fruitful action. This is not to deny that Wesley indicates that the clearest mark of a true Methodist is not fruitful action by itself but rather the "love of God shed abroad in the heart by the Holy Ghost given unto him."[5] Nevertheless, Wesley steadily encourages followers of Christ to carry out this method for fruitful action. It should be a part of any person's pursuit of the highest end of ethics. Carrying out such a method is itself an expression of God's gift.

An Encounter with John Wesley

Suppose that a sincere follower of Christ who is fairly new to the Christian religion approaches John Wesley and says, "Mr. Wesley I have learned your scriptural teachings of the way of salvation, the roadmap of the Christian life, and I understand that humankind's highest end is to love God and neighbor. But as someone who is otherwise unacquainted with the Methodists, I want to know what can I do in order to serve God and pursue Christian love? How am I to live my life? Please give me specific steps." How would Wesley respond to such questions? The answer is certainly a key part of Wesley's ethics, as it involves the matter of how to respond to God's grace by exercising one's liberty—one's power of choosing—in order to perform fruitful action.

---

[4] For discussions of the early usages of this term, see chapter 1 of Heitzenrater, *Mirror and Memory*.

[5] Wesley, 'The Character of a Methodist,' *Works* (Jackson), 8:341.

Over the course of this chapter, a basic answer—not an exhaustive one—to these questions will be provided on behalf of Wesley. A first point that can be offered in response to the sincere person's questions is that one must approach the need for fruitful action with diligence and constancy. Evidence for such a need is found in scripture. Consider the following comment from Wesley based on 1 Tim. 6:12 and 1 Tim. 1:18: "seeing ye are continually under the eye of your captain, how zealous and active should you be to 'fight the good fight of faith, and lay hold on eternal life', 'to endure hardship as good soldiers of Jesus Christ', to use all diligence, to 'war a good warfare', and to do whatever is acceptable in his sight!"[6] Other scriptures that Wesley uses in support of this point include but are not limited to: Galatians 6:10,[7] Titus 3:8,[8] and 1 Cor. 15:58.[9] The call for diligent fruitful action is also inspired by Phil 2:12, "work out your own salvation with fear and trembling,"[10] and the greatest commandment to love God with all one's heart, soul, mind and strength. It is also inspired by Isaiah 1:16-17, which we will consider in more depth below.

As part of his answer to the sincere person's question, Wesley would recommend his method for fruitful action, that is, what he recommends to his Methodist followers. This method involves three general parts: choose Christian fellowship, follow the *General Rules*, and obey God's moral commandments as found in the Bible. Of course, there is overlap in these three points. Nevertheless, these three points provide a general outline for Wesley's answer. Each of these recommended steps involves an array of fruitful actions. For the rest of this chapter, we will explore each one of these steps.

In addition to these three points, institutional reform and promoting correct forms of government are also important concerns for Wesley. However, these latter matters are secondary concerns. Unlike the pressing issue of discipleship on the level of a small group, achieving institutional reform and influencing government policy are often not easily within one's reach. This is not to deny that to "reform the nation"[11] is

---

[6] Wesley, 'On the Omnipresence of God,' *Works* (BE), 4:47.
[7] Wesley, 'The Signs of the Times,' *Works* (BE), 2:533.
[8] Wesley, 'Journal,' *Works* (Jackson), 1:280.
[9] Wesley, 'On Working Out Our Own Salvation,' *Works* (BE), 3:206.
[10] Wesley, 'On Working Out Our Own Salvation,' *Works* (BE), 3:199.
[11] Wesley, 'Minutes of Some Late Conversations Between the Rev. Mr. Wesley and Others,' *Works* (Jackson), 8:299.

one of Wesley's visions for Methodism, and this is not to deny that Wesley understands government politics to be related to the salvation and eschatology of the cosmos. Rather, it is to underscore a somewhat prior need for giving attention to the level at which a small group can "work out their own salvation" according to the graces available. In many ways, the success of the secondary concerns (institutional reform, government policy, etc.) depends on the success of the first concern. This chapter will explore Wesley's ethics mostly on the level of an individual, local church, and/or small group but touches a little on those matters that are also important but more out of reach, namely the macroscopic level (institutions, government matters, etc.).

Before we begin a closer examination of Wesley's method for fruitful action, we will clarify his understanding of what he calls the "means of grace." This is important because fruitful actions are in fact means of grace.

The Means of Grace

Fruitful actions are examples of what Wesley calls the "means of grace." This is true, despite the fact that not all means of grace are fruitful actions.[12] Wesley says, "By 'means of grace' I understand outwards signs, words, or actions ordained by God, and appointed for this end—to be the ordinary channels whereby he might convey to men preventing, justifying, or sanctifying grace."[13] Wesley bases his view of the means of grace in part on Acts 2:44 and 2:42: "'all that believed were together, and had all things common,' 'they continued steadfastly in the teaching of the apostles, and in the breaking of bread, and in prayers.'"[14] The spectrum of possible fruitful actions includes all active means of grace. See diagram 8.1. When a fruitful action is performed, one is responding to the grace of God. Such an action itself is an expression of grace and serves as a channel through which additional grace is conveyed to a person.

Included under this concept of the means of grace are instituted, prudential, and general means of grace.[15] The instituted means of grace

---

[12] Something can be true without its converse being true. For example: all runners are athletes but not all athletes are runners.

[13] Wesley, 'The Means of Grace,' *Works* (BE), 1:381.

[14] Wesley, 'The Means of Grace,' *Works* (BE), 1:378.

[15] This typology is an interpretation offered by Henry Knight. See Henry

include what Wesley speaks of on one occasion as certain "particular" means of grace.[16] The instituted means of grace also include what Wesley at times describes as certain "ordinances."[17] As described in the large minutes, the instituted means of grace typically include prayer, searching the scriptures, the Lord's Supper, fasting, and what Wesley calls Christian conference.[18] For Wesley, baptism is also a means of grace but he does not frequently list it with these others.

The prudential means of grace involve a wider range of activity. They involve the application of prudence, which is a Spirit-led process of reasoning in which general rules derived from scripture are applied to particular circumstances.[19] According to Henry Knight, Methodist classes and Methodist bands are examples of prudential means of grace.[20] The concept of a prudential means of grace is so broad that it may in fact refer to any creative action of a person whatsoever that in at least some small way advances the kingdom of God.[21] It can refer to rules for growing in grace and any kind of art of holy living.[22] It can also refer to those

---

Knight, *The Presence of God in the Christian Life* (Oxford: The Scarecrow Press, Inc., 1992), 3-6.

[16] Wesley, 'Minutes of Some Late Conversations between the Rev. Mr. Wesley and Others,' *Works* (Jackson), 8:286.

[17] See, for example, Wesley, 'The Nature, Design, and General Rules of the United Societies,' *Works* (Jackson), 8:271. However, it is possible that on other occasions, Wesley has a broader understanding of ordinances.

[18] Wesley, 'Minutes of Several Conversations Between the Rev. Mr. Wesley and Others,' *Works* (Jackson), 8:323.

[19] See, for example, Wesley's discussion of prudence here: Jackson, editor, *The Works of John Wesley*, 8:254, 255, and 259.

[20] Knight, *The Presence of God in the Christian Life*, 5; Wesley, 'Minutes of Several Conversations Between the Rev. Mr. Wesley and Others,' *Works* (Jackson), 8:323.

[21] Consider the comment: "God *can* give the end without any means at all; but you have no reason to think he will. Therefore constantly and carefully use all these means which he has appointed to be the ordinary channels of his grace. Use every means which either reason or Scripture recommends as conducive (through the free love of God in Christ) either to the obtaining or increasing any of the gifts of God" (Wesley, 'The Nature of Enthusiasm,' *Works* (BE), 2:59-60). Prudential means include those means that reason recommends as conducive for seeking God's love, even if these means are not necessarily specifically mentioned in scripture. Of course, if such means of grace are not found in scripture, they may not contradict scripture.

[22] Wesley, 'Minutes of Several Conversations Between the Rev. Mr. Wesley and Others,' *Works* (Jackson), 8:323.

actions that are indifferent in some contexts but are judged to bring spiritual benefit at the time and manner of their use.[23]

A third type of the means of grace of which Wesley speaks is the "general" means of grace. For Wesley, this includes keeping all the commandments of scripture, denying oneself, and taking up one's cross daily.[24] The prudential means of grace may possibly include some if not all of the general means of grace, but Wesley seems not to be entirely clear on this matter.[25]

As mentioned above, fruitful actions are active means of grace, including instituted, prudential, and general means of grace. We will now explore in more depth the three parts of Wesley's method for fruitful action: choosing Christian Fellowship, following the *General Rules*, and obeying the moral commandments of scripture. Each of the kinds of means of grace may be found in one or more of these parts.

Choosing Christian Fellowship

For Wesley, choosing to devote time to Christian fellowship is one of the most important kinds of fruitful actions. This type of action involves all categories of the means of grace: instituted, prudential, and general. In his writings, Wesley emphasizes that one has a liberty, a power of choosing, as to whether one opts to spend one's time in fellowship with Christians or with "people of the world," those who are not committed to Christian ends.[26] Too much fellowship with people of the world must be avoided because worldly ways are "infectious."[27] Allowing too much time with people of the world leads to self-indulgence, a reluctance to bear one's cross, and less resolve to deny oneself and use the other means of grace.[28]

It is highly preferable for one to invest much of one's time and energies in developing friendships with Christians. This is also more preferable than a lifestyle of living alone. Wesley says, "Christianity is essentially a social religion, and that to turn it into a solitary one is to

---

[23] Wesley, *Letters*, 1:93 and 1:114.
[24] Wesley, 'Minutes of Some Late Conversations between the Rev. Mr. Wesley and Others,' *Works* (Jackson), 8:286.
[25] See footnote in this section above.
[26] Wesley, 'On Friendship in the World,' *Works* (BE), 3:131.
[27] Wesley, 'On Friendship in the World,' *Works* (BE), 3:134.
[28] Wesley, 'On Friendship in the World,' *Works* (BE), 3:133-134.

destroy it."²⁹ He argues that this point is reinforced by Matt. 5:13-16 that advises one to give "light to all that are in the house" and to "let your light so shine before men that they may see your good works."³⁰ The greatest commandment and highest end of ethics is Christian love, and this requires giving time to be in the presence of the targets of this love, which are God and neighbors. Relationships of love cannot develop without choosing to give time for fellowship.

Joining the Methodist Society

One of Wesley's first pieces of counsel for a sincere inquirer would be to join a Methodist society. This provides much of the fellowship that one needs. A society is "a company of men [people] having the form and seeking the power of Godliness, united in order to pray together, to receive the word of exhortation, and to watch one another in love, that they may help each other to work out their own salvation."³¹ There were various sizes of Methodists societies, and their constituency was influenced partly by location. Although Anglicanism is Wesley's preferred tradition, he welcomes anyone from any cultural or religious background to seek admission to a Methodist society, as long as such a person is sincere in his or her quest for Christian faith working by love and desires to flee wrath and be saved from sins.³²

In order to become a member of a Methodist society, one must first become active in a "class," which is a division of the larger society.³³ A class is a group of around 12 people, grouped according to neighborhood of residence, that meets once per week, often for an hour, in order to carry on spiritually-directed activities.³⁴ A class is a kind of account-

---

²⁹ Wesley, 'Sermon on the Mount, IV,' *Works* (BE), 1:533.

³⁰ Wesley, 'Sermon on the Mount, IV,' *Works* (BE), 1:533.

³¹ Wesley, 'The Nature, Design, and General Rules of the United Societies,' *Works* (Jackson), 8:269.

³² Wesley, 'The Nature, Design, and General Rules of the United Societies,' *Works* (Jackson), 8:270.

³³ This point is evident in multiple places, including Wesley, 'On God's Vineyard,' *Works* (BE), 3:512.

³⁴ For the point that a class has about 12 people, see Wesley, 'The Nature, Design, and General Rules of the United Societies,' *Works* (Jackson), 8:269. For the point that a class meets usually once per week for about an hour, see Wesley, 'On God's Vineyard,' *Works* (BE), 3:512. For more information on the Methodist class, see Heitzenrater, *Wesley and the People Called Methodists*, 118 and Davies, editor, *The Methodists Societies* (BE), 9:12.

ability group. The task of the class meeting is for people to examine each other's soul with the assistance of the class leader, endeavor to work out their own salvation, clear up any quarrels and misunderstandings, provide advice and reproof where necessary, and put aside money for the poor.[35] The meeting is usually brought to an end with acts of prayer and thanksgiving.[36] A class meeting provides an avenue for friendship building that can be extended further outside of regularly-scheduled Methodist activities.

One also has the option of joining a band. The Methodist band often had some differences from a Methodist class.[37] Instead of being assembled based on location, bands were assembled based on age, sex, and/or marital status.[38] A band was usually smaller in size than a class.[39] While the regular participation in a class was required in order to maintain status as a member of a Methodist society, this was usually not the case for participating in a band.[40] Participation in a band was not as common as participation in a class. One of the primary purposes of a band was to allow band members to examine each other spiritually, confess faults to each other, and pray for each other.[41] Much of this could be done at a class meeting. However, bands tended to be stricter than classes in expectations for practicing Christian discipline, and often the former were composed of people who were more mature and/or serious about religion.[42] The Methodists often offered a "select band" for those who were more serious about discipleship or who wanted extra focus.[43]

---

[35] Jackson, editor, *The Works of John Wesley*, 8:253 and 8:270; Heitzenrater, *Wesley and the People Called Methodists*, 118-119.

[36] Wesley, 'A Plain Account of the People Called Methodists,' *Works* (Jackson), 8:254.

[37] Kevin Watson, *Pursuing Social Holiness* (Oxford: Oxford University Press, 2014), 66; Heitzenrater, *Wesley and the People Called Methodists*, 119.

[38] Henderson, *A Model of Discipleship: John Wesley's Class Meeting* (Nappanee, IN: Francis Asbury Press, c1997), 112; Heitzenrater, *Wesley and the People Called Methodists*, 119.

[39] Watson, *Pursuing Social Holiness*, 66; Heitzenrater, *Wesley and the People Called Methodists*, 119.

[40] For the necessity of attending a class for maintaining one's membership in a society, see, for example: Wesley, 'On God's Vineyard,' *Works* (BE), section 3 and paragraph 1.

[41] Wesley, 'Rules of the Band Societies,' *Works* (Jackson), 8:272.

[42] Heitzenrater, *Wesley and the People Called Methodists*, 119.

[43] Watson, *Pursuing Social Holiness*, 66. Heitzenrater, *Wesley and the People Called*

Upon visiting a class meeting for the first time, a person is supposed to receive his or her own copy of the *General Rules*, a document of moral principles written and published by Wesley for the purpose of guiding fruitful action.[44] Such a document includes many of the means of grace, which are examples of fruits meet for repentance, i.e. fruitful action. In order to join a Methodist society and remain a member, one must not only attend a Methodist class on a weekly basis, he or she must also show evidence of following these *General Rules*.[45] This includes performing the means of grace and works suitable for repentance. A new participant of a Methodist class is examined for a period of time before becoming a member of the society.[46] In many contexts, upon becoming a member of the Methodist society, the new member is given a ticket.[47] The new member must continue to show evidence of following the *General Rules* and must also attend his or her class each week. If this is not done, then in many cases, the ticket is taken and the member is not able to keep the same standing in the society.[48]

Methodists, 118.

[44] Wesley, 'Minutes of Several Conversations between the Rev. Mr. Wesley and Others,' *Works* (Jackson), 8:307.

[45] According to Wesley, one must show evidence of obeying the *General Rules* before becoming a member of a Methodist society (see paragraph 4 of Wesley, 'The Nature, Design, and General Rules of the United Societies,' *Works* (Jackson), 8:270 and III.1 of Wesley, 'On God's Vineyard,' *Works* (BE), 3:511). Wesley indicates that a first-time visitor of a class must be given the *General Rules* on his or her first visit and must then complete a trial before being offered membership (Wesley, Minutes of Several Conversations between the Rev. Mr. Wesley and Others, *Works* (Jackson) 8:307, Q. 14). In regard to the need of continuing to follow the *General Rules* after membership, Wesley says, "These are the *General Rules* of our societies"... "If there be any among us who observe them not, who habitually break any of them, let it be made known unto them who watch over that soul as they that must give an account. We will admonish him of the error of his ways; we will bear with him for a season: But then if he repent not, he hath no more place among us" (Wesley, 'The Nature, Design and General Rules of the United Societies,' *Works* (Jackson), 8:271). For the point that in order to become a member, one must attend a class every week, see Wesley, 'On God's Vineyard,' *Works* (BE), 3:512, section 3 and paragraph 1. Cf. Wesley, *Letters*, 6:208 and 6:238.

[46] Wesley, 'Minutes of Several Conversations between the Rev. Mr. Wesley and Others,' *Works* (Jackson), 8:307, Q. 14.

[47] Davies, editor, *The Methodists Societies* (BE), 9:12.

[48] For the point that often when one ceases to attend a class on a weekly

As we can see, Wesley, as leader of the Methodists, was attempting to encourage strict guidelines for Methodist conduct. Part of this was due to the difficulty he found in trying to uproot the spiritually crippling effects of practical antinomianism that continued to be seen in culture, including those claiming to be Christians. Even during his elderly life, Wesley continued to stress the importance of fruitful action and Christian discipline. Yet involvement in societies, classes, and bands were not the only means of fellowship that Wesley encouraged. He also encouraged participation in other modes of fellowship such as Methodist preaching services.

Early-Morning, Evening, and Outdoor Preaching Services

The Methodists of Wesley's time offered early-morning, evening, and outdoor preaching services. All people were encouraged to attend these. An early-morning preaching service would often take place around 5 or 6 A.M. on Sundays and at times during the week.[49] Throughout the final years of his life, Wesley continued to require that early-morning preaching take place on Sundays at 5 A.M. at the Foundery in London and that all the family in his house must consistently participate.[50] Evening preaching services were also frequently available at Methodist preaching

---

basis, the ticket is taken, see: Wesley, *Letters*, 6:208 and 6:238. For the point that in order for a person to maintain membership in the society, he or she must follow the *General Rules* and attend a class on a weekly basis, see the above footnote.

[49] In many contexts, there would be opportunities to attend early-morning preaching services during the week. In the Minutes of 1768, Wesley says, "Let the preaching at five in the morning be constantly kept up, wherever you can have twenty hearers. This is the glory of the Methodists" (Rack, editor, *The Methodist Societies* (BE), 10:361). Heitzenrater says that such meetings would usually take place at 5 A.M. or before people went to work (Richard Heitzenrater, "John Wesley's Principles and Practice of Preaching," *Methodist History*, 37 (1999): 94). There is no evidence that Wesley participated in such a service himself every day on a regular basis during every phase of his life. But it seems that in some places, a Methodist could have the opportunity to attend such an early-morning preaching service on a Sunday morning and on certain occasions during the week. On March 15, 1784, Wesley complained that this practice of early-morning preaching declined in some areas (Wesley, 'Journal,' *Works* (Jackson), 4:267).

[50] Wesley, 'Journal,' *Works* (Jackson), 4:406.

houses on Sundays and on various occasions during the week. Their frequency would depend in part on the location and on the time of year.

In addition to attending preaching services at Methodist preaching houses, Wesley would also encourage people to attend outdoor preaching events, commonly called "field-preaching." Field-preaching was a practice that was not common among other Anglican priests but was a well-known feature of the Methodist revival. After George Whitfield convinced Wesley that this practice was helpful for ministry, Wesley performed this practice quite regularly. Wesley led outdoor preaching events that took place on streets, on fields, in the marketplace, in rain, in snow, next to a house, next to a river, on a dock, under a tree, in a grove, in an amphitheater, and more.[51] Wesley's journal gives numerous accounts of him traveling and carrying on field-preaching all over Britain. Many of the Methodists of Wesley's time had opportunities each year to attend field-preaching events, and they were encouraged to do so.

The Covenant Service, The Love-Feast, the Watch-Night, and the Letter-Day

Other forms of fellowship also characterized Wesley's Methodists. One such activity is the annual covenant renewal service that Methodists would often hold on the first Sunday of each year.[52] This service invited each participant to re-commit oneself to the will of God.[53] Wesley would encourage people to attend the covenant service in addition to the events that occurred more frequently throughout the year such as watch-night services, love-feasts, and letter-day gatherings. The frequency of these latter kinds of services varied according to time and place. Usually, each one occurred at least once per quarter (once every three months). However, in some big societies such as the one in London, watch-nights services and love feasts each continued to be held on a monthly basis throughout Wesley's life.[54] Typically in such a setting, one would have

---

[51] For accounts of this in his journal see, for example, the following pages from volume 4 of Jackson, editor, *The Works of John Wesley*: 135, 150, 151, 152, 185, 186, 214, 234, 289, 313, 468, 469, 496.

[52] For sources that influenced Wesley's view on this practice, see Ward and Heitzenrater, editors, *Journals and Diaries IV* (BE), 21:23, footnote 82.

[53] Heitzenrater, *Wesley and the People Called Methodists*, 198.

[54] The "general love-feast" would occur quarterly (once per three months). However, in some societies, there was also a love-feast for only men and one for only women. Thus, each interval of three months would be: men's love-feast,

the opportunity to attend: (a) a watch-night service each month and (b) a love feast on two occasions out of every three months.[55]

The love-feast was an event that Wesley claims to have based on the practice of the early church.[56] In the early centuries of Christianity, Christians would practice what is called the "Agape," which was associated with Jesus' last supper. [57] In the Methodist societies, the love-feast was neither the formal practice of the Eucharist nor typically an elaborate meal with a wide range of the tastiest foods. Rather, it involved the eating of a piece of bread or biscuit and the drinking of tea or water.[58] The tea or water would be taken from a mug and passed around from person to person.[59] Each love-feast would commonly involve: hymn singing, prayer, distribution of bread, collection for the poor, circulation of the cup, address by a presiding minister, and testimonies.[60] Hymns selected for singing were sometimes those written by Charles Wesley.[61] As shown in John Wesley's journals, the time for the sharing of testimonies was one of the most powerful parts of the service.

In addition to attending love-feasts, one was also encouraged to attend watch-night services and letter-day events. The original watch-night services in the Methodist movement were designed in part to provide for young people an alternative to going to the alehouse and/or finding trouble.[62] Wesley liked the concept and decided to make it a standard Methodist activity.[63] Watch-night services would often occur on Friday

---

women's love-feast, and the general love-feast. Thus, each person would have an opportunity to attend a love-feast twice per every three months. The conference minutes from 1746-1747 show the monthly nature of love-feasts and watch-night services (Rack, editor, *The Methodist Societies* (BE), 10:185, 10:209). Meetings for January through May are not listed but seem likely to have occurred as Wesley says in 1746 that *general* love-feasts meet quarterly (implying that by the listed schedule in the minutes, the other meetings meet quarterly as well). For more information on this point, see Frank Baker, *Methodism and the Love-Feast* (London: Epworth Press, 1957), 14 and 41.

[55] See above footnote.
[56] Wesley, 'A Plain Account of the People Called Methodists,' *Works* (Jackson), 8:259.
[57] Baker, *Methodism and the Love-Feast*, 9.
[58] Baker, *Methodism and the Love-Feast*, 15.
[59] Baker, *Methodism and the Love-Feast*, 15.
[60] Baker, *Methodism and the Love-Feast*, 15.
[61] Baker, *Methodism and the Love-Feast*, 19.
[62] Heitzenrater and Ward, editors, *Journals and Diaries* (BE), 19:258. See footnote 50.

nights, often starting around 8:30 PM and continuing until a little passed midnight.[64] Such a service involved singing, prayer, praise, and thanksgiving.[65] Some of the songs included hymns by Charles Wesley.[66] At times, the watch-night service also involved a message from a preacher delivered usually sometime between 8 and 9 P.M.[67] The Methodists also held letter-day events. According to Heitzenrater, these were occasions in which recent accounts of religious experience were read to those present.[68] People often grew spiritually from the love feasts, watch-night, and letter-day events. In some places, the letter-day occurred once per month, and all sincere followers of Christ were encouraged to attend them.

In summary, Wesley helped to provide a number of avenues for fellowship: societies, classes, bands, preaching services, covenants services, love-feasts, watch-nights, and letter-day events. All sincere followers of Christ were encouraged to attend them. As mentioned before, in order to remain a member of a Methodist society (at least in many cases), one had to attend a class on a weekly basis and also show evidence of following the *General Rules*. Thus, the question arises: what are these *General Rules*? To this question we now turn.

Following *The General Rules*

Throughout Wesley's life, Wesley and the Methodists continued to use the *General Rules* as an important guide for Christian living. In the Large Minutes, Wesley advises the leaders of each class to "inquire how every soul in his class prospers; not only how each person observes the outward Rules, but how he grows in the knowledge and love of God."[69] From these comments, we observe that following the *General Rules* was

[63] Wesley, 'A Plain Account of the People Called Methodists,' *Works* (Jackson), 8:255.
[64] Heitzenrater and Ward, editors, *Journals and Diaries II* (BE), 19:258
[65] Wesley, 'A Plain Account of the People Called Methodists,' *Works* (Jackson), 8:256.
[66] See paragraph 7 of the introduction of: Hildebrandt and Beckerlegge, editors, *A Collection of Hymns* (BE), volume 7.
[67] Wesley, 'A Plain Account of the People Called Methodists,' *Works* (Jackson), 8:256.
[68] Heitzenrater, *Wesley and the People Called Methodists*, 146.
[69] Wesley, 'Minutes of Some Conversations between the Rev. Mr. Wesley and Others,' *Works* (Jackson), 8:301.

important, alongside of the need for growing in the love of God, the highest end of ethics.

The *General Rules* gives a list of fruitful actions that Methodists are expected to perform.[70] The ordering of the *General Rules* seems to reflect in part Isaiah 52:16-17: "Cease to do evil; learn to do well."[71] The *General Rules* are organized into three major categories: "doing no harm," "doing good," and "attending upon all the ordinances of God."[72] It should be evident that the first two categories resemble the commands from Isaiah. The third category resembles—if not fully, then at least in large part— Wesley's view of the *instituted* means of grace, derived from scripture. All of the *General Rules* appear to fall under Wesley's view of the means of grace. Many of the rules from the first two categories are prudential and/or general means of grace.[73] Although Wesley does at times make exceptions, his general expectation is for people to follow the *General Rules* on a regular basis.[74] We will now examine the content of the *General Rules*.

---

[70] Wesley, 'The Nature, Design, and General Rules of the United Societies,' *Works* (Jackson), 8:270.

[71] In his sermon *On Working out Our Own Salvation*, Wesley claims that these verses (from Isaiah 1:16-17) are the "general answer" to the question: "what are the steps which the Scripture directs us to take in the working out of our own salvation?" (Wesley, 'On Working out Our Own Salvation,' *Works* (BE), 3:205).

[72] Wesley, 'The Nature, Design, and General Rules of the United Societies,' *Works* (Jackson), 8:270-271. The first two of these, "doing no harm" and "doing good," are inspired by scripture (Wesley, 'On Working out Our Own Salvation,' *Works* (BE), 3:205). They are also important ethical principles that are widely discussed by various intellectuals from at least as far back as the ancient Greeks. Such principles are often related to a goal-oriented system of ethics that analyzes the pursuit of goals in consideration of the experience of pains and pleasures, or misery and happiness. In this way, for example, they are important for Aristotle's *Nicomachean Ethics*, Aquinas' "natural law" ethics, and many other versions of ethics before and during Wesley's life.

[73] The first two categories of the *General Rules*, "doing no harm" and "doing good" are examples of practicing the "general" means of grace, which includes "keeping all the commandments (Wesley, 'Some Late Conversations between the Rev. Mr. Wesley and Others,' *Works* (Jackson), 8:286)," including those cited here from Isaiah 52:16-17.

[74] See, for example, a case where a Methodist had trouble avoiding the need to work some on the Sabbath. Wesley granted him an exception. (Heitzenrater, *Wesley and the People Called Methodists*, 139).

Do No Harm

Rules for Doing No Harm

The first category is "do no harm."[75] Under this major category, Wesley begins by stating that one should "avoid evil of every kind." He then lists the following instructions: do not take the Lord's name in vain and do not profane the Lord's day by doing work. Also, one should not buy or sell on the Lord's day. He then goes on to list a number of other rules: there should be no drunkenness, "fighting, quarreling, brawling;[76] brother going to law with brother; returning evil for evil,[77] or railing for railing; the using many words in buying or selling; the buying or selling uncustomed goods; the giving or taking things on usury, that is, unlawful goods; uncharitable or unprofitable conversation, particularly speaking evil of Magistrates or of Ministers."[78] He then basically paraphrases the golden rule from Matt 7:12 and Luke 6:31: do not do to others those actions that one would wish are not done towards oneself. He then prohibits doing anything that does not lead to God's glory.

After the point concerning the golden rule, Wesley speaks some on the subject of dress, avoiding trivial activities, and abstaining from unnecessary indulgences. He says: do not put on gold or costly apparel. In another place in his writings, Wesley cautions against wearing ornaments such as rings, earrings, necklaces, laces, and ruffles.[79] The next rule prohibits diversions that cannot be used in the name of the Lord Jesus. At the same time, in his sermon "The More Excellent Way," Wesley does in fact allow certain contexts for fun activities such as sports, games, cultural fellowship activities, music, reading, and philosophical experiments.[80] The rules coming after this are: do not sing or read books that do not tend to the knowledge or love of God and do not have softness or needless self-indulgence. He elaborates on indulgence more in his other writings. Tobacco is a needless indulgence.[81] Also he cautions that too much sleep is indulgent and can lead to softness of tempers

---

[75] Wesley, 'The General Rules of the United Societies,' *Works* (Jackson), 8:270.
[76] Cf. Matt. 5:22-23.
[77] Cf. Matt 5:39.
[78] Cf. Matt 5:39.
[79] Wesley, 'Directions Given to the Band Societies,' *Works* (Jackson), 8:274.
[80] Wesley, 'The More Excellent Way,' *Works* (BE), 3:272-274.
[81] Wesley, 'Rules of the Band-Societies,' *Works* (Jackson), 8:273.

and becoming enslaved to bodily appetites.⁸² This is part of why he recommends that Methodists rise early in the mornings.⁸³

Managing Money

Wesley's next rule brings up his ethics of dealing with money: do not lay up treasures on earth. As one who is chief executive and chief financial officer for a movement involving thousands of people, Wesley carries much responsibility in dealing with money. He speaks of the moral significance of handling money fairly often in his writings.⁸⁴ He frequently gives caution concerning the danger of having a lot of money. The guiding principle for Wesley's economic ethics is to gain all one can in order to save all one can in order to give all one can.⁸⁵ One should not use more money for oneself than what is necessary for basic necessities. The rest of one's money should not be given for worldly materials or for selfish indulgence but should be invested in helping those in serious need. Wesley's final rule of the *General Rules* for the first category "do no harm" is related to money: do not borrow without a probability of paying back. This concludes the first category of the *General Rules*.

Do Good

Wesley's second category of the *General Rules* is: do good. In chapter 5, we discussed the distinction between "good works" and "doing good." The former refers to the action in itself and the latter refers to the effects. That is, Wesley makes a distinction for how some actions are not "good in themselves" on the one hand but are still "good and profitable to men" on the other hand.⁸⁶ By grace, all people can do good but only those who are born of God can do "good works," actions that are good in themselves. For this reason, one who is not yet justified cannot do good works but can "do good," as stated in the *General Rules*.⁸⁷ In summary, every person can "do good," regardless of where he or she is along the way of salvation but only some people (those born of God) can do good works.

---

[82] Wesley, 'On Redeeming the Time,' *Works* (BE), 3:328-333.
[83] Wesley, 'On Redeeming the Time,' *Works* (BE), 3:329.
[84] See, for example, Outler, editor, *Sermons* (BE), 2:263 and 3:227.
[85] Outler, editor, *Sermons* (BE), volume 2, sermon 50.
[86] Wesley, 'Justification by Faith,' *Works* (BE), 1:192.
[87] We know that it was in fact Wesley's expectation for those who are not yet justified to follow the *General Rules*. See chapter 8 for references.

"Doing good" may refer not only to the fruitful actions of the second category but also to all remaining categories of the *General Rules*.[88] For example, it seems that doing good may refer to the choice to avoid uncharitable conversation (under the first category, doing no harm) or the choice to search the scriptures (under the third category, to attend all the ordinances of God). For this section, we will turn our attention mostly to how "doing good" relates to the second category of the *General Rules*.

Under the category "doing good" in the *General Rules*, the first instructions listed are to be merciful according to one's power and to do good of every possible sort, as far as is possible to all people. These directions, along with the instruction to do good in general, are broad and seem to include in their intention the need to be obedient to the commandments of scripture. Implicitly, they also refer to the need to use creativity and practical reasoning in order to do good "of every possible sort," including for situations that are not specifically addressed by scripture or the *General Rules*.

In this category of rules, Wesley also encourages Methodist followers to do good to the bodies of other people and to their souls. We will now consider this last point in more depth, especially as it pertains to serving the needy.

Serving the Needy

A major focus of Wesley's ministry was serving the needy. This includes serving the poor. Service to the poor was a "hallmark" of Wesley's Methodist movement.[89] The majority of Methodists during Wesley's time were considered poor according to one account.[90] Wesley's program for ministering to the poor involved more than providing for immediate needs. It also involved incorporating the poor into the life and fellowship of the Methodists; providing an ongoing support system that helped

---

[88] See, for example, Outler, editor, *Sermons* (BE), 1:689 and 1:548. Wesley indicates that "good works" may refer to both works of mercy and works of piety (works that correspond with many of the ordinances of the third category of the *General Rules*). For more information on works of piety and works of mercy, see Wesley, 'The Repentance of Believers,' *Works* (BE), 1:343, including footnote 65.

[89] Richard Heitzenrater, *The Poor and the People Called Methodists* (Nashville, TN: Kingswood Books, c2002), 27.

[90] Heitzenrater, *The Poor and the People Called Methodists*, 27

them to grow in holiness of heart, improve in education, and strengthen in outward discipline.[91]

On one occasion, Wesley indicates that a goal of the Methodists is to "supply the present wants of all our poor, and put them in a way of supplying their own wants for the time to come."[92] The aim then, was not just to provide for the immediate needs of the poor but also educate them to know how to take care of themselves and even turn and give back to others who are in need.[93] Wesley and his followers did in fact have some success at this. Although there were some emerging problems, Wesley's program for the Methodists (including the poor) to show discipline, thrift, and responsibility sometimes led individual Methodists to make a great deal of financial gain.[94] Collins notes that for Wesley, such success in making and saving money is strongly rooted in having true religion understood as holiness of heart.[95] Many Methodists were effective at earning and saving money.[96]

Although the long-term goal of guiding the poor to learn self-sufficiency was important, the short-term goal of helping their immediate needs was also important. For the purpose of "doing good" in this way, Wesley lists throughout his writings a number of fruitful actions for Methodists to perform. Followers of Christ are encouraged to help give food to the hungry, clothes to the naked, and visit those that are sick and/or in prison. They are also encouraged to give help for widows and orphans. This may be done either by assisting the Methodist houses for widows and orphans[97] or simply by visiting them.[98] Wesley also encourages followers of Christ to help lodge the stranger, visit the afflicted, instruct the ignorant, be eyes to the blind, feet to the lame, encourage the well-doer, help out in Methodist-supported schools, and assist doctors in medical clinics.[99] They are also encouraged to help people struggling

---

[91] For a discussion of Wesley's commitment to serving the spiritual needs of the poor, see, for example, Collins, "The Soteriological Orientation of John Wesley's Ministry to the Poor," *Wesleyan Theological Journal*, 36, (2001): 25.

[92] Wesley, 'Causes of the Inefficacy of Christianity,' *Works* (BE), 4:93.

[93] Heitzenrater, *The Poor and the People Called Methodists*, 31.

[94] Heitzenrater, *The Poor and the People Called Methodists*, 36.

[95] Collins, "The Soteriological Orientation of John Wesley's Ministry to the Poor," 15.

[96] Heitzenrater, *The Poor and the People Called Methodists*, 37.

[97] Heitzenrater, *The Poor and the People Called Methodists*, 34; Jackson, *The Works of Wesley*, 4:449

[98] Wesley, 'Sermon on the Mount, XIII,' *Works* (BE), 1:695.

in business. Wesley attempted to increase employment by providing workers yarns for their looms and by establishing a loan system to help out people struggling in business.[100] He also established a publishing program that provided books to be given away for free for those in need.[101] All sincere followers of Christ were encouraged to help in these efforts.

Wesley's rules of action for helping the needy were examples of what he called "works of mercy." These are means of grace.[102] He teaches that it is best to show more zeal for works of mercy than works of piety such as searching the scriptures, prayer, the Lord's supper, and fasting.[103] He appears to base this point on Matt 9:13 and Matt 12:7, which is a quote of Hosea 6:6, in which God says: "I will have mercy and not sacrifice."[104] Wesley says "Whenever, therefore, one interferes with the other, works of mercy are to be preferred [over works of piety]. Even reading, hearing, prayer, are to be omitted, or to be postponed, 'at charity's almighty call'– when we are called to relieve the distress of our neighbor, whether in body or soul."[105]

The next rule that Wesley lists under the category rule "to do good" is for one to do good to other people's souls by reproving and exhorting all with whom one interacts. This can be done in class meetings or band meetings or wherever there is opportunity. One of the goals here is an effort to help save souls from death.[106]

Other Rules for Doing Good

Under the category of doing good in the *General Rules*, Wesley continues to list examples of what this means. The next rule is to trample on any doctrine or opinion that discourages people from performing fruitful actions before they receive the new birth. After this, Wesley adds: do "good especially to them that are of the household of faith, or groaning so to be; employing them preferably to others, buying one of another, helping each other in business; and so much the more, because the world

---

[99] Outler, editor, *Sermons* (BE), 1:573, 2:166, 3:191, 3:414; Heitzenrater, *The Poor and the People Called Methodists*, 34

[100] Heitzenrater, *The Poor and the People Called Methodists*, 34.

[101] Heitzenrater, *The Poor and the People Called Methodists*, 34.

[102] Wesley, 'On Zeal,' *Works* (BE), 3:313.

[103] Wesley, 'On Zeal,' *Works* (BE), 3:314.

[104] Cf. Wesley, 'On Zeal,' *Works* (BE), 3:314.

[105] Wesley, 'On Zeal,' *Works* (BE), 3:314.

[106] Wesley, 'On Zeal,' *Works* (BE), 3:319.

will love its own, and them only: by all possible diligence and frugality, that the gospel be not blamed: by running with patience the race that is set before them."[107] Here we observe encouragement to build relationships with other Christians and not too much with those with different and potentially harmful worldviews.

Self-Denial and Taking up the Cross

The *General Rules* also provide instructions for denying oneself and taking up one's cross daily. Wesley takes this commandment from Luke 9:23.[108] For Wesley, to deny oneself is to "deny our own will where it does not fall in with the will of God, and that however pleasing it may be."[109] The idea of taking up one's cross is similar to self-denial but goes a bit further: "taking up our cross goes a little farther than denying ourselves; it rises a little higher, and is a more difficult task to flesh and blood, it being more easy to forego pleasure than to endure pain."[110]

Self-denial and taking up one's cross are "absolutely, indispensably necessary, either to our becoming or continuing his [Christ's] disciples."[111] Pain is in fact necessary for eternal pleasure.[112] For Wesley, self-denial involves temperance in regard to eating, drinking, sex, and sleeping; and it involves abstaining from alcohol.[113] It also involves the denial of any other pleasure—including any remaining pleasures of sense,[114] pleasures of imagination[115] or the desire for human praise—, when this is in conflict with the will of God.[116] Self-denial is something that should be done on a *daily* basis, especially concerning having temperance in eating and sleeping. It also involves a willingness to follow

---

[107] Wesley, 'The Nature, Design, and General Rules of the United Societies,' *Works* (Jackson), 8:271.

[108] Wesley, 'Self-Denial,' *Works* (BE), 2:238.

[109] Wesley, 'Self-Denial,' *Works* (BE), 2:243.

[110] Wesley, 'Self-Denial,' *Works* (BE), 2:243.

[111] Wesley, 'Self-Denial,' (BE), 2:238.

[112] Wesley, 'Self-Denial,' (BE), 2:245.

[113] Wesley, 'Minutes of Several Conversations between the Rev. Mr. Wesley and others,' *Works* (Jackson); 8:324. The point about sex is implied in Wesley's statement concerning the need to deny one's pleasures of sense.

[114] See chapter 4 of this project for more information on Wesley's view of the pleasure of sense and pleasure of imagination.

[115] Ibid.

[116] Wesley, 'Minutes of Several Conversations between the Rev. Mr. Wesley and others,' *Works* (Jackson); 8:323.

the next rule of the *General Rules*: when necessary, submit to bear the reproach of Christ and endure when people "say all manner of evil of them falsely for the Lord's sake."[117]

Wesley explicitly indicates that taking up one's cross is a matter of choice.[118] It is a choice with moral significance; a fruitful action indeed. By choosing to take up one's cross, one is exercising one's liberty to follow in the ways of Christ rather than otherwise. Taking up one's cross does not mean it is necessary to inflict pain and suffering for its own sake,[119] but it refers primarily to those cases in which there is a choice between God's will and one's personal will.

In one of his letters, Wesley attempts to motivate and encourage a Methodist in regard to ministry by urging him to take up his cross. Wesley says, "You will fight and conquer; take up the cross until you receive the crown."[120] This concept of taking up the cross in order to receive one's crown is very much at the heart of Wesley's ethics. Throughout one's life, one must take up the cross and follow Christ's example and teachings until receiving the crown of the highest goal of ethics: love of God and neighbor, both in the world and in eternity.

Attend the Ordinances of God

Public Worship and Liturgy, the Ministry of the Word, and the Lord's Supper

Wesley's third category of the *General Rules* is to attend the ordinances of God. Under this category, the first rule is an instruction to participate in the public worship of God, which includes attending a public worship service on Sunday morning. In order to be Methodist, one did not have to attend the Anglican public worship service or be a member of the Church of England. However, even during the late part of his life, Wesley encouraged his followers to attend the Sunday morning public worship service of the Church of England, and he advised that services in Methodist preaching houses were not to replace this.[121] One of the purposes of the Methodist movement was to help renew the Church of England,

---

[117] Wesley, 'The Nature, Design, and General Rules of the United Societies,' *Works* (Jackson), 8:271.

[118] Wesley, 'Self-Denial,' *Works* (BE), 2:244.

[119] Wesley, 'Self-Denial,' *Works* (BE), 2:245.

[120] Wesley, *Letters*, 2:114.

[121] See paragraphs 2-4 in the answer to question 45 of the large Minutes (Wesley, 'Minutes of Several Conversations between the Rev. Mr. Wesley and Others,' *Works* (Jackson), 8:321).

and Wesley himself remained for his entire life an Anglican priest who was loyal to the Church of England and opposed separation from it.[122] As he said on one occasion within two years of his death: "The Methodists in general, my Lord, are members of the Church of England. They hold all her doctrines, attend her service, and partake of her sacraments."[123] Thus, in this way, Wesley encourages people to follow the traditions of the church of England.

Participating in the practices of Anglican liturgy outside of regular Methodist activities is not required for becoming a Methodist but it is encouraged. Wesley himself is committed to Anglican liturgy, including the Anglican *Homilies* and *Book of Common Prayer*. It is not the intention here to give an exhaustive portrait of Wesley's adherence to Anglican liturgy, but we will highlight some major features.

In many cases, a Methodist of Wesley's time who is loyal to the Church of England is expected to follow the guidelines provided by the *Book of Common Prayer*, an authoritative document for Anglican worship. This is true for activities such as baptism, confirmation,[124] marriage (if applicable), and burial. In the Eighteenth Century, the *Book of Common Prayer* also provides guidelines for many of the aspects of a typical Sunday morning public worship service of the Church of England. Such a service usually begins at 11 A.M.[125] and often includes public announcements,[126] prayer,[127] the singing of an anthem by the church choir,[128] the litany—which is a responsive reading between the priest and congregation—,[129] the singing of the congregation,[130] other readings from scripture, the administration of the Holy Communion with the reading of a collect (a type of prayer for Holy Communion), preaching, and possibly also public penances, public thanksgivings, and the reading of the banns of marriage.[131] Specific scriptures for the overall service and collects for

---

[122] Baker, *John Wesley and the Church of England*, 318-320.

[123] Baker, *John Wesley and the Church of England*, 318.

[124] This is despite the fact that Wesley dropped confirmation from the *Sunday Service* sent to the American Methodists.

[125] W.M. Jacob, *The Clerical Profession* (Oxford: Oxford University Press, c2007), 175.

[126] Jacob, *The Clerical Profession*, 173.

[127] Jacob, *The Clerical Profession*, 175.

[128] Jacob, *The Clerical Profession*, 188.

[129] Jacob, *The Clerical Profession*, 175.

[130] Jacob, *The Clerical Profession*, 187.

[131] Jacob, *The Clerical Profession*, 175.

Holy Communion must be read on specific days of the year, and this calendar is provided by the *Book of Common Prayer*.

In the Eighteenth Century, the *Book of Common Prayer* also provides instructions for how to participate in certain religious activities that were less frequent than occurring on a weekly basis. It provides the dates for each of the following important liturgical occurrences: Ash Wednesday, Lent, Easter, Rogation Days, Ascension Day, Whitsunday (Pentecost), Advent, and Christmas.[132] Various sorts of public services of worship were often practiced in celebration of these days and/or seasons. In his writings, Wesley makes reference to having celebrated each of these days and seasons. The *Book of Common Prayer* makes references to other special days of the liturgical calendar, but Wesley mentions these other events less often. Wesley was supportive of Methodists participating in Sunday morning public worship services of the Church of England and observing special days and seasons of the Anglican calendar. Such fruitful actions contribute positively to the formation of one's Christian identity and to growing in holiness of heart and life.

After giving instruction concerning public worship, the *General Rules* gives an instruction concerning the ministry of the word and the Lord's Supper. It seems that one may follow the first of these by attending any kind of social function with preaching and/or interaction with the scriptures.

The rule concerning the Lord's Supper is crucial. Wesley calls this one of the "works of piety."[133] In his sermon, "The Duty of Constant Communion," Wesley teaches that it is one's duty to take communion (the Lord's Supper) constantly and as often as one can.[134] When taking the Lord's Supper, one should approach this fruitful action with "a firm purpose to keep all the commandments of God, and a sincere desire to receive all his promises."[135] Participating in the Lord's Supper is a "chief" means of grace,[136] and it is a practice that is important to Wesley's ethics.

The origin of the Lord's Supper is tied to the scriptures' portrayal of the last supper, as in Luke 22:19 from the *NT Notes*: "And he took bread, and gave thanks, and brake it, and gave to them saying, 'This is my body which is given for you; do this in remembrance of me.'" Although the

---

[132] *The Book of Common Prayer* (Oxford: T. Wright and W. Gill, 1772).
[133] Wesley, 'On Zeal,' *Works* (BE), 3:313.
[134] Wesley, 'The Duty of Constant Communion,' *Works* (BE), 3:428.
[135] Wesley, 'On the Wedding Garment,' *Works* (BE), 4:141.
[136] Wesley, 'The Means of Grace,' *Works* (BE), 1:381.

Book of Common Prayer requires that the Lord's Supper be given on a weekly basis in an Anglican Church, it also says that if there is not adequate attendance, then the priest may reduce the frequency of offering it.[137] In the eighteenth century, Anglican parishes in towns often administered communion once per month, and those in small villages often administered it three or four times per year.[138] However, Wesley stresses that a person should take the Lord's Supper as often as possible, preferably at least once per week.[139]

Also, there would be intervals of time in which Wesley would recommend that the Lord's Supper be given *every* day during this period. One example of this is the "Octave," following Easter Day. Wesley says, "During the Octave, I administered the Lord's supper every morning, after the example of the Primitive Church."[140] Another example is the Twelve Days of Christmas, presumably around December 25 – January 5. Wesley speaks of celebrating the Lord's Supper each of these days, as "a little emblem of the Primitive Church."[141] Wesley recommends that a sincere follower of Christ should take the Lord's Supper on these occasions and on any other occasion when an opportunity arises.

Prayer, Searching the Scriptures, and Fasting

The next rule of the *General Rules* is to participate in family and private prayer. This is another example of the "works of piety."[142] This is something that Wesley advises to be done *daily*, both morning and evening.[143] There are a number of scriptures that Wesley uses in support of the need of prayer, including: "pray without ceasing; In every thing, give thanks" (1 Thess 5:17-18).[144] Prayer may be any of the following forms: private, family, or public.[145] It should include deprecation, petition, in-

---

[137] Jacob, *The Clerical Profession*, 183.
[138] Jacob, *The Clerical Profession*, 184-185.
[139] Wesley, 'Directions Given to the Band Societies,' *Works* (Jackson), 8:274. This is implied by the point that Wesley believes that everyone should join a band.
[140] See Wesley's journal entry for March 30, 1777, Ward and Heitzenrater, editors, *Journals and Diaries VI* (BE), volume 23. See also footnote 14.
[141] Wesley, 'Journal,' *Works* (Jackson), 4:38.
[142] Wesley, 'On Zeal,' *Works* (BE), 3:313.
[143] Wesley, 'Minutes of Some Conversations Between the Rev. Mr. Wesley and Others,' *Works* (Jackson), 8:322.
[144] Wesley, 'The Great Privilege of Those that Are Born of God,' *Works* (BE), 1:443

tercession, and thanksgiving.[146] Prayers may be read or they may be extemporaneous (spoken without prior preparation).[147] They can be silent or vocal.[148] Following William Law, Wesley advises that one should examine one's inward and outward spiritual state before praying and adjust one's prayers accordingly.[149] One should also pray before meals, and in general, pray at every opportunity.[150]

After the rule concerning prayer, there is the rule concerning searching the scriptures. This is another one of the "works of piety."[151] Studying the scriptures is an example of a fruitful action that should be performed every day.[152] Wesley believes that the scriptures are the supreme guide for the beliefs and practices of Christians. He says: "We believe, indeed, that 'all Scripture is given by the inspiration of God;'"… " We believe the written word of God to be the only and sufficient rule both of Christian faith and practice."[153] In support of this point, he cites scripture itself (2 Tim. 3:17): "All scripture is inspired of God, and is profitable for doctrine, for reproof, for correction, for instruction in righteousness; that the man [person] of God may be perfect, thoroughly furnished unto every good work."[154] He says it is important to read, meditate, and hear the scriptures; that one should use the commentary of the *NT Notes* as an aid; and that one should immediately practice what one learns.[155]

---

[145] Wesley, 'Minutes of Some Conversations Between the Rev. Mr. Wesley and Others,' Works (Jackson), 8:322.

[146] Wesley, 'Minutes of Some Conversations Between the Rev. Mr. Wesley and Others,' Works (Jackson), 8:322.

[147] Wesley, 'Minutes of Some Conversations Between the Rev. Mr. Wesley and Others,' Works (Jackson), 8:321. Prayers are commonly read in Anglican liturgy. Also, Wesley provides written prayers for families to be read during their prayer time, if they so choose. See Jackson, *The Works of Wesley*, 11:237.

[148] See Wesley's commentary on Ephesians 6:18 in the *ENNT*.

[149] Wesley, 'The More Excellent Way,' Works (BE), 3:268.

[150] Outler, editor, *Sermons* (BE), 3:270 and 1:570.

[151] Wesley, 'On Zeal,' Works (BE), 3:313.

[152] Wesley, 'Minutes of Several Conversations between the Rev. Mr. Wesley and Others,' Works (Jackson), 8:323.

[153] Wesley, 'The Character of a Methodist,' Works (Jackson), 8:340.

[154] See, for example, a reference to this verse in his journal entry, Wesley, *Journal* (Jackson), 1:278.

[155] Wesley, 'Minutes of Several Conversations Between Mr. Wesley and Others,' Works (Jackson), 8:323.

Wesley's final rule of the *General Rules* is to perform fasting or abstinence. This is another instance of the "works of piety."[156] For those who were not able to fast due to health, such people could simply practice "abstinence" as a substitute. Abstinence means "eating little; the abstaining in part; the taking a smaller quantity of food than usual."[157] However, fasting was the preferred course of action, if health permitted. Fasting is not an end but a means to an end, and when performed with prayer, it is a means for many blessings.[158] After the revival grew large and Wesley became elderly, he continued to stress that Methodists should fast at least on Fridays of each week.[159]

Following the Moral Commandments of Scripture

If in fact the need to obey all of the moral commandments of scripture is implied by the *General Rules*, not all of these commandments are specifically listed here. As mentioned above, Wesley's view of the "general" means of grace includes the need to follow and obey all of the moral commandments of scripture.[160] Many of Wesley's writings deal with the seriousness of this. For example, he published over 15 sermons devoted to considering the law and the moral commandments found in the Sermon on the Mount.[161] Wesley's recommendation to sincere followers of Christ is for them to do their best, by grace, to follow all of the moral commandments of scripture. The capacity for this is highest when the doer has the transformed heart of the new birth or perfect love. Wesley teaches that Christians are called to imitate Christ, and this is done by exemplifying both inward and outward holiness, including obedience to the moral law and commandments of scripture.

For Wesley, the moral law is a "copy of the eternal mind" and the "transcript of the divine nature." He describes the law as the "immutable rule of right and wrong."[162] "Immutable" means unchanging, and un-

---

[156] Wesley, 'On Zeal,' *Works* (BE), 3:313.

[157] Wesley, 'Sermon on the Mount, VII,' *Works* (BE), 1:595.

[158] Wesley, 'Sermon on the Mount, VII,' *Works* (BE), 1:593; 1:602.

[159] Wesley, 'Minutes of Several Conversations Between the Rev. Mr. Wesley and Others,' *Works* (Jackson), 8:323.

[160] Wesley, 'Minutes of Some Late Conversations between the Rev. Mr. Wesley and Others,' *Works* (Jackson), 8:286.

[161] See, for example, sermons 20-36 of Outler, editor, *Sermons* (BE).

[162] Wesley, 'The Original, Nature, Properties, and Use of the Law,' *Works* (BE), 2:13.

changing means that the moral commandments of scripture are not arbitrary or utterly contextual. Rather, these commandments are in some way, normative for all times and places.

Wesley stresses based on Matt. 5:17-20 that Christ came not to abolish but to fulfil the law.[163] As Paul indicates, much of the ceremonial law of the Old Testament—such as circumcision, details concerning the temple, and the dietary codes—are not applicable to Christians.[164] However, Christ has come to fulfil the moral law, including the Ten Commandments and other moral teachings of the Bible.[165] Christ fulfils the law because through his life, death, and resurrection, he provides the power of salvation, through which one has the freedom and power of a transformed heart directing one to follow the moral law at a high level. Christ also fulfils the law by providing an example for imitation. Fruitful action includes obedience to all the moral commandments of scripture, including those that Christ exemplifies and teaches. For those having experienced the new birth with the love of God shed abroad in the heart, such obedience comes easier. This is because for them, the law is written on their hearts, as prophesied in Jeremiah.[166]

For Wesley, nothing less than the power of sanctification, with the transforming love of God shed abroad in the heart and the resulting fruitful action, is what is necessary for a person to obey fully the moral law and commandments of scripture. Wesley says, "the righteousness of a Christian exceeds all this righteousness of a scribe or Pharisee by fulfilling the spirit as well as the letter of the law, by inward as well as outward obedience."[167] Inward righteousness includes the possessing of holy passive inward tempers and affections.[168] When a person has both inward and outward righteousness, he or she imitates Christ at a higher level than one acting as a Pharisee. The holy tempers and affections of one who has received sanctification provide a strong inclination that motivates a person to actively obey the law with more ease than before. Yet, even after the new birth, one retains the ability to sin. For any person, regardless of his or her location along the way of salvation, perform-

---

[163] Wesley, 'Sermon on the Mount, *Works* (BE), 1:551.
[164] See, for example, Outler, *Sermons*, 1:551.
[165] See, for example, Outler, *Sermons*, 1:551.
[166] Wesley, 'An Earnest Appeal to Men of Reason and Religion,' *Works* (Jackson), 8:22. Cf. Jeremiah 31:33.
[167] Wesley, 'Sermon on the Mount, V,' *Works* (BE), 1:568.
[168] Wesley, 'Sermon on the Mount, V,' *Works* (BE), 1:568.

ing fruitful action is a choice. For Wesley, performing fruitful action in obedience to the commandments of scripture (involving the moral law) is something that one must steadily do throughout one's life.

Recommended Action Concerning Slavery and Government

In addition to providing a plan of action for the need of working out one's own salvation on the level of an individual and small group, Wesley voices his views on some pressing issues of his day such as slavery and government. Furthermore, the former (working out one's own salvation) is related to the latter issues.

Wesley opposed both slavery and revolting from the established political order of England. In his essay "Thoughts Upon Slavery," he summarizes why he thinks slavery is wrong.[169] Furthermore, Wesley argues that freedom from slavery is a "right" which "derives from the law of nature."[170]

Thus, for these reasons and others, Wesley argues that there is no justification in forcibly taking Africans from their homes in Africa. In a letter to William Wilberforce, Wesley says, "Go on, in the name of God and in the power of his might, till even American slavery (the vilest that ever saw the sun) shall vanish away before it."[171] In addition to supporting politicians such as Wilberforce, Wesley urges captains, merchants, and planters to avoid slavery.[172] According to Wesley, it is the will of a loving God to set slaves free.

In regard to government, Wesley's view was to support the King of England and the established order. As David Hempton points out: "Wesley's support for the established order in the period of 1772-82 was based not only on his residual and suitably amended Toryism, but also on his appreciation of the rights enjoyed by the free-born Englishman."[173] During this period and after, Wesley believed that the English political system already offered the most crucial freedoms, including: the liberty to choose one's religion (whether orthodox Anglican, unorthodox Anglican

---

[169] Wesley, 'Thoughts Upon Slavery,' *Works* (Jackson), 11:59.
[170] Wesley, 'Thoughts Upon Slavery,' *Works* (Jackson), 11:79.
[171] Jackson, editor, *The Works of John Wesley*, 13:153.
[172] Wesley, *Thoughts Upon Slavery* (Jackson), 11:76.
[173] David Hempton, *The Religion of the People* (New York: Routledge, 1996), 82.

or any other religion that is allowable under the status of a dissenter) or not to have a religion at all; and the liberty to manage one's goods, fortunes, property, and life according to one's pleasure.[174]

Thus, for Wesley, there is no reason to change the established political order. Furthermore, Wesley gives some reasons for how a monarchy can be a more preferred form of government than a democracy and aristocracy.[175] He was against the American Revolution. In defense of the established political order of Britain, Wesley devoted extra attention to these matters in his writings between 1768 and 1782. His aim was to encourage others to support the King and the established political order of Britain. Yet, for Wesley, the success of the American Revolution did not slow his goal for ethics. While many of the ingredients for Wesley's prescribed method for fruitful action for Americans would remain the same as before, some revisions would have to be made to suit the changing circumstances in America.

For matters such as government and slavery, Wesley provides full-length publications that focus only on these matters. For other matters such as war, marriage, and women in ministry, he does not provide as much of a discussion. Yet, these matters and others are still of high importance and are worthy of much consideration on another occasion.

Summarizing this Chapter

Over the course of this chapter, we explored Wesley's method for fruitful action. It was shown that such a method involves a fairly wide range of activities including participating in Christian fellowship, following the *General Rules*, and obeying the moral commandments of scripture. Wesley also opposed slavery and supported the British political order. Again, it is not the purpose of this project to give an exhaustive list of Wesley's view of fruitful action but to present many of the most crucial examples. Furthermore, we showed that it is possible to gather a sense of how frequently certain actions should be performed in Wesley's view. When integrating the frequency of these prescribed actions, one is able to form a basic approach for fruitful action that does in fact have some flexibility.

On a daily basis, one is encouraged to pray, search the scriptures, practice self-denial, take up one's cross, and be careful to obey the commandments of scripture as they apply. Wesley himself also kept a daily

[174] Wesley, 'Some Observations on Liberty,' *Works* (Jackson), 11:92.
[175] Wesley, 'Some Observations on Liberty,' *Works* (Jackson), 11:105

diary partly in order to assist himself in reflecting on his own spiritual condition. There are not many written occasions in which he encourages others to do the same, but it seems that he would have been encouraging of others to carry on this practice as it assists self-examination concerning one's spiritual condition. Fasting, public worship, and attending a class meeting should be performed on a weekly basis. Preferably, one should also be involved in a band. If circumstances allow, then at least once per week, one should also partake of the Lord's Supper and attend early-morning and evening preaching services. One should also plan some time for serving the poor and those in serious need, especially since works of mercy often take priority over works of piety.

In addition, one should attend at least once per quarter (if not around once per month) a love-feast, watch-night service, and letter-day meeting. One should also attend gatherings for field-preaching when these are available. On a yearly basis, one should attend the covenant service and observe events relating to one's church tradition. Although Wesley welcomed people of other church traditions into the Methodist classes, his own preferred tradition was Anglicanism. For this reason, he would encourage followers of the Anglican tradition to participate in events relating to special days and seasons such as Ash Wednesday, Lent, Easter, Rogation Days, Ascension Day, Whitsunday (Pentecost), Advent, and Christmas.

Other remaining fruitful actions should be performed when there is time and opportunity. In addition, by grace, a person should use prudence or creativity to determine the right course of action for situations in which guidance from scripture is not altogether clear. Building loving relationships with God and one's neighbors should be an intentional goal for each sincere follower of Christ, and the performance of each of the fruitful actions above should be viewed as a means for pursuing this goal.

Of course, this method for fruitful action is not the essence of religion. For Wesley, the essence of religion is Christian faith working by love, a love that must have some type of fruitful action that flows from it if there is time and opportunity. In theory—even from Wesley's point of view—, one can neglect fruitful actions and still be at least temporarily blessed with Christian faith working by love. Nonetheless, with scripture as his supreme source, Wesley teaches that these fruitful actions should be diligently and constantly performed, regardless of one's point along the way of salvation. Without such effort, one is prone to the spiritual sickness of practical antinomianism, unhappiness, and backsliding.

It is easy for critics of Wesley's view of religious experience to call such religious experience (relating to the new birth, assurance, perfection, etc.) enthusiasm or something that is not verifiable for many. But the powerful challenge that Wesley has to offer is: "What have you done to seek God?" "Have you worked out your own salvation by performing fruitful actions in these ways?" The arguments of a critic of religious experience cannot hold until the critic tries these fruitful actions with sincerity, diligence, humility, and an open mind. Yet, the performance of these fruitful actions is nothing a person does alone. As discussed in chapter 5, fruitful action is made possible by the grace of God "preventing, accompanying, and following" every fruitful act.[176] Indeed, the performance of each specific fruitful action is a testimony to the tremendous presence of the Holy Spirit in one's life. Each specific fruitful action is an expression and pure example of God's gift. It is a gift available to all people. As one performs these fruitful actions and strives for the greatest end of ethics, God's gifts shine forth.

---

[176] Wesley, 'On Working Out Our Own Salvation,' *Works* (BE), 3:209.

CHAPTER 9

HEART ETHICS FOR TODAY

In this work, we have explored John Wesley's view of ethics. Ethics involves a consideration of the features of the soul and how they work together as an agent performs right action and pursues the highest end of human living. John Wesley's heart ethics focuses on the spiritual development of the heart and the pursuit of a highest goal, which is to love God and neighbor to the fullest extent possible. The thesis of this project was to argue that according to the view of John Wesley, a person's pursuit of the greatest end of ethics is an expression of God's gift and that the giftedness of this blessing is illuminated by a critical examination of the work of the Spirit with respect to the active and passive dimensions of a human being. We will now summarize the course we took in exploring Wesley's ethics in depth and defending this thesis.

The first task of this project was to clarify the features of the soul. These features of the soul are the essential constituents of the spiritual nature and natural image of God. Since Wesley's view of the soul involves a conceptual distinction between active and passive, we began by illuminating exactly what is meant by active and passive. Illustrations were used to clarify the meaning of each of these concepts. In chapters 2-3, we clarified Wesley's view of the features of the soul, which includes understanding, will, and liberty. In chapter 4, we looked at Wesley's view of the heart and understanding. We showed how the heart is of key importance for Wesley's ethics.

In chapter 5 - 7, we carried out the second task of this project. The second task was to consider in more depth how the features of the soul relate as an agent performs right action and pursues the highest end of ethics. In other words, we explored Wesley's view of ethics for each stage of the spiritual journey, from beginning to end. In chapter 5, we explored Wesley's understanding of the role of the Holy Spirit in moral action, specifically "fruitful action." In chapters 6 and 7, we considered Wesley's ethics in depth for each stage of spiritual growth. We examined his view of ethics for the servant of God, child of the new birth, child of perfect love, and inhabitant of heaven. For each stage, we showed that for Wesley, a person's pursuit of the greatest end of ethics is an expression of God's gift and that the giftedness of this blessing is illuminated by a critical examination of the work of the Spirit with respect to the active and passive dimensions of a human being. In chapter 8, a more detailed account of ethical action was considered. We considered the content of Wesley's method for fruitful action, highlighting the specific ways in which God's gift shows itself. In these ways, the thesis of the project was affirmed.

The next question to consider is "how does Wesley's ethics apply to people today?" In his book *John Wesley's Moral Theology*, D. Stephen Long offers the following point: "Wesley's ongoing relevance for 'today' arises from his irrelevance for 'today.'"[1] We will offer a somewhat different approach, one a bit more sympathetic to the approaches of figures such as Albert Outler and others. The approach here may be expressed by the simple idea: Wesley's heart ethics has relevance for today.

The project of showing convincingly why Wesley's voice should be welcomed more among the participants of contemporary academic theology and theological ethics is beyond the reach of this current work. Yet I would like at least to *begin* to reflect on this question of whether Wesley's theology and ethics should be welcomed more often into academic theological conversations of the highest priority both inside and outside Wesleyan Studies. To this purpose, we will now briefly put Wesley in dialogue with Stanley Hauerwas, one of the leading Christian ethicists of the present time.

Is Hauerwas the John Wesley of Today?

On some levels, John Wesley and Stanley Hauerwas are comparable. Wesley is the founder of the Methodist tradition, and Hauerwas grew up Methodist and spent much of his life as a member of the United Methodist Church. It is too early now to begin to assess the level of impact that Hauerwas will have on theology and the church in the centuries ahead. What is evident is that like John Wesley for his time, Hauerwas has had some impact. In 2001, *Time Magazine* described him as "America's Best Theologian" and "contemporary theology's foremost

---

[1] Long, *John Wesley's Moral Theology*, xvi.

intellectual provocateur."[2] In 2005, Jeffrey Stout of Princeton University says: "Stanley Hauerwas is surely the most prolific and influential theologian now working in the United States."[3] Hauerwas has published over 40 books and hundreds of articles. He has produced what is widely considered some of the most influential work in contemporary theological ethics.

With respect to their theological views, Hauerwas and Wesley have much in common. They both prefer an account of moral action that regards an agent's character and convictions. The thought of both may be described as a "virtue ethic" with a teleology, a goal-oriented perspective.[4] They both value the ecumenical creeds and stress that Christian community and Christian practices are important for the Christian life. Both of their theologies show that ethics must concern in some way ecclesiology, the sacraments, liturgy, and church tradition. Also, they both strongly and explicitly oppose a common trait of Enlightenment thought that divorces ethics from Christian theology. Hauerwas and Wesley also oppose subsequent approaches to ethics that maintain such a divorce.

One point of focus for Hauerwas is his advocacy for pacifism. Although unlike Hauerwas, Wesley did not write extensively on the subject of war, it is clear that Wesley supported efforts to avoid war.[5] Yet, according to Theodore Weber, there is no evidence Wesley forbids Christians from participating in justifiable wars.[6]

While there are points of resemblance between Hauerwas and Wesley, there are also some notable points of difference. As Hauerwas has lived several hundred years after Wesley, the former's thought has been influenced by figures that Wesley has never read. For example, Hauerwas' thought is deeply indebted to figures living after Wesley such as Ludwig

[2] Jean Bethka Elshtain, "Theologian Christian Contrarian," *Time Magazine*, September 2001.

[3] Jeffrey Stout, *Democracy and Tradition* (Princeton, NJ: Princeton University Press, c2004), 140.

[4] Nonetheless, remember that for Wesley, one becomes capable of virtue only after experiencing the new birth, the effect of the work of God alone. Wesley's model does not allow that one becomes virtuous only by doing right action.

[5] Ronald Stone, *John Wesley's Life and Ethics* (Nashville, TN: Abingdon Press, c2001), 137. Stone also claims that there is evidence that shows that Wesley is not a pacifist (p. 139).

[6] Theodore Weber, *Politics in the Order of Salvation, Transforming Wesleyan Political Ethics* (Nashville, TN: Abingdon Press, c2001), footnote 74, p. 465.

Wittgenstein, Karl Barth, Hans Frei, Alasdair MacIntyre, and John Howard Yoder. In what follows, we will not provide an exhaustive account of how Hauerwas and Wesley compare. Rather, we will highlight some basic differences between the two and begin to consider how this may have bearing on Wesley's relevance to contemporary academic theology and theological ethics. We will explore differences regarding scripture, experience, truth, and moral choice.

The Authority of Scripture

Wesley and Hauerwas differ in their understanding of the role of scripture in theology in part because of differing views they have in regard to Catholicism. Although Hauerwas grew up Methodist and has been active in the United Methodist church for much of his adult life, he has a stronger appeal than Wesley for Roman Catholic theology. Hauerwas is marked as a Roman Catholic thinker but will not convert to Catholicism as long as the Catholic church will not recognize what he calls his wife's priesthood in the Methodist tradition.[7]

Related to Hauerwas' closer affiliation with Catholicism, Hauerwas seems to ascribe a higher authority to tradition and community and less authority to scripture than Wesley does.[8] Consistent with this point, Richard Hays argues that Hauerwas' view of scripture is most suitable to Roman Catholic thought,[9] and William Cavanaugh argues that Hauerwas' view of scripture is suitable to either Roman Catholic thought or Eastern Orthodox thought.[10] In any of these cases, it is clear that Hauerwas tends to ascribe a higher authority to tradition and a lower authority to scripture than do Protestants and Anglicans such as John Wesley.

Of course, Wesley, unlike Hauerwas, takes the position that the Bible is the supreme authority for matters of faith and Christian living. In this way, Wesley's theology is more faithful to the *Articles of Religion* of the Church of England and United Methodist Church and to the doctrine of any other church that sees the Bible as the supreme authority for

---

[7] Berkman and Cartwright, editors, *The Hauerwas Reader* (Durham, NC: Duke University Press, c2001), 24.

[8] C.f. Berkman and Cartwright, editors, *The Hauerwas Reader*, 639-642, 645.

[9] Richard Hays, *The Moral Vision of the New Testament* (San Francisco: HarperSanFrancisco, c1996), 265.

[10] Berkman and Cartwright, editors, *Hauerwas Reader*, 641.

matters of faith and Christian living.[11] Thus, how to view the authority of scripture is one key difference between Wesley and Hauerwas.

Regard for Religious Experience

Wesley's regard for religious experience is a key part of his ethics. It is also part of what makes it possible for his ethics to be a practical science. Albert Outler describes Wesley's ethics as a practical science. He says, "Wesley's concept of theology as a scientia practica had always meant to him that evangelical doctrine entailed a series of ethical imperatives which issued, in turn, from clear conceptions of sound doctrine."[12] For Wesley, such sound doctrine must be grounded in scripture, which as discussed in the last section, is the highest authority for matters of faith and Christian living. Scripture itself deals directly with religious experience. Furthermore, according to Wesley, for the purpose of pastoral guidance, it is also useful to regard people's experiences for matters where scripture is not clear.[13]

One of the strengths of Wesley's ethics is that it is informed by a vast collection of experiences from his ministry. Wesley draws from a larger database of observations and testimonies of people in the life of the church than that of most other major theologians throughout history. In the beginning part of his ministry, Wesley did not have a full understanding of the difference in regard to human experience between the scriptural levels of a servant of God, newborn child, and perfected child. His experience in ministry guided him to understand more clearly what he believed that the scriptures teach regarding these stages. With time, Wesley saw more convincingly how each stage corresponds to a unique collection of spiritual events and religious experiences.

---

[11] See article VI of the *Articles of Religion* of the Anglican Church and article V of the *Articles of Religion* of the *Book of Discipline of the United Methodist Church*.

[12] Outler, editor, *Sermons* (BE), 2:236.

[13] C.f. Don Thorsen, "Experimental Method in the Practical Theology of John Wesley," *Wesleyan Theological Journal*, 24, (1989). Wesley did not believe that his inductive method fell short of its purpose. Yet, Maddox is correct that Wesley did not merely develop his theology from empirical analysis of contemporary Christian piety and life in a manner like Troeltsch. Wesley begins his experimental method with the prior assumption that Anglican doctrines and the supreme authority of scripture are truthful. See Randy Maddox, "John Wesley—Practical Theologian?", *Wesleyan Theological Journal*, 23, (1988): 128.

Hauerwas' concern is that Wesley's emphasis on religious experience can lead to narcissism.[14] For Hauerwas, the preferred level of theological focus is not the individual and his or her feelings or experiences (such as the direct witness of the Spirit, the fruits of the Spirit, the love of God shed abroad in the heart, etc.). Rather it is the Body of Christ as manifest in the narrative and politics of the Christian community. Such a narrative involves concrete practices and helps to shape human characters. It is in this setting, that God introduces the divine life to a person, while God is building and enriching the Christian narrative. Wesley would appreciate many of these insights. Like Hauerwas, Wesley shows interest in human character,[15] but the latter gives more attention to how character relates to religious experience.

A person may defend Wesley's emphasis on religious experience by showing that Wesley is simply being faithful to the teachings of the scripture. As shown in chapters 6 and 7 of this work, religious experiences such as those regarding the witness of the Spirit, the fruits of the Spirit, the love of God shed abroad in the heart, and even the experience of perfect love, are points of teaching in the scriptures. Furthermore, neglecting the scriptural teaching of the love of God shed abroad in the heart is no small oversight. It is missing the fundamental meaning of what it means to be born of God. From Wesley's perspective, Hauerwas' ongoing recommendation for concrete practices without any reminder of the importance of scriptural heartfelt experience can at times come across as Pharisaic. It promotes the form of religion, not the power of religion. Wesley's concern for religious experience is not narcissistic and for its own sake. Rather, such a concern is for the sake of gauging a person's own spiritual progress and to help people protect against a misunderstanding of one's own spiritual state. Wesley's ethics is outward directed and focuses on loving God and neighbor.

Truth and Ethics

Another crucial difference between Wesley and Hauerwas is in regard to their views of truth. For some, it may be surprising to learn the degree

---

[14] Berkman and Cartwright, editors, *The Hauerwas Reader*, 267.

[15] See Wesley, 'The Character of a Methodist,' *Works* (Jackson), 8:339. Wesley says "A Methodist is one who has 'the love of God shed abroad in his heart by the Holy Ghost'" (p. 341).

to which Hauerwas' view of truth is influenced by his interpretation of the later writings of Ludwig Wittgenstein, which holds that much of truth—if not all truth— is confined to a "language game."[16] Yet, the problem sometimes goes deeper. Hauerwas' view of truth is given by some the charge of relativism. This is not a position that Hauerwas openly embraces. However, whether or not he is guilty of such a charge depends on who is being asked. For example, J. Wesley Robbins says, "If Hauerwas' pure narrative theory of moral rationality were to be adopted, the results would include an unavoidable acceptance of moral relativism."[17]

Hauerwas' view of the nature of truth is not one that he holds alone but has a considerable following in the field of theological ethics, not to mention other academic fields, including some with non-Christian perspectives. In regard to his view of truth, Hauerwas shares much in common with Christian philosopher Alasdair MacIntyre.

What then is this interpretation of the nature of truth that Hauerwas and MacIntyre share and with which Wesley would disagree? It is simply the rejection of what we will call "PremiseT." "PremiseT" is the claim that there is such thing as objective truth that is universally accessible and that the basis of much of this truth exists completely independently of particular human communities. As we will show, figures such as Hauerwas and MacIntyre reject this claim while figures such as Wesley and Alvin Plantinga accept it. Indeed, that Hauerwas and MacIntyre reject PremiseT might seem a bit shocking to some.

In regard to the matter of truth, Hauerwas contends that there is "no way to deal with the question of 'truth as such' but only the question of

---

[16] Hauerwas denies that truth is confined to a language game that is self-validating (Brad Kallenberg, *Ethics as Grammar* (Notre Dame, Indiana: University of Notre Dame Press, c 2001), 241), but he seems to affirm that truth is confined to a language game understood as a narrative context of a particular community. In other words, for Hauerwas, "self-validating" is the wrong phrase for describing Hauerwas' belief that truth is utterly dependent on the linguistic context of a particular community. In his book *Ethics as Grammar*, Brad Kallenberg attempts to illuminate Hauerwas' work with Wittgenstein. Kallenberg says that for Hauerwas, "there appears no way to evaluate truth claims in Enlightenment fashion, which is to say, in isolation from a particular community (p. 240-244)." Concerning Hauerwas' view of truth, see also below, including footnotes.

[17] J. Wesley Robbins, "Narrative, Morality, and Religion," *Journal of Religious Ethics*, 8, (1980): 175.

this or that claim."[18] Also, evidence from Hauerwas' writings suggests that he rejects PremiseT.[19] Sharing sympathy with this point by Hauerwas, MacIntyre gives a glowing assessment of Nietzsche's diagnosis of the problem with an Enlightenment way of thinking, especially in regard to morals: "For it was Nietzsche's historic achievement to understand more clearly than any other philosopher...not only that what purported to be appeals to objectivity were in fact expressions of subjective will, but also the nature of the problems that this posed for moral philosophy."[20] In other words, what MacIntyre is claiming is that people who claim to show the objective truth of PremiseT do not show universal truth in the manner that they are presuming but are rather no more than promoting a view that depends on a particular social location and is not accessible to all people.

It is here that MacIntyre opens himself up to the same types of charges of relativism and postmodernism that have been directed at Hauerwas.[21] MacIntyre even admits that charges of relativism directed at his book *After Virtue* are not scarce but are "repeated."[22] Like Hauerwas, MacIntyre attempts to escape the charge of a certain notion of relativism. However, MacIntyre openly admits to being a relativist as such

[18] Stanley Hauerwas, *Christian Existence Today* (Durham, NC, Labyrinth Press, 1988), 8. Also, see the footnote below for more on Hauerwas' view of truth.

[19] Hauerwas indicates that truth is not something that is "'out there' waiting to be seen" (Stanley Hauerwas, "Ethics and Ascetical Theology," *Anglican Theological Review*, 61, (1979). 97). Hauerwas acknowledges that some scholars have raised concerns regarding his view of truth. For example, he says, "Jenson, as usual, goes to the heart of the matter by challenging not only me but also anyone who, like Milbank, accepts the critique of 'foundational' accounts of knowledge. *Many* think that our willingness to assume the contingency of our own convictions means that we must abandon all attempts to claim Christian beliefs as true." (Italics are added, Stanley Hauerwas, *Wilderness Wanderings* (Boulder, Colo.: Westview Press, 1997), 188). My aim is to offer that Hauerwas may go a bit too far in the view that truth depends on the linguistic context of a particular community. See also Hauerwas, *Christian Existence Today*, 8 and the footnote above concerning how he is influenced by his interpretation of the later writings of Wittgenstein. See also Hauerwas' section "Ethics and the Demand for Absolutes" in chapter 1 of *The Peaceable Kingdom* (Notre Dame: University of Notre Dame Press, c1983) and his section "On the 'Tonto' Principle," p. 214 of *Schooling Christians* (Grand Rapids, Michigan: W.B. Eerdmans, c1992).

[20] MacIntyre, *After Virtue*, 113.
[21] MacIntyre, *After Virtue*, xii.
[22] MacIntyre, *After Virtue*, xii.

is understood in a certain way: MacIntyre says that there are times when "it is possible to discover no rational way to settle the disagreements between two rival moral and epistemological traditions, so that positive grounds for a relativistic thesis would emerge. But this I have no interest in denying."[23]

It is not the purpose here to prove that Hauerwas and MacIntyre are in fact relativists. Even if they succeed in convincing some people that they are not relativists, their epistemology may still be problematic if it fails to account adequately for the objective truth of PremiseT. There are certain objective truths that can be known in basically the same manner for a person of any linguistic community in any time period. Examples of such objective truths are apparent from concepts such as "night is followed by day," "each person has a brain," and "a person with a XY chromosome has some traits that are different from a person with a XX chromosome." There are also objective truths even in regard to moral matters. Examples of these include: "it is preferable for a person to have breathable air," "in general, one should avoid severe heat that produces pain and injury," and "food and water are necessary for survival, and so in general, obtaining at least some level of these is preferable." We are not claiming here that there is no such thing as truth that fully depends on a particular language community. Rather, we are avoiding the claim that all truth has such a full dependence.

An epistemology that recognizes objective truth as mentioned in PremiseT may also recognize the powerful ways in which the practices and life of a community with a tradition shape epistemology. Hauerwas and MacIntyre are correct and insightful in much of how they show that practices and the life of a community with a tradition (a particular social location) shapes epistemology and greatly fashions a person's character, convictions, and beliefs. They are also correct in their portrayal of Kant's neglect of how history shapes identity and how proponents of the Enlightenment too often purport claims of universal truth that are in fact no more than views that derive from their social location and are not accessible to all people. Furthermore, they are right to combat the problems that too often arise from this principle. For example, it would be good to oppose universalists who impose their ideas on others in a way that causes harms and resembles a kind of epistemic imperialism.

---

[23] MacIntyre, *After Virtue*, 277.

MacIntyre is correct in observing that on some important moral issues there are deep differences in views from one moral tradition to another. He is also correct in showing that adherents of the Enlightenment and/or its descendants—logical positivism, foundationalism, and certain forms of analytic philosophy—who believe in objective truth as mentioned in PremiseT, cannot come to full agreement on what many objective truths are, especially as these objective truths concern morals. However, of course, the failure of various parties to come to full agreement on some matters does not logically necessitate the conclusion that there are no such objective truths at all. Perhaps there is more agreement among people and different communities than appears on the surface, as scholars tend to get bogged down and entangled in conceptual detail. It is because of the objective truth of PremiseT that people of different narratives have the potential to communicate at some level, to build relationships, and to function in harmony with one another (rather than disconnect at 100 percent).

If Hauerwas and MacIntyre do in fact claim that truth is fully dependent on a particular narrative context, and if this claim is correct, then this serves as more support for those who argue that John Wesley's theology cannot and should not serve as a guide for today. According to such an epistemology, Wesley's theology is only fully intelligible in the English-speaking Eighteenth Century, and today we can only consider perhaps derivatives of parts of his theology. The rest is hidden behind an immovable barrier of time. However, if we presuppose the possibility for the objective truth of premiseT, then many of Wesley's insights concerning the Christian life could potentially offer much of the same value for any social location or language community in any period of history.

As discussed above, Hauerwas and MacIntyre share opinions about epistemology that has led to charges of relativism. Of course, in regard to the issues considered here, there are in fact alternative approaches to epistemology that are academically rigorous. Such alternatives are framed in such a way that they are not as disposing to charges of relativism. Furthermore, many of such alternative epistemologies provide a defense for PremiseT. It is well beyond the scope of this project to argue why an alternative epistemology is more helpful than one that confines truth only to social location. Nonetheless, we will observe briefly *candidates* for providing helpful resources in support of such an alternative approach.

In his essay "Are Concept-Users World-Makers?," distinguished Christian Philosopher Nicholas Wolterstorff offers a critique of some of the cousins of Hauerwas and MacIntyre's epistemology. These cousins are not mirror reflections of the epistemologies of Hauerwas and MacIntyre, but the fact that they share with Hauerwas and MacIntyre a rejection of PremiseT is significant. In critique of one such an epistemology that was at least temporarily held by Hilary Putnam, Wolterstorff says,

> We wanted to know what the anti-realist means in saying that 'existence' and 'truth' are relative to conceptual schemes, and why he insists on the propriety of describing concepts with his world-making metaphors. One would have guessed that Putnam's theory of concepts tells us something relevant. That expectation is dashed. Nothing in the theory—so far as I can see, at any rate—makes these metaphors seem at all appropriate, or explains why 'truth' and 'existence' are relative.[24]

This statement sheds light on one of the larger purposes of Wolterstorff's essay, which is to reject an epistemology of relativism that is grounded on the view that truth depends on concepts that are confined to local context, whether linguistic or however it may be posed. One of Wolterstorff's conclusions in this essay is that "What we count as an object of this or that sort was there all along awaiting our counting it as that."[25] In other words, there is such thing as the objective truth of premiseT, independent of local context.

Another critique of the family of epistemologies that reject PremiseT is offered by Geoffrey Wainwright. In reference to George Lindbeck's narrative theology, Wainwright says,

> To begin with: his theory of truth appears inadequate, at least to the claims Christians have traditionally thought they were making for their message and teaching. Lindbeck sounds like a consensualist (pp. 18, 47f, 63f), and what has just been suggested about a continuing 'active receptivity' certainly implies epistemological significance for consensus. But what matters is what we consent *to* and *in*. A consensus theory of truth–leaving aside the philosophical objection of the possibility universal delusion—is of no use to Christianity without a *veridical* God.[26]

[24] Nicholas Wolterstorff, "Are Concept-Users World Makers?," *Philosophical Perspectives*, 1, (1987): 248.

[25] Wolterstorff, "Are Concept-Users World Makers?," 264.

[26] Geoffrey Wainwright, "Ecumenical Dimensions of Lindbeck's 'Nature of Doctrine,'" *Modern Theology*, 4, (1988): 124.

Here, Wainwright is clearly showing disapproval of what he interprets as Lindbeck's rejection of PremiseT. What Wainwright calls a "consensualist" outlook is the view that truth fully depends on linguistic context. In other words, truth is no more than the consensus of a linguistic community. Under such a consensualist view, if a community decides that there is no God, then there really is no God. Wainwright's response is to stress that there is a God that exists completely independent of linguistic context and consensus and that the existence of such a God is "veridical" and truthful, as truth is represented in PremiseT. Consistent with this point, Thomas Noble says, "For all the insights of George Lindbeck and 'postliberalism,' Nicene Trinitarian theology is not just concerned with laying down rules for theological grammar, but with assertions or truth claims about the reality of the Living God."[27]

Another candidate for providing helpful resources in support of premiseT is drawing from the thought of Christian philosopher Alvin Plantinga.[28] In his essay "Christian Philosophy at the End of the 20th Century," Plantinga says "Clearly one of the deepest impulses in Christian thought is the idea that there really is such a person as God, who has established the world a certain way: there really is a correct or right way of looking at things; this is the way God looks at things. Furthermore, things are the way God sees them for everyone, quite independently of what they might think, say, or wish."[29] Note again the last line, "things are the way God sees them for everyone, quite independently of what they might think, say, or wish."

In other words, what we observe here is support of the truth of PremiseT, that there is some objective truth that has its basis completely independent of human language communities. In similar fashion, Plantinga affirms the truth that certain things exist, such as horses for example, completely independently of people's way of talking, seeing or

---

[27] Thomas Noble, "To Serve the Present Age: Authentic Wesleyan Theology Today, The 2010 WTS Presidential Address," *Wesleyan Theological Journal*, 46, (2011): 79.

[28] As a side note, in his book, *Aldersgate and Athens*, William Abraham briefly compares John Wesley and Alvin Plantinga. See, for example, William Abraham, *Aldersgate and Athens* (Waco, Texas: Baylor University Press, c2010), 31.

[29] Alvin Plantinga, "Christian Philosophy at the End of the Twentieth Century," *The Analytic Theist* (Grand Rapids, Michigan: W.B. Eerdman's Publishing Company, c1998), 334.

existing.[30] Plantinga is in support of Hauerwas' and MacIntyre's rejection of classical foundationalism, but unlike these others, Plantinga accepts a revised foundationalism.[31] Such a foundationalism is an example of one way of thinking that aims to be compatible with affirming the truth of premiseT.

Wesley stresses the importance of a right understanding of truth in his analysis of virtue. For Wesley, virtue requires both "love" and "truth."[32] The reality of "Christian love" already presupposes the right notions of truth. However, in the context of his ethical debate with Hutcheson, Wesley had to emphasize the importance of truth because he believed that Hutcheson's account of ethics neglected this.[33] In a response to Hauerwas and MacIntyre, a similar type of need is apparent. Like Wesley, Hauerwas would reject Hutcheson's account of ethics. Yet, for Wesley, Hauerwas' account of truth may not be adequate. Theological ethics cannot stand on a view that truth is utterly dependent on local context, as has been charged to Hauerwas and MacIntyre by those noted above. Rather, Christian thought must rest on the view that there is such truth as the type premiseT, such as that there is a God that exists completely independent of local context. While there is a diversity of cultures in the world and a variation in how people experience God, there also must be some common ways across all local contexts in which God is known and the gospel is offered. The essence of such truth does not depend on factors that are limited to a particular local context.

Choice as Gift

Wesley and Hauerwas also somewhat differ in their understanding of moral choice. Much of Hauerwas' critique of choice is a response to his interpretation of the Enlightenment. According to Hauerwas, the problem with the ethics of the Enlightenment, is that it wrongly presupposes that it is possible for a moral agent to make correct moral decisions in a way that is reliant on reason and is disconnected from history and human character. Alasdair MacIntyre, Hauerwas' ally in ethics in regard

---

[30] Plantinga, "Christian Philosophy at the End of the Twentieth Century," 333.

[31] Plantinga, "Christian Philosophy at the End of the Twentieth Century," 333.

[32] Wesley, 'An Israelite Indeed,' *Works* (BE), 3:289.

[33] Wesley, 'An Israelite Indeed,' *Works* (BE), 3:279.

to this subject, offers that Kant, the epitome of Enlightenment ethics, fails to show that human reason alone is sufficient for providing a justification for moral choosing.[34]

The problem with Hauerwas' and MacIntyre's treatment of choice is not their disapproval of how they interpret modernist ethics. The problem begins with how their view of moral choosing is an example of something that is once again entangled in their problematic view of truth. They argue that a person can never step outside of local context and make a choice based on what is an objectively right way of acting. This is because it seems that for them, all truth and seeing are utterly dependent on local context.

Wesley offers a different theology of choice that does not share all of the same assumptions as those of Hauerwas and MacIntyre. For Wesley, one *can* in some cases step outside of local context, identify what is objectively right and wrong, and make what is objectively the right choice. For Wesley, this is possible because God has given by prevenient grace to *every* person, regardless of culture and local context, a conscience and some knowledge of the moral law.[35] Such a gift gives every person the power to choose between good and evil. It also gives every person a power to choose between different narratives such as, for example, between serving God or the world.

It seems that Hauerwas' reluctance to affirm such freedom of choice is because he thinks that such a view leads to the undermining of one of the central messages of Christianity—that salvation is God's gift. According to Hauerwas' concern, for a person to choose the way of salvation seems to give to a person—rather than God— credit for salvation. It seems that it is from this concern that Hauerwas portrays a stark polarity (opposition) between God's gift and human choosing.[36]

---

[34] See for example, MacIntyre, *After Virtue*, 47.

[35] As discussed in chapter 6, Wesley teaches that every person starts with some degree of conscience due to the effects of God's supernatural prevenient grace. Prevenient grace is universal. Such prevenient grace provides every person a degree of the power to know the difference between good and evil and the power to choose either good or evil. See Wesley, 'On Conscience,' *Works* (BE), 3:481-484; Wesley, 'Some Remarks on Mr. Hill's 'Review'', *Works* (Jackson), 10:392.

[36] For example, Hauerwas says, "since we are God's good creation, we are not free to choose our own stories. Freedom lies not in creating our lives but recognizing our lives as gift" (Stanley Hauerwas, "Preaching as Though We Had Enemies," *First Things*, 53, (1995): 48). Like Hauerwas, Wesley would reject the

With this concern in mind, there are two points that must be considered on Wesley's behalf. First, Wesley avoids disconnecting choice from character and history in the manner that is charged to Kant. As shown in Appendix A, in a manner comparable to the "middle view" of Samuel Clarke, Wesley's view of choosing is internally consistent with his view of the importance and *necessity* of holy character for virtue. For Wesley, the active power (the power of choosing) and passive inclinations of one's character (tempers and affections of the heart, etc.) are both essential for virtue and are not designed, in a person's ideal state, to be opposing forces. This makes Wesley a bit different from modern figures such as Kant and Reid.

The second point is that for Wesley, Hauerwas is wrong to claim that there must be a polarity between God's gift and human choice. Wesley is commonly misunderstood on this matter, as he is sometimes accused of being a Pelagian or semi-Pelagian. It has been the hope of this project to show that for Wesley, right choosing (and the corresponding fruitful action) demonstrates the opposite of Hauerwas' worry. Right choosing *is* a pure expression of God's gift. This is *not* to say that right choosing is the only relevant gift to human salvation or is the most important gift that is relevant. Nonetheless, as shown in this project, right human choosing is itself a gift and for Wesley, it must be recognized as such![37]

In this section, we have compared Wesley and Hauerwas on some selected matters relating to scripture, experience, truth, and moral choice. Hauerwas is considered an important figure in contemporary academic theology and theological ethics. Therefore, for the task of *continuing* to consider the relevance of Wesley's theology and ethics for academic theology of today, one possible avenue is to put him in conversation with Hauerwas. It has been offered here that there are some advantages to Wesley's view in regard to the points of differences discussed. Neverthe-

---

"creating" point of this statement. Yet, Wesley's model of moral choosing seems preferable. Wesley's model is as follows: without invitation, God first works alone on the human soul by passive operations. Also, the offer of the gospel itself is the work of God alone. As was argued in this project, the choice to respond to such passive operation is itself also an expression of God's gift. Gift and choice do not have to be made antithetical as Hauerwas seems to suggest. For more of Hauerwas' discussion of ethics and choosing, see his section "Living and Fragments: The Insufficiency of Ethics" in chapter 1 of *The Peaceable Kingdom*.

[37] Many of Wesley's statements in support of this point are cited in chapter 5.

less, while Wesley and Hauerwas have some differences in view, there are important ways in which their thought is compatible. Overall, Wesley and Hauerwas are probably best viewed as allies. As mentioned, they both promote virtue ethics, value the creeds and the importance of community and Christian practices; they both cherish ecclesiology, sacraments, liturgy, and church tradition; and they both oppose divorcing Christian thought from ethics. These reflections are only a beginning. There would be much value in future scholarship that compares or draws from Wesley and Hauerwas.

Volf and Wesley

There are some similarities in the theological concerns of John Wesley and Mirsolav Volf. Miroslav Volf is currently a chaired professor of theology at Yale University. He was born in Croatia and completed doctoral studies in Germany under the supervision of Jürgen Moltmann. Like Wesley, Volf's work has devoted special attention to areas in practical theology, ethics, and social justice. Volf is a member of the Evangelical Church in Croatia and Episcopal Church (U.S.A.), a tradition with roots to Wesley's Anglicanism. As evident in some of his books, Volf, like Wesley, has explored and emphasized the role of the Holy Spirit in human action and the importance of gift in ethics and theology.[38] Resources from Volf and Wesley offer potential for future constructive theology and work in ecumenism.

At times, Wesley's theology is put in conversation with the views of other theologians. This can be useful. It is also possible to consider Wesley's theology on its own and from this, offer relevance to the life of the church today. Some scholars have already made remarkable efforts in promoting Wesley's theology for today in various ways. We will now turn to a consideration of some such examples.

John Wesley's Theology for Today

There have been some debates with respect to how Wesley's theology

---

[38] In his book *Free of Charge*, Volf offers a view of gift drawing some from the views of Luther. Volf examines the co-operating nature of good action in his book *Work in the Spirit*. Volf, *Free of Charge*, 37 – 51; Miroslav Volf, *Work in the Spirit*, (New York: Oxford University Press, 1991), 114; Miroslav Volf and Dorthy C. Bass, editors, *Practicing Theology: Beliefs and Practices in Christian life* (Grand Rapids: Eerdmans, 2002).

should be authoritative for today. William Abraham of Southern Methodist University argues that although he thinks of John Wesley as a "spiritual father in God," Wesley's theology should not be regarded as authoritative.[39] Abraham entitles one of his critiques of Wesleyan theology as "Whose Wesley? Which Wesleyan Tradition?," echoing the approach of Alasdair MacIntyre as evident, for example, in MacIntyre's book *Whose Justice? Which Rationality?* Abraham argues that in Wesleyan Studies today, there are numerous conflicting accounts of Wesley's thought that reflect much about Wesley's interpreter and fail to offer an objective interpretation of Wesley.[40] But this approach seems to repeat the same error that postmodernists and extreme post-liberals sometimes make when they dwell on and become entangled in small differences rather than recognize major points of overlap.

In his essay, "The End of Wesleyan Theology," Abraham argues that "John Wesley is not some norm of truth"[41] and that "an appeal to Wesley... cannot operate as a criterion of credibility or truth."[42] Perhaps surprisingly to some, the major reason that Abraham gives for these claims is because Wesley views scripture as the highest authority. Abraham says, "the ultimate test of truth in theology for Wesley was Scripture. This immediately undercuts any idea of appeal to Wesley as a warrant in theology."[43] Abraham's whole project in theology rests on the assumption that scripture is not the ultimate test of truth in the manner that Protestants tend to make it. Abraham openly disavows allegiance to Protestant and Catholic theology,[44] and so in this way, it seems that he would admit that at this time, he has a limited following.[45]

---

[39] William Abraham, "The End of Wesleyan Theology," *Wesleyan Theological Journal*, 40, (2005): 24.

[40] Abraham, "Whose Wesley, Which Wesleyan Tradition?," *Wesleyan Theological Journal*, 46, (2011): 149; Abraham, "The End of Wesleyan Theology," 8 and 13.

[41] Abraham, "The End of Wesleyan Theology," 24.

[42] Abraham, "The End of Wesleyan Theology," 18.

[43] Abraham, "The End of Wesleyan Theology," 18.

[44] Abraham says, "We are at the end of the line where Protestant theology is concerned; five hundred magnificent years of theology have come to an end. Epistemology has destroyed us from within" and in footnote 40 of the same page, he says, "Nor can we be saved by turning to Roman Catholicism, for Roman Catholicism, as we know it today, is simply one more effort to fix the Protestantism it inevitably spawned" (Abraham, "The End of Wesleyan Theology," 21).

Over the last 70 years, there have in fact been some notable efforts to argue that Wesley's theology is both relevant and applicable to the lives of Christians today. Examples of this include but are not limited to writings by Colin Williams, Albert Outler, Theodore Runyon, Kenneth Collins, and Randy Maddox. Like some of these others, Outler was not only a major figure in Wesleyan Studies but also in the field of academic theology as a whole. As president of the American Theological Society, Outler delivered an address to this society that argues that Wesley may in fact be viewed as a kind of theologian.[46] One of the major points of this address was to argue that Wesley's "methodology and motifs are still significant for contemporary theology."[47] Outler says that he himself takes Wesley as a "mentor and a guide" and that concerning Wesley's views of grace and human consciousness—which regard the way of salvation (his roadmap for the Christian life)—, "his basic insights are still as pertinent as any I know, in the whole history of Christian thought or in the new frontiers of psychotherapy."[48]

Recent efforts to argue for the relevance of John Wesley's theology for today include work by Randy Maddox and Kenneth Collins. In the last decade of the Twentieth Century, Maddox produced a number of articles on the relevance of John Wesley's theology for today, in addition to his widely-read book *Responsible Grace*. In many of his writings on this matter, Maddox observes how "practical theology" has become increasingly influential in the academic discipline of theology as a whole.[49] For Maddox, Wesley's theology has relevance for today in part because of how it fits well into this notion of practical theology.[50] For Maddox, it

---

[45] For an example of a critical response to Abraham, see Kenneth Collins, "Is 'Canonical Theism' a Viable Option for Wesleyans?," *Wesleyan Theological Journal*, 45, (2010).

[46] Outler, "Towards a Re-Appraisal of John Wesley as a Theologian," *The Wesleyan Theological Heritage* (Grand Rapids, Michigan: Zondervan Publishing House, c1991), 39.

[47] Outler, "Towards a Re-Appraisal of John Wesley as a Theologian," 40.

[48] Outler, "John Wesley as Theologian—Then and Now," *The Wesleyan Theological Heritage* (Grand Rapids, Michigan: Zondervan Publishing House, c1991), 57 and 71.

[49] See for example, Maddox, "John Wesley—Practical Theologian?," 126; see also Randy Maddox, "The Recovery of Theology as a Practical Discipline," *Theological Studies*, 51, (1990).

[50] Randy Maddox, "Reading Wesley as a Theologian," *Wesleyan Theological Journal*, 30, (1995): 18.

is preferable to approach Wesley's theology through the guide of an "orienting concern"—which for him is responsible grace— rather than build a systematic theology.[51]

More recently, Kenneth Collins has published a widely-read book called *The Theology of John Wesley, Holy Love and the Shape of Grace*. In this project, Collins follows Outler's perspective that Wesley's theology is "conjunctive" in nature. Collins' axial theme of focus is the conjunction of holiness and grace.[52] In Collins' portrait of Wesley, although there are some offered differences, we find much of the same as what is found in the portraits of Wesley offered by Outler and Maddox. For example, in all such portraits, we observe that Wesley has a way of salvation that includes in some way original sin, total depravity, prevenient grace, repentance, Christian faith, the new birth and justification, the witness of the Spirit, Christian perfection, etc. These major points of agreement between Outler, Maddox, and Collins, contradict an argument similar to Abraham's that Wesleyan scholars cannot agree on the important aspects of Wesley's theology. Collins concludes each chapter with a section entitled, "today and tomorrow," in which he offers the relevance of Wesley's theology for today.

In 2009, Sarah Lancaster et al. published an article entitled "What Makes Theology Wesleyan?," in which they summarize five approaches to Wesley's theology for today. The range of approaches goes from one end of a spectrum, at which point Wesley is viewed as a model theologian with a theology that is prescriptive for today, to the end of the other side of the spectrum, at which point Wesley's theology is believed to be irrelevant for today.[53] Lancaster et al. observe that many scholars in Wesleyan studies take an approach that falls somewhere in this spectrum. One of the overall aims of Lancaster et al. is to consider "Phase IV" of Wesleyan Studies, which they summarize as follows: Phase IV is "moving beyond Wesley Studies per se to apply the results of research in the area more broadly to the constructive theological work that is now being carried out in the life and thought of the body of Christ (and not only in those church traditions having a historical connection to John and Charles Wesley)."[54]

---

[51] Maddox, "The Recovery of Theology as a Practical Discipline," 670.
[52] Collins, *The Theology of John Wesley*, 6.
[53] Sarah Lancaster et al., "What Makes Theology Wesleyan?," *Methodist Review* (online), 1, (2009): 10.
[54] Lancaster et al., "What Makes Theology Wesleyan?," 7. Two examples of

I will now make a distinction concerning terminology. For this project, "Wesley's theology" refers to Wesley's theology as it is. "Constructive Wesleyan theology" refers to a project that aims to develop and expand Wesley's theology or use a modification of it in some way. Constructive Wesleyan theology refers to what Lancaster et al. describe as "Phase IV" of Wesleyan Studies and pertains to several of the five approaches to Wesley's theology listed by them. On the other hand, the primary focus of this work so far, regarding Wesley's heart ethics, has been on "Wesley's theology."

As mentioned above, Wesley's heart ethics is theological and an aspect of his overall theology. Therefore, for those who are open to Wesley's theology as relevant for today, we can consider some ways in which his heart ethics is relevant for today. We will now offer three important ways in which this is true. Although these three approaches overlap, we will consider them one at a time. For each approach, it will be shown that Wesley's theology may be applied by itself or applied as some form of a constructive Wesleyan theology.

John Wesley's Heart Ethics for Today

Approach 1: Academics

John Wesley's heart ethics, by itself or part of a constructive Wesleyan theology, has relevance to academic discussions. It offers important matters of consideration for many different kinds of academic groups and societies across the world. It is something that may offer helpful discussion both inside and outside "Wesleyan Studies" in various continents. Wesley's heart ethics can be put in dialogue with a wide range of approaches in theology. It can be considered in light of systematic theology, narrative theology, feminist theology, ethnic theologies, liberation theology, various kinds of hermeneutics or other kinds of theology. It can be considered in respect to other academic disciplines such as philosophy, social science, natural science, and more.

Wesley's heart ethics (by itself or part of a constructive Wesleyan theology) has especially important relevance to academic work that is con-

---

constructive theology in Wesleyan studies are work by Thomas Noble and Jason Vickers. See, for example, Noble, "To serve the Present Age: Authentic Wesleyan Theology Today, the 2010 WTS Presidential Address;" Noble, *Holy Trinity: Holy People*; and Jason Vickers, "Albert Outler and the Future of Wesleyan Theology: Retrospect and Prospect," *Wesleyan Theological Journal*, 43, (2008).

cerned with practical living. Practical theology should not completely replace speculative theology, nor is it disconnected from it, but for some, it takes priority over it. Although practical theology is related to speculative theology, much of practical theology may function well in a way that is independent of many of the efforts of speculative theology.[55]

Approach 2:
Determining Relevance to One's Church Tradition

Another approach for considering the relevance of Wesley's heart ethics for today (either by itself or as a Wesleyan constructive theology) is considering its relevance to and compatibility with one's specific church tradition. For those who are strongly committed to the doctrine of their tradition, the degree of the relevance of Wesley's ethics will somewhat depend on which church tradition that one has chosen to follow.

Wesley's heart ethics has at least some degree of compatibility with many church traditions in the World Methodist Council, which includes now over 70 church traditions worldwide, including over 80 million people in over 130 countries.[56] It also has a degree of compatibility with some holiness and Pentecostal churches that are not in the World Methodist Council but have roots in the Methodist tradition.[57] For those people who are strongly committed to the doctrine of any of the traditions in the World Methodist Council or related church traditions, they will find that Wesley's heart ethics has at least some relevance for today.

The United Methodist Church is an example of a tradition for which we now find strong convergence with Wesley's theology. For example, *The Book of Discipline of the United Methodist Church* shows that many of

---

[55] Consider the following comment by Wesley in which he argues for the importance of studying the Trinity in a way that has practical significance: "Mr. Jones's book on the Trinity is both more clear and more strong, than any I ever saw on that subject. If anything is wanting, it is the application, lest it should appear to be a merely speculative doctrine, which has not influence on our hearts or lives; but this is abundantly supplied by my brother's Hymns." Jackson, editor, *The Works of John Wesley*, 13:30.

[56] See the website for the World Methodist Council.

[57] See, for example, Bishop Ithiel Clemmons discussion of the view of sanctification held by the Church of God in Christ. This can be found in Ithiel Clemmons, *C.H. Mason and the Roots of the Church of God in Christ* (Bakersfield, CA: Pneuma Life Pub., 1996).

Wesley's sermons and his *Explanatory Notes Upon the New Testament* are authoritative for theology.[58] Wesley's *General Rules* is actually fully quoted in this *Book of Discipline* and is a doctrinal standard.[59] Also, in the "Articles of Religion" and "The Confession of Faith," the *Book of Discipline* recognizes the authority of many of Wesley's doctrines such as Christian perfection.[60] In this way, we observe how the United Methodist Church is one example of how Wesley's heart ethics has strong compatibility with a church tradition. Wesley's heart ethics may also have a strong compatibility with many "nondenominational" churches of today. Wesley is considered a forefather of the "evangelicalism" that characterizes many nondenominational churches.[61]

Many of the traditions outside of the World Methodist Council have less compatibility with Wesley's heart ethics. Yet, even for many of these, scholars have traced and highlighted important points of overlap. For those traditions with perhaps the least compatibility, there is even still a degree of relevance because Wesley's theology, or at least parts of it, is widely considered to be an important resource for Christian ecumenism. Christian ecumenism involves the efforts of different church traditions to come closer together in theology and practice. Among supporters of Christian ecumenism, there has been vast interest in using Wesley's theology as a resource. Albert Outler was a distinguished supporter of this effort. Other contributions include but are not limited to work by people such as Geoffrey Wainwright, Don Thorsen, Edgardo Colon-Emeric, Kenneth Loyer, and many more.

Thomas Noble makes the following comment that sheds some light on *why* Wesley's theology is an important resource for ecumenical dialogue:

> Particularly it is in this ecumenical context of catholic and evangelical

[58] This is clearly evident from the section "Doctrinal Standards and Our Theological Task" in the *The Book of Discipline of the United Methodist Church: 2008-2012* (Nashville, TN: United Methodist Publishing House).

[59] This is clearly evident from the section "Doctrinal Standards and Our Theological Task" in the *The Book of Discipline of the United Methodist Church: 2008-2012* (Nashville, TN: United Methodist Publishing House).

[60] See for example, the article in the Book of Discipline entitled "Sanctification and Christian Perfection."

[61] Cf. Kenneth Collins, *The Evangelical Moment* (Grand Rapids, Michigan: Baker Academic, 2005), 70; and Mark Noll, *The Rise of Evangelicalism* (Downers Grove, IL: Intervarsity Press, 2003).

theology that we need to demonstrate that Wesley, the 'conjunctive' thinker (as Kenneth Collins has argued), the one who produced a synthesis of the evangelical theology of the Reformation and the ancient catholic spirituality of Christian perfection, is a pivotal figure for today's global church.[62]

Wesley's theology is "conjunctive" in many ways, including, for example, how it brings together the Protestant doctrine of justification by faith alone, the Catholic emphasis on the importance of works and liturgy, and the view of the early church—followed later especially by Eastern Orthodox and Roman Catholic traditions—that the Christian life involves a potential for growth in character. In this way and in other ways, if nothing more than for ecumenical considerations, Wesley's heart ethics has a degree of relevance to church traditions quite different from the World Methodist Council. Thus, in summary, Wesley's heart ethics has compatibility with or at least relevance to people of a vast range of church traditions.

Approach 3: Planning and Acting

Over the course of this project, we explored Wesley's heart ethics, understood as a practical academic work. Wesley's heart ethics provides a guide for Christian living. This guide prescribes planning and acting. We will call this guide for acting "applied heart ethics." Heart ethics helps to produce applied heart ethics, and yet there is a difference between the two. A key difference is that everyone, even those who are uncomfortable with academics, can use applied heart ethics.

Wesley's applied heart ethics is simple. It is simply that any person can follow the way of salvation, a scriptural roadmap for the Christian life, by applying a scriptural method of action (Chapters 6 and 7 give an account of Wesley's way of salvation, and chapter 8 gives an account of Wesley's method for fruitful action; diagrams 6.1, 7.1, and 8.1 provide summaries). In this way, Wesley's applied heart ethics may be thought of as following a plan of discipleship or method of psychotherapy. Any person of any time period or culture can give this a try. Of course, it is evident that Wesley believes that any person who gives applied heart ethics a try will find much benefit. Furthermore, it is apparent that not many of the critics of this approach have ever given it a serious try.

---

[62] Noble, "To serve the Present Age: Authentic Wesleyan Theology Today, the 2010 WTS Presidential Address," 87.

We are not promoting here an individualist mindset that excludes an essential need for relationships and community. As shown in chapter 8, Wesley's method for fruitful action requires relationship building and involvement in fellowship and community. Applied heart ethics strongly promotes a group mindset, including a regard for the local community, nation, world, etc. However, it also recognizes that a group mindset is only possible by means of the cooperation of individual mindsets. Shaping a group mindset is not always much within one's reach. However, to a significant degree, individual planning and acting are always within one's reach. Not all avenues of ministry (outdoor preaching services, the Lord's Supper, etc.) are always available to a person, but one is always free to do one's best with what is available. For this reason, applied heart ethics has much to offer to an individual with respect to planning and acting.

For anyone who appreciates Wesley's applied heart ethics but wishes to develop it some or modify it, turning to a constructive Wesleyan theology is also an option. Such a constructive ethics could then serve as a guide for planning and acting.

Wesley's applied heart ethics offers some guidance but also underscores inescapable mystery. God is far beyond human understanding, and there is much that is unpredictable and unknown about the Christian life. Nevertheless, it is helpful to follow as best as possible the guidance that is available, especially from scripture. Wesley's applied heart ethics is not confined to a few people but is available to all. God's invitation for love and happiness extends forth, undefeated. "Nor height, nor depth, nor any other creature shall be able to separate us from the love of God, which is in Christ Jesus our Lord."[63] Such love is the highest end of ethics. It is the promised blessing of "whosoever will" seek it.[64] Those who decide to seek God's blessings must give God all the glory because such efforts, like so much else, are the expressions of God's gift.

---

[63] This is Romans 8:39 from Wesley's *ENNT*.
[64] The phrase "whosoever will" is being quoted here from Wesley's notes underneath the Biblical text of Revelation 22:17. See Wesley's *ENNT*.

Diagram 2.1
Meanings of Passive

Mode of Human Consciousness	Libertarian View[1]	Necessitarian View
Choice	Active	**Active in one Sense** *Choice is active in the sense that from the standpoint of human consciousness, it is different in nature from other forms of consciousness such as inclination. As one necessitarian acknowledges: choosing to eat an apple is itself different from the feeling of hunger for the apple **Passive in another Sense** *Choice is passive in the sense that each choice is *fully* caused by the strongest motive, which is the effect of a chain of causes and effects that originates from external forces of one path of history * "typeX" meaning of passive
Inclination (Also called a motive. Examples include a feeling of hunger or a feeling of love)	Passive ("the first meaning of passive")	Passive ("the first meaning of passive")
Affections and Tempers that Spring from an Inclination (Joy, meekness, anger, hatred, envy, jealousy, etc.)	Passive	Passive
All Remaining forms of Human Consciousness that are Not Active (Feelings of hotness or coldness, all sensations of five senses, all sensations from spiritual sense such as the direct witness of the Spirit)	Passive	Passive

---

[1] It is offered that the libertarian example of this chart characterizes the view of John Wesley. For other libertarians such as Andrew Michael Ramsay, some choices are in a sense fully passive while others are no For example, for Ramsay, when a person is presented with two options and one of these is a clearly known greater good, a person must by necessity choose the clearly known greater good. See Appendix A for more information.

Diagram 3.1

Views of the Will

Name of Thinker	Name for the Affections, etc. (passive dimension)	Name for the Power Of Choosing (active dimension)
John Wesley	**will** (properly speaking)	**liberty** (properly speaking) * = Wesley's second meaning of will, which is used colloquially not in formal definitions * = "free will" Note: Although "free will" and liberty appear equivalent, Wesley seems to prefer the language of "liberty" instead of "free will" after 1774 * is "neither more nor less than" the will, as understood by Wesley in his old typology of "understanding, will, and affections" * is so broad that it even applies to animal action
Jonathan Edwards	**will**	**will** * Describes himself as an opponent to free will in the libertarian sense
Augustine	**will**	**will** * = free will, but opposes free will in the libertarian sense?
John Duns Scotus	**will**	**will** * = free will (in libertarian sense)
Jean Burlamaqui	**will**	**will** * The will clearly includes the active power. Liberty does not apply to all instances of the will (action), such as when there are two options with one being a clearly-known greater good.
Samuel Clarke	**will**	**liberty/will** * For Clarke, liberty and the active component of the will appear completely interchangeable in most if not all contexts.
Thomas Reid	**affections, etc.** * Reid clearly rejects using the name "will" for this. This is a growing trend in modern philosophy.	**will** * For Reid, the will pertains to the active power, both in animals and humans. Liberty requires reason, and so only humans have liberty. Also, liberty does not apply to all instances of human action such as choice that follows from the force of habit.

Diagram 4.1

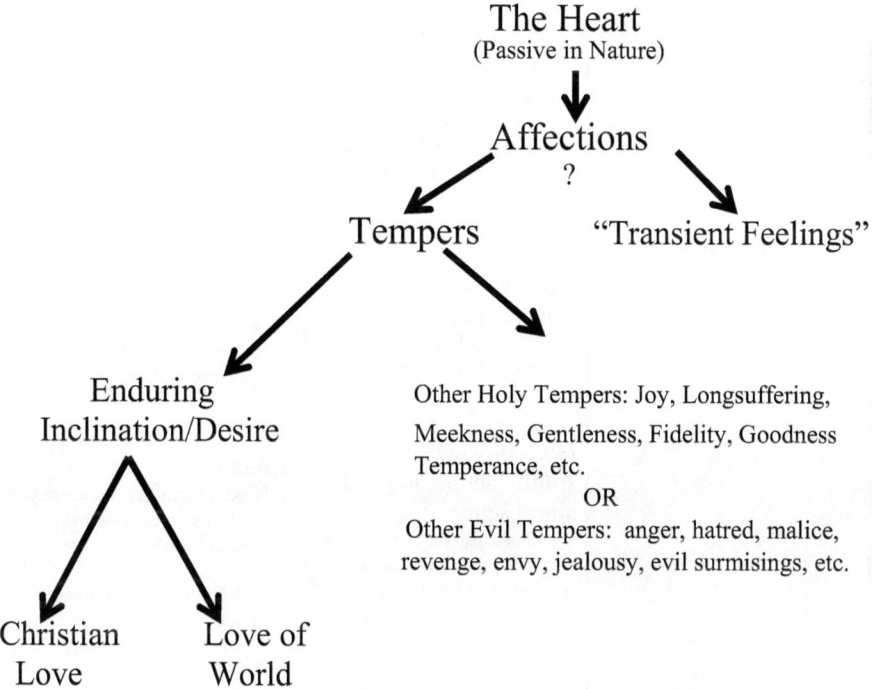

Diagram 5.1

Contrasting Two Views of Fruitful Action

Type of Choosing/Acting	John Wesley's View	Necessitarian View
Fruitful action	Active with respect to consciousness Does not demonstrate "typeX" meaning of passive *The choice to perform fruitful action does not have to follow the strongest motive Does not demonstrate absolute necessity *History has many possible trajectories God co-operates in fruitful action, unlike for sinful action *Perhaps one could argue that this is yet another sense of passiveness. In any case, it does not demonstrate the typeX meaning of passive *An agent has liberty, which is a power that is in some ways mysterious and beyond human understanding (A person, without God, is the doer of sinful action. A person is accountable for sinful action)	Active in one sense (see Diagram 2.1) Passive in another sense Demonstrates the "typeX" meaning of Passive *Choice is passive in the sense that each choice is *fully* caused by the strongest motive, which is the effect of a chain of causes and effects that originates from external forces of one path of history Demonstrates absolute necessity *History has only one possible trajectory God is the doer of all human action *God determines human action by determining external forces, which determine the strongest motive, which determines human action (Since there is only one possible path of history, God is implicitly the author of sinful human actions. Humans are not accountable for sin. There is no possibility of virtue, vice or ethics.)

Diagram 6.1
"The Way of Salvation"
According to John Wesley

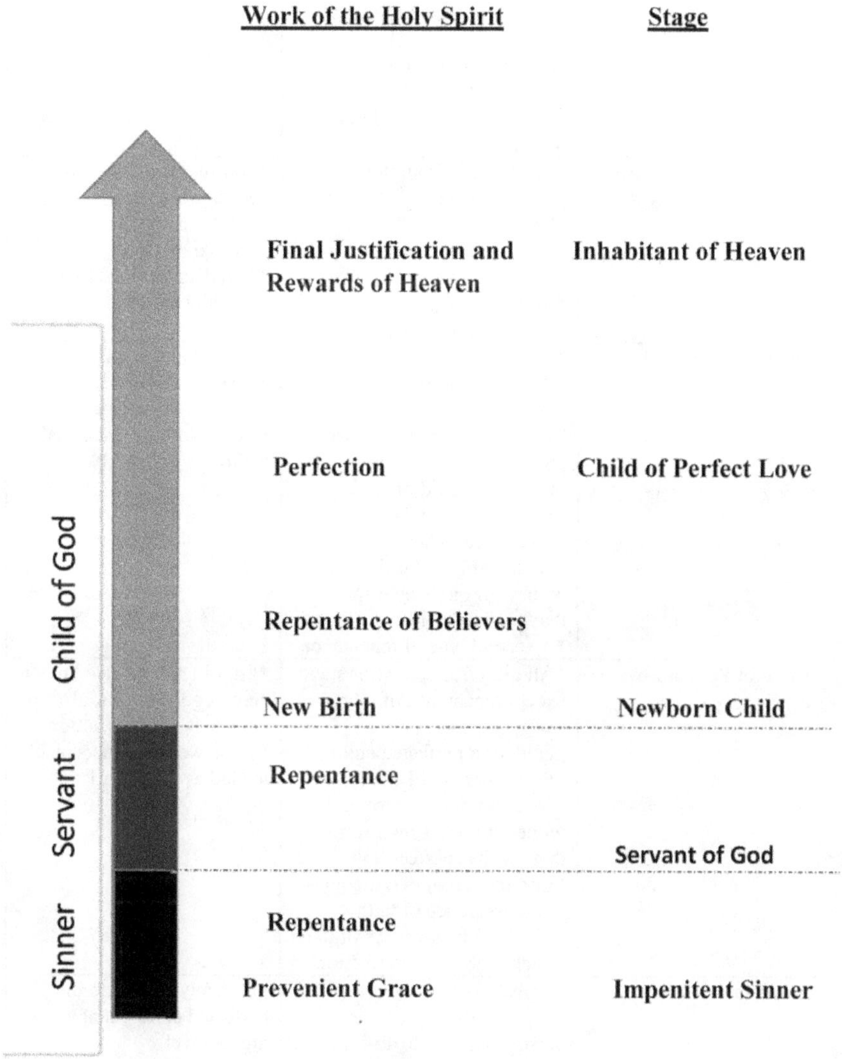

Work of the Holy Spirit	Stage
Final Justification and Rewards of Heaven	Inhabitant of Heaven
Perfection	Child of Perfect Love
Repentance of Believers	
New Birth	Newborn Child
Repentance	
	Servant of God
Repentance	
Prevenient Grace	Impenitent Sinner

Sinner — Servant — Child of God

Diagram 7.1

Stage	Spiritual Gifts	Type of Action
Impenitent Sinner	*Prevenient grace *Conscience *Some awareness of moral law *Conviction of wrong *Slight touch on the heart *Power to choose right or wrong	*Fruitful action in a weak sense
Servant of God	*All the gifts from the previous stage *Fear of God *Faith of a servant *Accepted by God *No wrath of God *Sustained repentance	*Fruitful action, also known here as works of righteousness that are accepted by God *God does not recognize this action as good works
Child of the New Birth	*Conscience *Power to choose right or wrong *Justification and new birth *Sanctification Begins *Faith of a child of God *Spirit of Son and of adoption *Love shed in heart *Witness of the Spirit and witness of one's own spirit that one is a child *A second type of repentance	*Fruitful action, also known here as good works, also known as virtuous action *Good works are acceptable to God as good works.
Child of Perfect Love	*All gifts from the prior stage, except repentance of inbred sin *Faith of a perfected child *Pure Heart and Perfect Love * Witness of the Spirit and witness of one's own spirit that one has perfect love *Elimination of evil thoughts *Full assurance of faith *Maybe full assurance of hope *Lacks "absolute perfection"	*Fruitful action, also known here as good works, also known as virtuous action *Good works are acceptable to God as good works.
Inhabitant of Heaven	*Probably all of the gifts of the previous stage, except this person is nearer to absolute perfection *Final Justification *The Rewards of Heaven	*Probably similar to the perfected child but at a higher level

Diagram 8.1

A Method For Fruitful Action
(Good works and Limitedly Good Works)

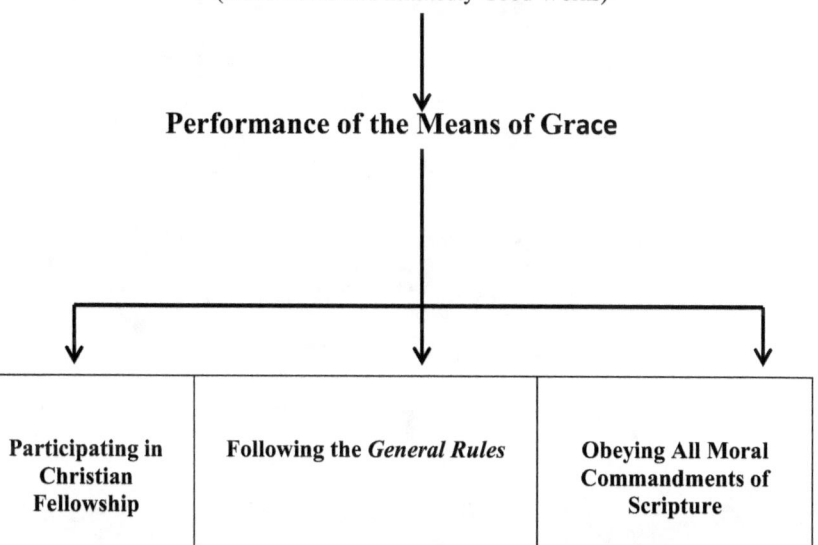

Appendix A

Responding to Interpretations of John Wesley's View of Liberty

In this appendix, interpretations of John Wesley's view of moral liberty offered by Albert Outler and D. Stephen Long will be critically considered. In *The Bicentennial Edition of the Works of John Wesley*, in a footnote concerning Wesley's comments on liberty in his sermon "The General Deliverance," Albert Outler makes the claim that Wesley's view of moral liberty "had been directly influenced by Locke" regarding Locke's *An Essay Concerning Human Understanding*.[1] It is clear that Wesley read Locke and may have been influenced by Locke in a number of ways. However, the above statement implies that Wesley's *view of liberty*, understood as moral choosing, was directly influenced by Locke's view. Outler's analysis of liberty in this context is not a major concern for him, and he seems to be off track. He does not provide adequate support for this claim.[2] After closer consideration, there is much evidence that suggests that Outler's claim on this particular matter is misleading, if not entirely off target.

One point of consideration here is what Outler means by "influence." If what he means by "influence" is no more than that Wesley has read Locke's view of liberty, then Outler is correct. But even here, Outler is being misleading because Wesley has read over 20 figures who have written on philosophical liberty, including Thomas Reid whose work on liberty Wesley describes as a "strong and beautiful treatise on moral liberty."[3] Outler does not acknowledge that Wesley has read these others.

---

[1] Wesley, 'The General Deliverance,' *Works* (BE), 2:440.
[2] Even in regard to the "liberty of conscience," it is not clear that Wesley was influenced by Locke. The "liberty of conscience" was a common phrase in the eighteenth century, and it was used before Locke was born.
[3] *The Arminian Magazine*, 14, (1791) 14:3

If what Outler means by "influence" is that Wesley's view of liberty resembles Locke's view, then Outler's claim is clearly off target. Wesley's view of liberty more closely resembles the views of other figures that Wesley has read. For example, Wesley's theology is not identical to the thought of Samuel Clarke, but his view of liberty is more similar to Clarke's view than it is to Locke's view.

Wesley publishes an extract of Locke's *An Essay Concerning the Human Understanding* in bits, starting in the 1782 volume of the *Arminian Magazine* and continuing for the next two years.[4] Among these many pages, Wesley includes some of Locke's most important discussions of philosophical moral liberty. In the final posthumous edition of Locke's *Essay* (published before Wesley was born), a paragraph is added to Locke's work that gives Locke's thought a closer resemblance to the recommendations of an Arminian interlocutor named Philipp van Limborch.[5] This paragraph is included in the portion of the work that Wesley opts to include in the *Arminian Magazine*.[6] As we shall see, it is more likely that Wesley included this more because he wants to include a variety of different views on moral liberty in the *Arminian Magazine* and less because he shares in any way Locke's view of moral liberty.[7]

Although leading contemporary commentators on Locke consider him most likely a necessitarian or compatibilist,[8] it is possible that the addition of this paragraph led some during Wesley's time to believe that Locke was a libertarian. By "libertarian," I mean one who holds the doctrine of free will as opposed to the philosophical necessity that is presupposed in absolute predestination.[9] For a libertarian, a human is free, in at least some cases, to choose for or against the perceived strongest motive. A "necessitarian" is one whose system of thought presupposes that every human choice must be caused by a strongest motive, which

[4] *The Arminian Magazine*, volumes 5 - 7, (1782-1784).

[5] Harris, *Of Liberty and Necessity*, 34.

[6] *The Arminian Magazine*, 6, (1783): 6:136.

[7] As we shall explore, Wesley also publishes in the *Arminian Magazine* work on moral liberty by Joseph Fisher, Paul Ramsey, Thomas Reid, and others.

[8] Daniel Garber and Michael Ayers, editors, *Cambridge History of Seventeenth Century Philosophy* (Cambridge: Cambridge University Press, 1998), 1245; Harris, *Of Liberty and Necessity*, p. 21, footnote 5.

[9] Exploring the concept of "libertarian" and "necessitarian" is one of the major tasks of James Harris in *Of Liberty and Necessity, The Free Will Debate in Eighteenth Century British Philosophy*, published by Oxford University Press. For an account of what is meant by a "libertarian" and "necessitarian," see p. 7.

in turn is the effect of a chain of causes and effects that originates from outside of a person.

The theory of absolute predestination is an example of necessitarianism. A "compatibilist" is a necessitarian who argues that moral responsibility is consistent with necessitarianism. Even after the final revision of Locke's work, Locke was not clear on his position concerning the debate of free will v. necessity, and so there was widespread dissatisfaction with regard to Locke's lack of clarity on this point.[10] It is possible that some of the libertarians of the eighteenth century who Wesley has read such as Andrew Michael Ramsay and Isaac Watts are indebted to Locke's view of the liberty of suspension, but it is difficult to prove that their views are identical to Locke's.[11]

In any case, what we shall find upon closer examination is that Wesley's view of liberty is not the same as Locke's, not even near to the same. If Locke were a necessitarian or compatibilist as leading contemporary commentators argue,[12] then Wesley would surely disagree with him, as Wesley is a strong libertarian. But let us suppose for a moment that Wesley read Locke as a libertarian. It must be emphasized that even in this case, the differences between Wesley and Locke with respect to liberty remain crucial. The first crucial difference is with respect to naming. It is true that Locke and Wesley share an emphasis on the difference between liberty and will.[13] However, they define each of these terms differently. Unlike Locke, Wesley uses the term "will" properly speaking to represent the ideas of affections and passions.[14] Unlike Wesley, Locke uses the term "will" to represent only the idea of choice. Locke says "the Will in truth, signifies nothing but a power, or ability, to prefer or chuse."[15]

[10] Harris, *Of Liberty and Necessity*, 12.

[11] Related comments by Andrew Michael Ramsay are found in *The Arminian Magazine*, 8, (1785): 8:316; Watt's "An Essay on The Freedom of Will in God and in Creatures," 380. See also *The Arminian Magazine*, 9, (1785): 9:30.

[12] Garber and Ayers, *Cambridge History of Seventeenth Century Philosophy*, 1245; Harris, *Of Liberty and Necessity*, p. 21, footnote 5.

[13] Wesley, 'What is Man?,' *Works* (BE), 4:23; *The Arminian Magazine*, 5, (1782): 5:476.

[14] Wesley, 'The General Deliverance,' *Works* (BE), 2:439 and 2:442; Wesley, 'The End of Christ's Coming,' *Works* (BE), 2:474; Wesley, 'On the Fall of Man,' *Works* (BE), 2:401; Wesley, 'On Divine Providence,' *Works* (BE), 2:540.

[15] "Extracts from Locke on Human Understanding with Short Remarks," *The Arminian Magazine*, 5, (1782): 5:529.

For Locke, the term "liberty" represents the idea of the absence of exterior restraint or compulsion.[16] Consider the following illustration to clarify Locke's understanding of this meaning of liberty. Suppose a man leads his companion into a room. The companion's name is John. He takes John inside the room and tells John that he will leave John here alone for a few minutes. He tells John that John is free to leave the room any time John chooses. The man leaves, and after a few minutes, John becomes impatient and chooses to leave the room. However, John is not able to act out his choice because to John's surprise, after turning the knob and pulling on the door, John discovers the room is locked from the outside. To his surprise, John discovers it is a prison. According to Locke's view, in this scenario, choice occurs, but liberty is absent. Liberty is absent here because there is a restraint: John is in a prison and cannot exit. This shows how, according to Locke, choice can take place *without* liberty.[17] As Locke says "there may be will [choice], there may be volition, where there is no liberty."[18] *For Locke, there is no liberty in this scenario, but for Wesley there is*. For Wesley, there is liberty in this scenario because Wesley, unlike Locke, defines liberty as choice itself.[19] In this illustration, John was free to attempt to leave the room or not attempt to leave. For Wesley, his choice to attempt to leave the room is an exercise of liberty. This is a key difference in meaning between Locke's view of liberty and Wesley's view of liberty.

Locke has an additional sense of liberty. Humans have "a power to *suspend* the execution and satisfaction of any of his Desires, and so all, one after another, is at liberty to consider the objects of them; examine them on all sides and weight them with others."[20] Locke indicates this

---

[16] "Extracts from Locke on Human Understanding with Short Remarks," *The Arminian Magazine*, 5, (1782): 5:415.

[17] Locke's wording can be tricky. A reader must see the difference in Locke's intended meaning between: "choosing" and "the power to act out what one chooses." Liberty, for Locke, refers only to the latter. Hopefully this illustration helps to show this.

[18] "Extracts from Locke on Human Understanding with Short Remarks," *The Arminian Magazine*, 5, (1782): 5:415. I add choice in brackets since, as shown above, Locke defines the will as the power of choice.

[19] Outler, editor, *Works* (BE), 2:439, 2:440, 2:475, 2:401, 2:6, 2:399, and 2:489.

[20] "Extracts from Locke on Human Understanding with Short Remarks," *The Arminian Magazine*, 5, (1782): 5:646.

is liberty.[21] In a moment, more will be said on how this meaning of liberty compares to Wesley's view.

The most crucial difference between Locke and Wesley with regard to their views of liberty concerns their understanding of choice. As shown above, for Wesley, choice and liberty are equivalent. This is not true for Locke. For Locke, liberty does not apply to a person's power to will [choose]. Locke himself put this point in italics: "a man in respect of willing [choosing], or the Act of the volition, when any action in his power is once proposed to his Thoughts, as presently to be done, cannot be free."[22] He also says "a Man, in respect of the Act of Willing [choosing], is under a Necessity, and so cannot be free."[23] These remarks are included by Locke after completing the final revision of his work. In a later section, after repeating the point that there is no freedom in choice, he claims that there is a case of exception to the larger rule. This point is made in a paragraph (section 56) that is added to Locke's book after this death.[24] It will be assumed here for Wesley's purposes, that Locke intended to include this paragraph. Wesley includes this paragraph in his extract of Locke's book for the *Arminian Magazine*.[25]

In order to consider what Locke means by this exceptional case for when a person has freedom with respect to willing [choosing], we will consider another analogy. Suppose a woman comes across a horse that she really likes. The thought of purchasing the horse comes to her mind. Here is where Locke would allow there to be freedom of willing [choosing]. There is freedom of the will here in this sense. Since it is not at first clear to her whether to purchase the horse is the greater good, the woman is free to purchase hastily the horse right away without further thought. Or she is free to suspend the act of purchasing in order to think through and weigh all the objects of her desires and potential outcomes that relate to this situation.

Suppose that the woman decides to make such a suspension. After such thinking, the woman realizes she cannot afford the horse and so wills [chooses] not to buy the horse. Thus, returning to the beginning

[21] Ibid., 5:646.
[22] Ibid., 5:532.
[23] Ibid., 5:533.
[24] "Extracts from Locke on Human Understanding with Short Remarks," *The Arminian Magazine*, 6, (1783): 6:136. Harris, *Of Liberty and Necessity*, 34.
[25] "Extracts from Locke on Human Understanding with Short Remarks," *The Arminian Magazine*, 6, (1783): 6:136.

of the scenario, the woman was free to act in one of several ways: either to choose to purchase the horse right away (before carefully weighing her options) or to choose not to purchase it after deliberation. Yet, the will [the power of choosing] of the woman is no longer free after deliberation. At this point, as in Locke's regular cases of willing [choosing], the woman is necessitated to reject the horse. In other words, if deliberation leads the woman to conclude that rejecting the horse is clearly the greater good, she cannot choose otherwise. In this case, she must choose not to buy the horse.

Unlike Locke, Wesley believes that the power of choice is always free. For Wesley, there is no need to make special exceptions to a general rule. And for this reason, Wesley, unlike Locke, is able to define the power of choice itself as liberty. Another crucial point of difference regarding choice is that for Locke, the choice of a person is "always determined by that which is judged good by his [or her] Understanding."[26] This claim echoes scholastic intellectualism.[27] It is a claim that Wesley rejects. For Locke, it is not possible for a person to choose an evil when it is clearly known that such an evil act is in conflict with an available alternative option believed to bring immediate happiness.[28] This point is in clear contrast to Wesley who argues that liberty as moral choice is by definition the power to choose either known good or known evil.[29] For Wesley, because of the gift of conscience, every person has some knowledge of what is good and evil, and every person has the power to choose either of these options. And for Wesley, happiness does not have to be chosen by necessity.[30] For Locke, the choice of evil results in large part from misjudgement, which sometimes results from a person not using his or her power of suspension to deliberate more about the situation. For Wesley, a person, whether unsaved or perfected, always has the power to use liberty (a power of choice) to select any option, whether an agent rejects a

---

[26] Ibid., 6:137.

[27] An argument is made in *The Cambridge History of Seventeenth Century British Philosophy* (p. 1252) that Locke's thought resembles intellectualism, even after revision of his work.

[28] "Extracts from Locke on Human Understanding with Short Remarks," *The Arminian Magazine*, 6, (1783): 6:197.

[29] This point is made on just about every occasion that Wesley discusses liberty. See, for example, Wesley, 'The End of Christ's Coming,' *Works* (BE), 2:475.

[30] See the discussion above on conscience. See also: Wesley, 'Thoughts Upon Necessity,' *Works* (BE), 13:544.

known greater good or accepts it, whether an agent rejects a certain means for happiness or accepts it.[31]

Thus, it appears that Wesley's view of liberty does not resemble Locke's view. Consistent with this claim, there appears to be no place in Wesley's writings where he indicates that his view of liberty resembles Locke's view. Wesley gives his first extensive treatment of this type of liberty in his "Thoughts Upon Necessity," which is published in 1774, eight years before the publishing of his extract of Locke in the Arminian *Magazine*. There is no mention of Locke in Wesley's diary or journal near around 1774. It is true that Locke had a large impact on philosophy in the eighteenth century for both proponents of necessity and libertarianism.[32] In this way, it could be considered that Wesley's thought is *indirectly* influenced by Locke. Some of those who Wesley reads in regard to liberty are responding to Locke, modifying, and/or developing Locke's ideas

Let us now consider a second important treatment of John Wesley's view of moral liberty. In his book *John Wesley's Moral Theology, The Quest for God and Goodness*, D. Stephen Long discusses Wesley's view of liberty. Long attributes the liberty of indifference to Wesley. Long believes Wesley's primary motive for accepting the liberty of indifference is protecting his thought from absolute predestination and necessity. Long concludes that the result is that Wesley's theology is internally inconsistent. The charge is that there is an internal contradiction in Wesley's thought because the doctrine of the liberty of indifference and Wesley's commitment to aspects of the Thomistic-Aristotelian tradition are not compatible.[33] In this section, we will consider whether Long's charge of Wesley holding the liberty of indifference is fair. It will be shown, against Long, that Wesley's view of liberty more closely resembles what James Harris calls a "middle way," a position in *between* the liberty of indifference and determinism. For this reason, Long does not succeed in showing conflict in Wesley's thought.

The first concern regarding Long's argument is that he does not make adequately clear what he means by the liberty of indifference. From the medieval period to the time of Wesley, there are a variety of articulations of the liberty of indifference. How one defines the "liberty of

---

[31] See, for example, Wesley, 'Thoughts Upon Necessity,' *Works* (BE), 13:544.

[32] Harris, *Of Liberty and Necessity*, 18.

[33] See, for example, D. Stephen Long, *John Wesley's Moral Theology, The Quest for God and Goodness* (Nashville, TN: Kingswood Books, 2005), 64 – 65.

indifference" has bearing on whether or not the doctrine of the liberty of indifference is in fact clearly contradicting other parts of Wesley's thought.

Let us first consider several articulations of the liberty of difference that Wesley clearly rejects. First, Wesley's view of liberty is not like Long's representation of Locke's liberty of indifference. Long says, "The emphasis on the liberty of indifference provides the basis of the modern notion of the freedom of the will, which John Locke developed and to which John Wesley appeals whenever he explains anthropology."[34] Later in the book, Long says, "Wesley... affirms Locke's liberty of indifference."[35] There are several problems with these comments. First, Locke does not have a notion of the liberty of indifference in this way. For Locke, "indifferency" refers to that which may come only after the final judgment and *after* the exercise of the will.[36] Locke's liberty of indifference does not refer to choice, but it refers to a state in which there are no restraints or compulsions in circumstances that are exterior to a person. Second, Wesley's view of liberty is different from Locke's.[37]

There is a second view of the liberty of indifference that Wesley rejects. Wesley's view of liberty is not like the story of Buridan's ass.[38] In this story, a donkey is placed midway between two bales of hay and has no reason to choose one or the other. While the donkey is unable to choose a bale of hay, a human being in the same situation can. This is because, according to the story, humans have an arbitrary power to choose, which is a liberty of indifference. While Wesley might allow such a liberty of indifference in neutral matters, this type of liberty is not compatible with Wesley's view of liberty concerning the choice between virtue and vice. For Wesley, the power of liberty as choosing virtue is only possible in response to a previously perceived motivating influence from the heart provided by the Spirit.[39] Such motivation from the heart does

---

[34] Long, *John Wesley's Moral Theology*, 41.

[35] Long, *John Wesley's Moral Theology*, 61.

[36] Harris, *Of Liberty and Necessity*, 19 and 33. See the analogy in chapter 3 concerning a man named John who was led to prison. See also Peter Nidditch, editor, *An Essay Concerning Human Understanding* (Oxford: Oxford University Press, 1975), 283-284.

[37] The evidence for this point will be presented in chapter 3.

[38] C.F. Long, *John Wesley's Moral Theology*, 39.

[39] See chapters 5-7.

not necessitate choosing virtue. However, choosing virtue is not possible without it.

A third view of the liberty of indifference that Wesley rejects is the model of liberty provided by Anglican Archbishop William King. It is clear that Wesley as a young adult has read King's comments on the liberty of indifference, as Wesley summarizes such parts of King's *Origin of Evil* in a letter to his father in 1731.[40] In a letter to Thomas Taylor in January of 1791, Wesley seems to imply that he thinks Thomas Reid's discussion of moral liberty is "far better" than William King's.[41] For King, one chooses a thing not because it is expected to bring pleasure. Rather the chooser is pleased with the thing only because it is chosen.[42] For Wesley this is not the case. For Wesley, one's choice to serve God and neighbor is done after an awareness of one's motivation, which derives in large part from feeling the tempers of the heart to love God and neighbor. The pleasure that comes from loving God and neighbor is not the consequence of the human choice in isolation but rather a fulfilment of the desires of the heart, forces of motivation that were perceived before choosing.[43] King argues that one's chief happiness is from one's elections or choices, and the more one resists appetites, senses, and reasons, the better.[44] Wesley differs on both these points. For Wesley happiness includes feeling the love of God in one's heart in relationships; it is not confined to only choice. Secondly, for Wesley, what is stressed in a definition of virtue is not resisting inclinations but rather affirming them. Virtue is choosing to follow the motivation from the heart that is di-

---

[40] Wesley, 'Letters from the Reverend John Wesley to Various Persons,' *Works* (BE), 25:264.

[41] Wesley, *Letters*, 8:254. Note that the editor references Wesley's affirmation of Reid's view of moral liberty, suggesting that this is that to which Wesley refers when Wesley says "a far better tract."

[42] Wesley, 'Letters from the Reverend John Wesley to Various Persons,' *Works* (BE), 25:265 - 267.

[43] See chapters 3-7.

[44] Wesley, 'Letters from the Reverend John Wesley to Various Persons,' *Works* (BE), 25:265 – 267.

rected at loving God and neighbor.⁴⁵ Such a heart-founded account of virtue is not found in King's view of ethics.⁴⁶

Wesley does speak of a freedom of "indifference" in his sermon "The Image of God," published in 1730.⁴⁷ However, one reason that we cannot take this portrayal of liberty as his standard view is because it is published in 1730, before the time in which Wesley himself says that his thought is consistent. Near his death, Wesley says: "To conclude, I defy any man living to prove that I have contradicted myself at all in any of the writings which I have published from the year 1738 to the year 1788."⁴⁸ In 1730, Wesley's thought had not yet been influenced by his relationship with the Moravians and his experience at Aldersgate.

James Harris, a prominent scholar regarding eighteenth century British philosophy, remarks that a number of defenders of free will shift away from holding the liberty of indifference. One such example is the case of Samuel Clarke. Harris says:

> King is a defender of the liberty of indifference: he believes that freedom is most purely realized in the exercise of a capacity to choose to act in a certain way regardless of the recommendations of the understanding. Clarke, like Locke, believes that to define freedom in this way is a serious mistake; and, following Bramhall, he seeks to negotiate a middle way between the indifference of the will, on the one hand, and the literal determination of the will by motives, on the other. This notion of 'moral necessity', as distinct from 'literal' or 'physical necessity' is at the heart of Clarke's theory of freedom. It allows him to connect free choice with

---

⁴⁵ For example, see Wesley, 'An Israelite Indeed,' *Works* (BE), 3:280; Wesley, "Justification by Faith,'" *Works* (BE), 1:192; Wesley, 'On Zeal,' *Works* (BE), 3:320; Wesley, 'Upon Our Lord's Sermon on the Mount, V,' *Works* (BE), 1:568; Wesley, 'Upon Our Lord's Sermon on the Mount, VI,' *Works* (BE), 1:573; Wesley, 'Heaviness through Manifold Temptations,' *Works* (BE), 2:232. Wesley sometimes also uses the word "virtue" to refer to qualities that do not involve choice. See for example, Wesley, 'Circumcision of the Heart,' *Works* (BE), 1:403, in which he uses "virtue" to refer to fruits such as faith and humility.

⁴⁶ It is clear that for Wesley, virtue often requires choice. This is evident from his frequents statements that without choice (liberty), there would be no virtue and vice. Yet, for Wesley, virtue properly understood presupposes the possession of Christian faith with the love of God shed abroad in the heart. In these cases, virtue requires both right tempers and right choice.

⁴⁷ Wesley, "The Image of God,' *Works* (BE), 4:295.

⁴⁸ Wesley, *Letters*, 8:179.

rationality (and goodness) without conceding that, at any one time, the influence of the understanding makes only one choice possible.[49]

Samuel Clarke holds a view of ethics that, following Harris, I will describe here as "a middle way." According to Harris, this view is not the "liberty of indifference," as we see in the case of King. And yet it is not the same as a necessitarian view, in which an agent's choice must be determined by the strongest motive. In other words, according to the view of Clarke, one has the power to choose *against* what is perceived as the strongest motive and/or known greater good.[50] At the same time, motives are not ignored as in the case of the liberty of indifference. The strongest motive influences a person and is usually followed. This is what is meant by "moral necessity."[51]

An abundance of evidence suggests that Wesley has read Clarke's comments on these matters.[52] As mentioned by Sean Greenberg, Clarke is "one of the chief advocates of libertarian freedom."[53] But regardless of whether or not Wesley consciously inherits his view directly from Clarke, one conclusion remains clear: Wesley holds this "middle way" of moral liberty. Wesley's view of liberty is not the liberty of indifference as in the case of King or Buridan's ass, and it is not an absolute necessitarian scheme such as say Hobbes. For Wesley, motives in the form of tempers and affections play an important and indispensably helpful role for ethics.[54] Virtuous action is when the choice of an agent follows the

---

[49] Harris, *Of Liberty and Necessity*, 13.

[50] See, for example, Alexander, editor, *The Leibniz-Clarke Correspondence*, 45. Harris says that for Clarke, "We retain the capacity to ignore what the understanding tells us, and to choose the worse thing, while knowing the better." Harris, *Of Liberty and Necessity*, 51.

[51] See, for example, Clarke, *A Demonstration of the Being and Attributes of God*, 73; Clarke, *Remarks Upon a Book Entitled Enquiry Concerning Human Liberty*, 16 and 23-24.

[52] Through a correspondence with Randy Maddox, it was confirmed that Wesley records in his Oxford diaries that he read *A Demonstration of the Being and Attributes* in September of 1725. He recommends it to clergy in his *Address to the Clergy* (Wesley, 'Address to the Clergy,' *Works* (Jackson), 10:492). Wesley mentions his reading of the Leibniz-Clarke correspondence in his journal on May 22, 1775. See Wesley, 'Journal,' *Works* (BE), 22:451.

[53] Sean Greenberg, "Liberty and Necessity," in *The Oxford Handbook of British Philosophy in the Eighteenth Century*, ed. James Harris (Oxford: Oxford University Press, 2014), 249.

[54] See chapters 3-7.

suggestion of motivational input from the holy tempers and affections of the heart.

If what Long means by the "liberty of indifference" is the view of King or the above illustration concerning Buridan's ass, then Long's charging Wesley for the liberty of indifference is unfair. However, if what Long means by the "liberty of indifference" is what is summarized here as the "middle way" of moral liberty, that which is between absolute necessitarianism and certain types of liberty of indifference, then Long's interpretation is correct but a bit awkward since the middle way does not refer to typical notions of indifference. But Long does not make clear what he means.

The question is now whether Long is correct in claiming that Wesley's view of liberty is in conflict with other aspects of Wesley's thought that may resemble the Thomistic-Aristotelian tradition. The brief answer is that Long has not demonstrated such an inconsistency in Wesley's thought in part because he has not tested an adequate interpretation of Wesley's view of liberty. The "middle way," unlike the liberty of indifference, requires that the tempers and affections have a central role in ethics (as claimed by Aquinas, Aristotle, and others), without demonstrating necessitarianism. Wesley's view of liberty and his view of the central role of the affections in moral action are held together in harmony. Aquinas' intellectualism, something that Wesley rejects, is not required for this harmony.[55] There still seems to be room in Wesley's thought for the doctrine of participation, the connection between God and goodness, and much of what Long thinks is at stake. The conclusion that we offer from this discussion is that Wesley's understanding of ethics, specifically his understanding of liberty, exemplifies a "middle way," more similar to

[55] For Aquinas, one cannot choose against a clearly known option for the greatest good and thus, Aquinas is the epitome of intellectualism (Lagerlund and Yrjonsuuri, *Emotions and Choice: from Boethius to Descartes*, 14). For Wesley, unlike for Aquinas, it is possible to choose a clearly known evil instead of the clearly known highest good. This is indicated in his view that by conscience, one knows the difference between good and evil and has the liberty to choose either one. It is also implied in his view that a perfected person has the choice to backslide. Also, see Wesley, 'Thoughts upon Necessity,' *Works* (BE), 13:544. In this way, Wesley's view of ethics is different from Aquinas. For many commentators, it seems that for Aquinas, evil is only possible through an error in judgment. In other words, when wrong is chosen it is because the chooser did not sincerely know ahead of time that it is wrong (Lagerlund and Yrjonsuuri, *Emotions and Choice: from Boethius to Descartes*, 136).

Harris' portrait of Clarke than to common notions of the liberty of indifference such as that of King.

Appendix B

Consistency in Wesley's Thought

When carrying out a study of the thought of Wesley, it is helpful first to consider the question of whether or not Wesley's thought is consistent throughout his life. In answering this question, a first point to consider is what Wesley himself thought on this matter. Throughout his ministry, Wesley dealt with numerous people who were attempting to understand his thought and whether or not it was consistent. Wesley repeatedly claimed throughout his life that his thought is in fact consistent after 1738. Within several years of his death, Wesley says, "I have been uniform both in doctrine and discipline for above these fifty years."[56] Several months before this, he says, "To conclude, I defy any man living to prove that I have contradicted myself at all in any of the writings which I have published from the year 1738 to the year 1788."[57] These are some of the latest statements that Wesley makes regarding his consistency, but he makes many other such statements all throughout his adult ministry after 1738.[58]

Wesley argues that his view on justification is consistent after 1738. In March 1790, Wesley says, "Only about fifty years ago, I had a clearer view than before of justification by faith: and in this from that very hour I never varied, no not an hair's breadth."[59] Throughout his entire adult life after 1738, Wesley continues to affirm the doctrine of justification

---

[56] Wesley, *Letters*, 8:196.

[57] Wesley, *Letters*, 8:179.

[58] For some of the most notable attempts by Wesley to show consistency in his own thought, see "Some Remarks on Mr. Hill's 'Review of all the Doctrines Taught by Mr. John Wesley,'" and "Some Remarks on Mr. Hill's 'Farrago Double-Distilled,'" *Works* (BE), 13:429ff and 13:488ff.

[59] Wesley, "On the Wedding Garment," *Works* (BE), 4:147. See also Wesley, "Some Remarks on Mr. Hill's 'Review'" (BE), 13:474.

by grace through faith alone (sola fide) as expressed in the scripture by Paul in Romans 4:5. As we will explore more in chapter seven of this project, Wesley understands this view to be in harmony with his view that there is a second justification. This second justification is by works as mentioned in James 2:24 and Matthew 12:36-37.

Of course, Wesley's claim that his thought is consistent after 1738 does not deny that he adds many clarifications and important nuances after 1738. For Wesley, these added nuances are not contradictions to what he has said after 1738.[60] For him, such additions generally show an expansion of his thought (a sort of development) rather than a retraction of any of his previous views.

Several prominent Wesleyan scholars have made comments regarding Wesley's consistency. Albert Outler says, "Between 'Circumcision of the Heart' and 'On the Wedding Garment' lie six lively decades of theological development. And yet, when they are read together, these two descriptions of the Christian life do not differ on any essential point."[61] Randy Maddox says, "Moreover, the dynamic theological consistency that I believe unites the phases of Wesley's life and ministry is often most evident in his very process of nuancing disputed issues. As such, consideration of the *whole* Wesley is necessary to understand his mature position adequately."[62] Maddox and Outler offer that it is possible to consider three periods in Wesley's thought: the early Wesley (1733-1738), the middle Wesley (1738-1765), and the late Wesley (1765-1791).[63] It seems that they offer this three-stage model as a guide for nuancing rather than as a guide for arguing against consistency in Wesley's thought. Choosing 1765 as the division between the middle and late Wesley is debatable because there are many significant developments all throughout Wesley's ministry after 1738.[64]

[60] Wesley, *Letters*, 8:179. In 1768, Wesley says, "During these last thirty years, I may have varied in some of my sentiments or expressions without observing it." He cites the difficulty of having to respond to so many different objectors. He says in the same letter, "I believe there will be found few, if any, *real* contradictions in what I have published for near thirty years [between 1738 and 1768]." Wesley, *Works* (BE), 9:375.

[61] Outler, editor, *Works* (BE), 1:66.

[62] Maddox, "Reading Wesley as a Theologian," 25.

[63] Outler, editor, *Works* (BE), 1:42, footnote 55; Maddox, "Reading Wesley as a Theologian," 23; Maddox, *Responsible Grace*, 20.

[64] In an email sent to me, Randy Maddox indicates that the year 1765 is chosen as a division between stages because this was the year of Wesley's publication

In regard to a model that tests the consistency in Wesley's thought, Wesley's own self-understood model of having general consistency from 1738 onwards probably remains as authoritative for his theological interpretation as any other model available. For example, many of Wesley's theological views—including his view of many of the features of the way of salvation such as prevenient grace, repentance, the new birth, justification by grace through faith alone, the faith of a child of God, the witness of the Spirit, Christian perfection, the encouraged role of fruitful action throughout the entire course, etc.—are consistently held after 1738.

One of the most research-intensive essays regarding Wesley's nuances is "Great Expectations: Aldersgate and the Evidences of Genuine Christianity" by Richard Heitzenrater. In this essay, one of Heitzenrater's conclusions is that in regard to Aldersgate, Wesley modified "nearly every aspect of his perception and explanation of the event at the time."[65] Although this may be a bit of an overstatement (especially in Wesley's eyes!), Heitzenrater has helpfully shown that Wesley added some important nuances after his Aldersgate experience between 1738 and 1740. These include the following views: there are degrees of faith and degrees of assurance, the means of grace should be encouraged prior to assurance, assurance of justification does not necessarily entail constant freedom from doubt and fear, assurance of justification does not necessarily accompany fully developed loving tempers of the heart, and assurance is not final salvation.[66]

However, there are some major points regarding Wesley's view of Aldersgate that remain fixed from 1738 onwards. One such point is Wesley's inextricable conjoining of the first experiences of the following: the new birth, the entering of Christ into the heart, the love of God shed abroad in the heart, the Spirit of adoption, the witness of the Spirit that one is a child of God, and the faith of a child of God.[67] Furthermore,

---

of the "Scripture Way of Salvation." However, as Maddox is of course aware, there are many other important points of theological nuancing for other years after 1738.

[65] Heitzenrater, "Great Expectations," *Aldersgate Reconsidered* (Nashville, TN: Kingswood Books, 1990), 149.

[66] Heitzenrater, "Great Expectations," 147.

[67] See paragraph II:4 and II:7 of the sermon "Salvation by Faith," published in June 1738 and compare this with paragraph I:12 of 'On Faith' published in 1788 and paragraphs 13 and 14 of 'On the Discoveries of Faith' published in

some scholars have argued that throughout the rest of Wesley's life, Wesley consistently claims that other spiritual events are also inextricable with this package. These include justification in a Christian sense and the fulfilment of what it means to be a "real Christian."

In this project, we are in fact assuming, as Wesley did, that there is a general consistency in Wesley's thought after 1738. Wesley continues to maintain throughout his life that the way of salvation is a universal model for Christian living.[68] Yet, from Wesley's perspective, there is much mystery involved and such a model is far from an exhaustive explanation of the Christian life. Also, Wesley teaches that from person to person, there is diversity in how people experience the Christian life.[69] While there is diversity in experience, there is also a common sharing in experience. For example, Wesley appears to hold that to an important degree, his experience of Aldersgate holds true for people in general. This includes how the following aspects of the new birth first occur together: the entering of Christ into the heart, the love of God shed abroad in the heart, the Spirit of adoption, the witness of the Spirit that one is a child of God, and the faith of a child of God.

Clearly in this way, for people in general, there is a potential to have a perceptible experience of God's love. Every aspect of the experience of God's love is not the same for all people but there is something in common in the experience for everyone (just as the taste of sugar is not ident-

---

1708. Wesley also makes the point in 1772 regarding his comments in 1738: "Although I did not clearly see that we 'are saved by faith' till the year 1738, I then published the sermon on 'Salvation by Faith,' every sentence of which I subscribe to now" (Wesley, 'Remarks on Mr. Hill's "Review,"' *Works* (BE), 13:474). In regard to Wesley's view of assurance, Heitzenrater rightly points out that Wesley says that some who have not yet experienced the new birth experience a consciousness of God's favor ("Great Expectations," top of page 144). However, such a consciousness of God's favor is something different from the witness of the Spirit that one is a child of God. This latter kind of witness involves the impression "that Jesus Christ hath loved me, and given himself for me; that all my sins are blotted out, and I, even I, am reconciled to God" (Wesley, 'The Witness of the Spirit, I,' *Works* (BE), 1:274). There is no evidence that for Wesley, the former type of consciousness of divine favor includes this.

[68] See, for example, see Outler, editor, *Works* (BE), 2:155-169, 3:497-498, 4:34-38.

[69] See, for example, paragraph 15 of Wesley, 'The General Spread of the Gospel,' *Works* (BE), 2:491 and Wesley, 'The Imperfection of Human Knowledge,' *Works* (BE), 2:584.

ical for everyone, but everyone has a common aspect of the experience). For some people, the new birth is experienced strongly and energetically while others experience it faintly and calmly. Nevertheless, in every case— except perhaps for people with certain psychological abnormalities—, something is perceivable at the new birth.

For Wesley, there is a commonality of perception, not only in the first moments of the new birth, but also in other features of Wesley's way of salvation. It is Wesley's view that the consistency of human experience, in agreement with the authority of scripture (and secondarily other sources), allows for his model of the "way of salvation" to serve as a general guide for all sincere followers of Christ. As we show more in the chapters of this project, this point has relevance for Wesley's ethics.

In his essay, "The *Imitatio Christi* and the Great Commandment: Virtue and Obligation in Wesley's Ministry with the Poor," Heitzenrater claims that Wesley changes his mind with respect to his view of the role of good works before justification. Heitzenrater says that Wesley transitions from the "denigration of good works prior to justification" in the 1740s to "proclaiming the necessity of good works for salvation, even good works prior to justification, if given the time and opportunity" in the 1760s.[70] He cites p. 163 of volume 2 of Outler's *Sermons* as the evidence for this. Yet it seems that Wesley may be consistent here on one level. There is not a place in Wesley's writings where Wesley argues that good works are necessary for first justification if there is time and opportunity. The key word is the adjective "good" in reference to the works in themselves. Wesley consistently argues that good works are only after the new birth and justification. This allows him to remain consistent in his commitment to article 13 of the Articles of Religion of the Church of England, "Of Works Before Justification."[71] Heitzenrater is correct that for Wesley in the 1760s, *fruitful* action (fruits meet for repentance) are necessary prior to justification if there is time and opportunity. But such fruitful action is not good works. Furthermore, this point about fruitful action is not a new development. Wesley makes this point clear in his disagreement with Molther in 1739 and also in his *A Farther Appeal*

---

[70] Richard Heitzenrater, "The *Imitatio Christi* and the Great Commandment: Virtue and Obligation in Wesley's Ministry with the Poor," *The Portions of the Poor: Good News to the Poor in the Wesleyan Tradition*, editor Douglas Meeks (Nashville, TN: Kingswood Books, 1995), 62.

[71] Wesley, *Works* (Jackson), 8:54, 10:432 and 10:444.

to *Men of Reason and Religion* in 1744.[72] These distinctions are investigated in more depth in chapters 5 and 6 of this project.

---

[72] Wesley, *Works* (Jackson), 1:258, 8:47.

Bibliography

Works of John Wesley

The Works of John Wesley. Begun as "The Oxford Edition of The Works of John Wesley" Oxford: Clarendon Press, 1975-1983; continued as "The Bicentennial Edition of The Works of John Wesley." 35 volumes. Nashville: Abingdon Press, 1984–Frank Baker, Editor in Chief. Nashville, TN: Abingdon Press, 1984ff.

The Works of John Wesley, 14 vols. Thomas Jackson, editor. Grand Rapids: Baker Books, reprinted 1986.

Wesley, John, ed. *The Arminian Magazine*. vols. 1-14. London: Printed for the Editor, January 1778 – February 1791.

_____. *Explanatory Notes Upon the New Testament*. London: Printed for the Author, 1788.

_____. *The Letters of the Rev. John Wesley*. 8 vols. John Telford, ed. London: Epworth Press, 1931.

_____. *John Wesley's Prayer Book: The Sunday Service of the Methodists in North America*, ed. James White. Akron, Ohio: OSL Publications, reprinted 1991.

Works Originally Published Before John Wesley's Death (1791)

Aquinas, Thomas. *Summa Theologica*. Allen Texas: Christian Classics, 1981.

Aristotle. *Aristotle, Selections*, Terence Irwin and Gale Fine. Indianapolis: Hackett Publishing Company, Inc., 1995.

_____. *Nicomachean Ethics*, editor Roger Crisp. Cambridge: Cambridge University Press, 2000.

Arminius, James. *The Works of James Arminius*. Lamp Post Inc., 2008.

Augustine. *The City of God Against the Pagans*, editor R.W. Dyson, Cambridge: Cambridge University Press, c1998.

Augustine. *On the Free Choice of the Will, On Grace and Free Choice and Other Writings*, editor Peter King. Cambridge: Cambridge University Press, 2010.

Beattie, James. *Dissertations Moral and Critical*. London: Strahan and Cadell, 1783.

―――. *Essay on the Nature and Immutability of Truth in Opposition to Sophistry and Scepticism*. Edinburgh: A Kincaid & J. Bell, 1771.

The Book of Common Prayer and Administration of the Sacraments and other Rites and Ceremonies of the Church, According to the Use of the Church of England: Together the Psalter of Psalms of David, Oxford: T. Wright and W. Gill, 1772.

Bramhall, John. *Castigations of Mr. Hobbes in his las animadversions in the case concerning liberty and universal necessity wherein all his exceptions about that controversie are fully satisfied*. London: E.T., 1657.

Buddeus, Johann Franciscus. *Elementa Philosophiae Theoretica*. First edition. Halle: Glauche-Hallensis, 1706.

Burlamaqui, Jean. *The Principles of Natural Law in which the True Systems of Morality and Civil Government and the Different Sentiments of Grotius, Hobbes, Pussendorf, Barbeyrac, Locke, Clark, and Hutchinson Occasionally Considered*. London: J. Nourse, 1748.

Butler, Joseph. *The Analogy of Religion Natural and Revealed to the Constitution and Course of Nature*. London: Robert Horsfield, 1765.

Calvin, John. *Institutes of the Christian Religion*. Philadelphia: the Westminster Press, 1960.

Clarke, Samuel. *A Demonstration of the Being and Attributes of God*, editor Ezio Vailati. Cambridge: Cambridge University Press, 1998.

―――. *The Leibniz-Clarke Correspondence*, editor H.G. Alexander. Manchester: Manchester University Press, 1998.

―――. *Remarks upon a Book, Entituled A Philosophical Enquiry Concerning Human Liberty*. London: James Knapton, 1717.

Collier, Jeremy (1650–1726). *Essays Upon Several Moral Subjects*. Second edition, enlarged. London: R. Sare, 1697.

Collins, Anthony. *Philosophical Inquiry Concerning Human Liberty*. The Fourth Edition. Glasgow: R. Urie, 1749.

Cudworth, Ralph. *A Treatise Concerning Eternal and Immutable Morality with A Treatise of Free Will*. Cambridge: Cambridge University Press, 1996.

Descartes, Rene. *The Passions of the Soul*. Cambridge: Hackett Publishing Company, 1989.

Doddridge, Philip. *A Course of Lectures on the Principle Subjects of Pneumatology, Ethics and Divinity; with references to the most considerable authors on each subject*, editor SC. London: J. Buckland, 1763.

Duns Scotus, John. *Dun Scotus On the Will & Morality*, editor William Frank. Washington D.C.: The Catholic University of America Press, 1997.

Edwards, Jonathan. *A Treatise Concerning Religious Affections*. Nu Vision Publications, LLC: 2009.

———. *The Works of Jonathan Edwards*, volume 1, edited by Paul Ramsey. New Haven: Yale University Press, 1957.

Erasmus, Desiderius. "The Free Will." *Erasmus and Luther, Discourse on Free Will*, editor Ernst F. Winter. New York: Continuum, 2007.

Eustachius a Sancto Paulo [or Eustache Asseline]. *Ethica: sive summa moralis disciplinae, in tres partes divisa*. London: Roger Daniels, 1658.

Fisher, Joseph, *A Review of Dr. Priestly's Doctrine of Philosophical Necessity. The Arminian Magazine*, volumes 11-13, 1788-1790. London: Printed for the Editor.

Fletcher, John. *Works of John Fletcher*, ed. Joseph Benson. 10 Volumes. London: Richard Edwards, 1806.

Forbes, Alexander, Lord. *Essays, Moral and Philosophical, on several subjects:viz. A View of the Human Faculties, A Short Account of the World, Two Discourses on Decency, An Essay on Self-Love*. London: Osborn & Longman, 1734.

Goodwin, John. *Eirenomachia, the agreement and distance of brethren; or, A brief survey .. these important heads of doctrine: 1. Election & Reprobation, 2. The death of Christ, 3. the grace of God ..., e. the liberty or power of the will ..., 5. The perseverance of the saints*. London: Peter Parker, 1671.

Hale, Matthew. *Contemplations, Moral and Divine*. 2 vols. in 1. London: Printed for William Shrowsbury & John Leigh, 1682.

Hill, Richard. *A Review of all the Doctrines Taught by the Rev. Mr. John Wesley*. Second Edition. London: E. and C. Dilly, 1772

Hobbes, Thomas. *A Letter about Liberty and Necessity Written to the Duke of Newcastle*. London: J. Grover, 1676.

Hutcheson, Francis. *An Essay on the Nature and Conduct of the Passions and Affections, with Illustrations on the Moral Sense*. London: John Smith & William Bruce, 1728.

———. *An Inquiry into the Original of our Ideas of Beauty and Virtue; in two treatises, in which the principles of the late Earl of Shaftesbury are explained and defended against the author of the Fable of the Bees*. Third edition. London: J. Knapton,

———. *System of Moral Philosophy*. 3 vols.; London, 1755.

Jackson, John. *A Defense of Human Liberty*. London: J. Moon, 1730.

———. *A Vindication of Human Liberty*. London: J. Noon, 1730.

Kames, Henry Home, Lord. *Essays on the Principles of Morality and Natural Religion; with other Essays concerning the Proof of a Deity*. Edinburgh: A. Kinkaid & A. Donaldson, 1751.

King, William. *The Origin of Evil*. London: Knapton, 1731.

Langbaine, Gerard. *Ethices compendium*. Oxford: Richard Sare, 1714.

Locke, John. *An Essay Concerning Human Understanding*, editor Peter Nidditch. Oxford: Oxford University Press, 1975.

———. "Extracts from Locke on Human Understanding with Short Remarks," *Arminian Magazine*, volumes 5-7, London: Printed for editor, 1782-1784.

Lombard, Peter. *The Sentences*. Toronto: Pontifical Institute of Mediaeval Studies, c2007-2010.

Luther, Martin. "The Bondage of the Will." *Erasmus and Luther, Discourse on Free Will*. Ernst F. Winter. New York: Continuum, 2007.

———. *Luther's Works on C.D. Rom, American Edition*. Editors Jaroslav Pelikan and Helmut T. Lehmann. Fortress Press and Concordia Publishing House, 2004.

Malebranche, Nicolas. *The Search After Truth*, editor Thomas Lennon. Columbus: Ohio State University Press, Columbus, 1980.

———. *A Treatise of Morality*. London: Knapton, 1699.

More, Henry. *Enchiridion ethicum: praecipua moralis philosophiae rudimenta complectens, illustrata utplurimum veterum monumentis*. London: Benj. Tooke, 1690.

Norris, John. *The Theory and Regulation of Love; a Moral Essay in two parts. To which are added letters philosophical and moral between the author and Dr. Henry More*. Oxford: Sheldonian Theatre, 1688.

———. *A Treatise Concerning Christian Prudence; or the Principles of Practical Wisdom Fitted to the Use of Human Life, Designed for the-Better Regulation of It*. London: Samuel Manship, 1710.

Orders Belonging to a Religious Society: London: [n.p.] 1724.

Plato. *Plato, Collected Dialogues*. Edith Hamilton and Huntington, Cairns. Princeton: Princeton University Press, 1989.

Priestley, Joseph. *The Doctrine of Philosophical Necessity Illustrated*. London: J. Johnson, 1777.

Pseudo-Macarius. *The Fifty Spiritual Homilies; and, The great letter*, editor George Maloney. New York: Paulist Press, c1992.

Ramsay, Andrew Michael. "Of Human Liberty," *The Arminian Magazine*. Volume 8. London: printed for editor, 1785.

Reid, Thomas. *Essays on the Active Powers of Man*. Edinburgh: John Bell, 1788.

_____. *An Inquiry into the Human Mind on the Principles of Common Sense*. London: T. Cadell, 1769.

_____. "On the Liberty of Moral Agents," *Arminian Magazine*. volume 14. London: printed for the editor, 1791.

Rider, William. *A New English Dictionary or a Compleat Treasure of the English Language*. London: W. Griffin, 1759.

Seneca, Lucius Annaeus. *Seneca's Morals, abstracted in three parts: I. of benefits, II. of a happy life, anger, and clemency, III. a miscellany of epistles*, editor Roger L'Estrange. London: Henry Brome, 1679.

Watts, Isaac. *The Doctrine of the passions explained and improved, or, A brief and comprehensive scheme of the natural affections of mankind: to which are subjoined moral and divine rules for the regulation or government of them*. Third edition. London: Richard Hett & James Bracestone 1739.

Watts, Isaac. "An Essay on the Freedom of the Will in God and in Creatures." *The Works of the Late Reverend and Learned Isaac Watts*, London: T. and T. Longman and J. Buckland, 1753.

Whitehead, John. *An Essay on Liberty and Necessity: In Answer to Augustus Toplady's Tract*. London: R. Hawes, 1775.

Works Published after 1791:

Abraham, William. *Aldersgate and Athens, John Wesley and the Foundations of Christian Belief*. Waco, TX: Baylor University Press, c2010.

_____. "The End of Wesleyan Theology." *Wesleyan Theological Journal*, 40, no 1, (2005): 7-25.

_____. "Response: The Perils of a Wesleyan Systematic Theologian." *Wesleyan Theological Journal*, 17, no 1, (1982): 23-29.

_____: Whose Wesley?, Which Wesleyan Tradition? *Wesleyan Theological Journal*, 46, no 2, (2011): 142-149.

———— and James E. Kirby. *The Oxford Handbook of Methodist Studies.* Oxford: Oxford University Press, 2009.

Adams, Robert. *A Theory of Virtue: Excellence in Being for the Good.* Oxford: Oxford University Press, 2006.

Alexander, H.G., editor. *The Leibniz-Clarke Correspondence.* Manchester: Manchester University Press, 1998.

Aston, T.H. *The History of the University of Oxford.* Oxford: Clarendon Press, 1986.

Baggett, David and Jerry Walls. *Good God, the Theistic Foundations of Morality.* Oxford: Oxford University Press, 2011.

Baker, Frank. *John Wesley and the Church of England.* London: Epworth, 2000.

————. *A Union Catalogue of the Publications of John and Charles Wesley.* Second Edition. Stone Mountain, GA: George Zimmermann, 1991.

————. *Methodism and the Love-Feast.* London: Epworth Press, 1957.

Barrett, David, et al. *World Christian Encyclopedia.* New York: Oxford University Press, 2001.

Bartels, Laura. "The Political Image as the Basis for Wesleyan Ecological Ethics." *Quarterly Review,* 23, no 3, (2003): 294 - 301.

The Book of Discipline of the United Methodist Church: 2008 – 2012. Nashville, TN: United Methodist Publishing House.

Browder, Michael. *Pursuing Christian Love according to the Theology of John Wesley.* Dissertation at the University of Manchester, Manchester, England, 2017.

Carse, James. *Jonathan Edwards & The Visibility of God.* New York: Charles Scribner's Sons, 1967.

Cessario, Romanus. *The Moral Virtues and Theological Ethics.* Notre Dame: University of Notre Dame Press, 1991.

Clemmons, Ithiel. *C.H. Mason and the Roots of the Church of God in Christ.* Bakersfield, CA: Pneuma Life Pub., c1996.

Clapper, Gregory. "John Wesley's 'Heart Religion' and the Righteousness of Christ." *Methodist History,* 35, (1997): 148-156.

————. "John Wesley's Language of the Heart." *Wesleyan Theological Journal,* 44, no 2, (2009): 94 – 102.

————. *John Wesley on Religious Affections: his views on experience and emotion and their role in the Christian life and theology.* London: The Scarecrow Press, Inc., 1989.

_____. "Review of *John Wesley's Moral Theology: The Quest for God and Goodness.*" *Wesleyan Theological Journal.* Vol 40, no 2, (2006):256-259.

_____. "'True religion' and the affections: a study of John Wesley's abridgement of Jonathan Edwards' *Treatise on Religious Affections.*" *Wesleyan Theology Today.* Nashville, TN: United Methodist Publishing House, 1985.

Clough, David. *Ethics in Crises, Interpreting Barth's Ethics.* Aldershot, Hants, England; Burlington, VT: Ashgate Pub., c2005.

Collins, Kenneth. "Is 'Canonical Theism' a Viable Option for Wesleyans?" *Wesleyan Theological Journal*, 45, no 2, (2010): 82 – 107.

_____. *The Evangelical Moment, The Promise of an American Religion.* Grand Rapids, Michigan: Baker Academic, 2005.

_____. "John Wesley and the Means of Grace." *Drew Gateway*, 56, no 3, (1986): 26 – 33.

_____. *John Wesley: A Theological Journey.* Nashville: Abingdon Press, 2003.

_____. "John Wesley's Topography of the Heart: Dispositions, Tempers, and Affections." *Methodist History*, 36, no 3, (1998): 162-175.

_____. "The Promise of John Wesley's Theology for the 21st Century: A Dialogical Exchange." *The Asbury Theological Journal*, 59, no 1 – 2, (2004) : 171-180.

_____. "Real Christianity as the Integrating Theme in Wesley's Soteriology: a Critique of a Modern Myth." *Wesleyan Theological Journal*, 40, no 2, (2005): 52-87.

_____. *The Scripture Way of Salvation: The Heart of John Wesley's Theology.* Nashville, Abingdon Press, 1997.

_____. "The Soteriological Orientation of John Wesley's Ministry to the Poor." *Wesleyan Theological Journal*, 36, no 2, (2001): 7 – 36.

_____. The *Theology of John Wesley: Holy Love and the Shape of Grace.* Nashville, TN: Abingdon, c2007.

_____ and Christine Johnson. From the Garden to the Gallows: the Significance of Free Grace in the Theology of John Wesley, *Wesleyan Theological Journal*, 48, no 2, (2013): 7 – 29.

Colon-Emeric, Edgardo. *Wesley, Aquinas & Christian Perfection.* Waco, Texas: Baylor University Press, 2009.

Cooper, Allen. "John Wesley: A Study in Theology and Social Ethics," Ph.D. dissertation, Columbia University, 1962.

Copp, David. *Oxford Handbook of Ethical Theory*. Oxford: Oxford University Press, 2005.

Coppedge, Allan. *Shaping the Wesleyan Message*. Nappanee, Indiana: Asbury University Press, 1987.

Crisp, Roger. *The Oxford Handbook of the History of Ethics*. Oxford: Oxford University Press, 2015.

_____ and Michael Slote. *Virtue Ethics*. Oxford: Oxford University Press, 1997.

Curran, Charles and Lisa Fullam. *Virtue. Readings in Moral Theology*. Mahwah, NJ: Paulist Press, 2011.

Dihle, Albrecht. *The Theory of Will in Classical Antiquity*. Berkeley: University of California Press, c1982.

Dunning, H. Ray. "Ethics in a Wesleyan Context." *Wesleyan Theological Journal*, 5, no 1, (1970): 3 – 10.

Dunning, H. Ray. *Reflecting the Divine Image: Christian Ethics in Wesleyan Perspective*. Downers Grove, Ill: Intervarsity Press, c1998.

Elshtain, Jean Bethke. "The Christian Contrarian," *Time Magazine*, September, 2001.

Frank, William. "Duns Scotus on Autonomous Freedom and Divine Co-Causality." *Medieval Philosophy and Theology*, 2, (1992): 142 – 164.

Fujimoto, Mitsuru. *John Wesley's Doctrine of Good Works*. Ph.D. Dissertation, Drew University, 1986.

Gaines, Timothy. "Can Ethics be Wesleyan?: Moral Theology and Holiness Identity." *Wesleyan Theological Journal*. Vol 51, no 1, (2016): 155 – 167.

Garber, Daniel and Michael Ayers. *Cambridge History of Seventeenth-Century Philosophy*. Cambridge: Cambridge University Press, 1998.

Gill, Mary Louise, and James G. Lennox. *Self-Motion, from Aristotle to Newton*. Princeton, New Jersey: Princeton University Press, 1994.

Gill, Robin. *The Cambridge Companion to Christian Ethics*. Cambridge: Cambridge University Press, 2012.

Gill, Robin. *A Textbook of Christian Ethics*. London: T & T Clark, 2014.

Grant, W. Matthews. "Aquinas among Libertarians and Compatibilists: Breaking the Logic of Theological Determinism." *Proceedings of American Catholic Philosophical Association*, 75, (2001): 221 – 235.

_____. "Can a Libertarian Hold that Our Free Acts are Caused by God?" *Faith and Philosophy: Journal of the Society of Christian Philosophers.* 27, no 1, (2010): 22 – 44.

Grenz, Stanley. *The Moral Quest, Foundations of Christian Ethics.* Downers Grove, Ill: Intervarsity Press, c1997.

Gustafson, James. "The Sectarian Temptation: Reflections on Theology, The Church and the University." *Proceedings of the Catholic Theological Society of America,* 40, (1985): 83 - 94.

Gunter, W. Stephen et al. *Wesley and the Quadrilateral: Renewing the Conversation.* Nashville, TN: Abingdon, 1997.

Harris, James. *Of Liberty and Necessity: The Free Will Debate in Eighteenth-Century British Philosophy.* Oxford: Oxford University Press, 2005.

_____. *The Oxford Handbook of British Philosophy in the Eighteenth Century.* Oxford: Oxford University Press, 2014.

Harrison, Simon. *Augustine's Way into the Will, The Theological and Philosophical Significance of De Libero Arbitrio.* Oxford: Oxford University Press, 2006.

Hauerwas, Stanley. *Character and the Christian Life, A Study in Theological Ethics.* San Antonio: Trinity University Press, 1985.

_____. "The Church in a Divided World. The Interpretive Power of the Christian Story." *Journal of Religious Ethics,* 8, no 1, (1980): 55 – 82.

_____. *Christian Existence Today: Essays on Church, World, and Living in Between.* Durham, NC: Labyrinth Press, 1988.

_____. "Ethics and Ascetical Theology." *Anglican Theological Review,* 61, no 1, (1979): 87 – 98.

_____. *The Hauerwas Reader,* editors John Berkman and Michael Cartwright. Durham, NC: Duke University Press, 2001.

_____. *The Peaceable Kingdom*: a Primer in Christian Ethics. Notre Dame: University of Notre Dame Press, c1983.

_____. "Preaching as Though We Had Enemies." *First Things,* 53, (1995): 45 – 49.

_____. *Wilderness Wanderings: Probing Twentieth-Century Theology and Philosophy.* Boulder, Colo: Westview Press, 1997.

_____. *Working with Words, On Learning to Speak Christian.* Eugene, Oregon: Cascade Books, c2011.

_____ and Samuel Wells. *The Blackwell Companion to Christian Ethics.* Malden, MA: Blackwell Pub., 2004.

_____ and John Westerhoff. *Schooling Christians: "Holy Experiments" in American Education*. Grand, Rapids, Mich: W.B. Eerdmans, c1992.

Hays, Richard. *The Moral Vision of the New Testament: Community, Cross, New Creation: a Contemporary Introduction to New Testament Ethics*. San Francisco: HarperSanFrancisco, c1996.

Heitzenrater, Richard. "Great expectations: Aldersgate and the Evidences of Genuine Christianity." *Aldersgate Reconsidered*. Nashville, TN: Kingswood Books, 1990.

_____ "The *Imitatio Christi* and the Great Commandment: Virtue and Obligation in Wesley's Ministry with the Poor." *The Portion of the Poor: Good news to the Poor in the Wesleyan Tradition*. Nashville, TN: Abingdon Press, 1995.

_____. "John Wesley's Principles and Practice of Preaching." *Methodist History*, 37, no 2, (1999): 89 – 106.

_____. *Mirror and Memory: Reflections on Early Methodism*. Nashville, TN: Kingswood Books, c1989.

_____. *The Poor and the People Called Methodists*. Nashville, TN: Kingswood Books, c2002.

_____. *Wesley and the Oxford Methodists, 1725-1735*. Ph.D. Dissertation, Duke University, 1972.

_____. *Wesley and the People Called Methodists*. Nashville: Abingdon Press, 1995.

Helm, Bennett. "Freedom of the Heart." *Pacific Philosophical Quarterly*, 77, no 2 (1996), 71 - 87.

Hempton, David. *The Religion of the People*. London: Routledge, 1996.

Henderson, D. Michael. *A Model for Making Disciples: John Wesley's Class Meeting*. Nappanee, IN: Francis Asbury Press of Evangel Pub. House, c1997.

Henry, G. C. "John Wesley's Doctrine of Free Will." *London Quarterly and Holborn Review*, 185, (1960): 200 - 204.

Hooft, Stan Van. *The Handbook of Virtue Ethics*. Bristol, CT: Acumen, 2014.

Hursthouse, Rosalind. *On Virtue Ethics*. Oxford: Oxford University Press, 2001.

Hynson, Leon O. *To Reform the Nation: Theological Foundations of Wesley's Ethics*. Grand Rapids, Mich.: Francis Asbury Press, c1984.

_____. *The Wesleyan Revival, John Wesley's Ethics for Church and State*. Schmul Pub. Company, 1999.

Jackson, Nicholas D. *Hobbes, Bramhall and the Politics of Liberty and Necessity, A Quarrel of the Civil Wars and Interregnum*. Cambridge, England: Cambridge University Press, 2007.

Jacob, W.M. *The Clerical Profession*. Oxford, Oxford University Press, 2007.

Jenson, Robert. "Hauerwas Examined." *First Things*, no 25 (1992): 49 – 51.

_____. Systematic Theology, Volume 1, *The Triune God*. Oxford: Oxford University Press, 2001.

_____. Systematic Theology, Volume 2, *The Works of God*. Oxford: Oxford University Press, 1999.

Kallenberg, Brad. *Ethics as Grammar*. Notre Dame, Ind: University of Notre Dame Press, c2001.

Kent, Bonnie. *Virtues of Will, The Transformation of Ethics in the Late Thirteenth Century*. Washington, D.C.: Catholic University of America Press, 1995.

Kerr, Fergus. *Theology after Wittgenstein*. New York: Blackwell, 1986.

Kuhn, Thomas S. *The Structure of Scientific Revolutions*. Chicago: The University of Chicago Press, 1996.

Lagerlund, Henrik and Mikko Yrjonsuuri. *Emotions and Choice from Boethius to Descartes*. Dordrecht, The Netherlends: Kluwer Academic Publishers, 2002.

Lapsley, Daniel K. and F. Clark Power. *Character Pyschology and Character Education*. Notre Dame: University of Notre Dame, 2005.

Lancaster, Sarah, et al. "What Makes Theology 'Wesleyan?'" *Methodist Review* (Online), 1, (2009).

Leppin, Volker, editor. *The Bondage of the Will, 1525, The Annotated Luther Study Edition*. Minneapolis: Fortress Press, 2016.

Lindbeck, George. *The Nature of Doctrine: Religion and Theology in a Postliberal Age*. Philadelphia: Westminster Press, c1984.

Lindstrom, Harold. *Wesley and Sanctification*. New York, Abingdon Press, ~1946.

Long, Stephen. *John Wesley's Moral Theology: The Quest for God and Goodness*. Nashville: Kingswood Books, 2005.

Lovin, Robin. "Moral Theology." *The Oxford Handbook of Methodist Studies*. Oxford: Oxford University Press, 2009.

Lowery, Kevin Twain. *Salviging Wesley's Agenda: a New Paradigm for Wesleyan Virtue Ethics*. Eugene, OR: Pickwick Publications, 2008.

MacIntyre, Alasdair. *After Virtue*. Notre Dame: University of Notre Dame Press, c2007.
―――――. *A Short History of Ethics*. Notre Dame: University of Notre Dame Press, 1998.
MacIntyre, Alasdair. *The Tasks of Philosophy*. Cambridge: Cambridge University Press, 2006.
―――――. *Whose Justice? Which Rationality?* Notre Dame, Ind: University of Notre Dame Press, c1998.
Maddox, Randy and Jason L. Vickers. *Cambridge Companion to John Wesley*. Cambridge: Cambridge University Press, 2010.
Maddox, Randy Lynn. "A Change of Affections: The developments, Dynamics, and Dethronement of John Wesley's Heart Religion." *"Heart Religion" in the Methodist Tradition and Related Movements*, edited by Richard B. Steele. Lanham, MD: Scarecrow Press, 2001.
―――――. "Holiness of Heart and Life: Lessons from North American Methodism." *Asbury Theological Journal*, 51, no 1, (1996): 151-72.
―――――. "Gracious affection and True Virtue According to Jonathan Edwards and John Wesley." *Asbury Theological Journal*, 52, (1997): 67-58.
―――――. "John Wesley—Practical Theologian?" *Wesleyan Theological Journal*, 23, no 1 - 2, (1988): 122-147.
―――――. "John Wesley's Precedent for Theological Engagement with the Natural Sciences." *Wesleyan Theological Journal*, 44, 1, (2009): 23-54.
―――――. "Practical Theology: A Discipline in Search of a Definition." *Perspectives in Religious Studies* 18 (1991): 159-69.
―――――. "Reading Wesley as a Theologian." *Wesleyan Theological Journal*, 30, no 1, (1995): 7 - 54.
―――――. "Reconnecting the Means to the End: A Wesleyan Prescription for the Holiness Movement." *Wesleyan Theological Journal*, 33, no 2, (1998):29-66.
―――――. "The Recovery of Theology as a Practical Discipline." *Theological Studies*, 51, no 4, 650 - 672.
―――――, "Respected Founder/Neglected Guide: The Role of Wesley in American Methodist Theology." *Methodist History*, 37, (1999): 71-88.
―――――. *Responsible Grace: John Wesley's Practical Theology*. Nashville: Kingswood Books, 1994.
―――――. "Wesleyan Theology and Moral Psychology: Precedents for Continuing Engagement." *Wesleyan Theology and Social Science: The*

Dance of Practical Divinity and Discovery, editors, M. Kathryn Armistead, Brad D. Strawn, & Ronald W.Wright. Newcastle upon Tyne: Cambridge Scholars Publishing, 2010.

Matthews, D.K. *A Theology of Cross and Kingdom*. Eugene, Oregon: Pickwick Publications. 2019.

Marquardt, Manfred. *John Wesley's Social Ethics, Praxis and Principles*. Nashville, TN: Abingdon Press, c1991.

McClendon Jr., James. *Systematic Theology*, Vol. I - III. Waco, TX: Baylor University Press, 2012.

McGonigle, Herbert. *Sufficient Saving Grace: John Wesley's Evangelical Arminianism*. Carlisle, Waynseboro, GA: Paternoster Press, 2001.

Meeks, M. Douglas. *Portion of the Poor: Good News to the Poor in the Wesleyan Tradition*. Nashville, TN: Kingswood, Books: 1995.

Meilaender, Gilbert and William Werpehowski. *The Oxford Handbook of Theological Ethics*. Oxford: Oxford University Press, 2005.

Milbank, John. *The Suspended Middle, Henri de Lubac and the Renewed Split in Modern Catholic Theology*. Grand Rapids, Michigan: William B. Eerdmans Pub., 2014.

Murphy, Nancey and Brad Kallenberg. *Virtues & Practices in the Christian Tradition, Christian Ethics after MacIntyre*. Harrisburg, Pa: Trinity Press, International, c1997.

Noble, Thomas. *Holy Trinity; Holy People: The Historic Doctrine of Christian Perfecting*. Eugene, Oregon: Cascade Books, 2013.

_____. "John Wesley as a Theologian: An Introduction." The Evangelical Quarterly, 82, no 3, (2010): 238 - 257.

_____. "To Serve the Present Age: Authentic Wesleyan Theology Today, The 2010 WTS Presidential Address." *Wesleyan Theological Journal*, 46, no 1, (2011): 73 - 89.

Noll, Mark. *The Rise of Evangelicalism, The Age of Edwards, Whitefield, and the Wesleys*. Downers Grove, IL: Intervarsity Press, 2003.

O'Donovan, Oliver. *Resurrection and Moral Order, An Outline for Evangelical Ethics*. Grand Rapids, Michigan: Eerdmans, 1994.

Oord, Thomas. *Love, Wesleyan Theology, and Psychological Dimension of Both*. Journal of Psychology and Christianity, 31, no 2, (2012): 144 - 156.

Osborne, Kenan. *The History of Franciscan Theology*. St. Bonaventure, NY: Franciscan Institute, St. Bonaventure University, 1994.

Outler, Albert. *Psychotherapy and the Christian Message*. New York: Harper & Brothers, Publishers, 1954.

_____. *John Wesley*. Oxford: Oxford University Press, 1964.

_____ *The Wesleyan Theological Heritage*. Grand Rapids, Michigan: Zondervan, 1991.

Oxford Dictionary of National Biography. Oxford: Oxford University Press, 2004.

Pecknold, C.C. *Transforming Postliberal Theology: George Lindbeck, Pragmatism, and Scripture*. London: T & T Clark; Continuum, 2005.

Plantinga, Alvin. *The Analytic Theist: an Alvin Plantinga Reader*. Grand Rapids, Michigan: W.B. Eerdmans Pub. Co., c1998.

_____. *Where the Conflict Really Lies: Science, Religion, and Naturalism*. Oxford: Oxford University Press, 2011.

_____. *Warrented Christian Belief*. Oxford: Oxford University Press, 2000.

_____. *Warrant: the Current Debate*. Oxford: Oxford University Press, 1993.

_____. *Warrant and Proper Function*. Oxford: Oxford University Press, 1993.

Pyle, Andrew. *Dictionary of Seventeenth-Century British Philosophers*. Continuum, 2000.

Rack, Henry. *Reasonable Enthusiast: John Wesley and the Rise of Methodism*. Epworth Press, 2002.

Rakestraw, Robert. *The Concept of Grace in the Ethics of John Wesley*. Ph.D. Dissertation, 1985.

Ramsey, Paul. *Basic Christian Ethics*. Louisville, KY: Westminster, 1993.

Robbins, J. Wesley. "Narrative, Morality, and Religion." *Journal of Religious Ethics*, 8, no 1, (1980): 161 – 176.

Rodes, Stanley J. *From Faith to Faith, John Wesley's Covenant Theology and Way of Salvation*. Eugene, Oregon: Pickwick Publications, 2013.

Reist, Irwin W. "John Wesley's View of Man: A Study in Free Grace Versus Free Will," *Wesleyan Theological Journal*, 7 (1972): 23-35.

Runyon, Theodore. *The New Creation, John Wesley's Theology Today*. Nashville, TN: Abingdon Press, 1998.

Russell, Daniel C. *The Cambridge Companion to Virtue Ethics*. Cambridge: Cambridge University Press, 2013.

Simpson, J.A, and E.S.C. Weiner. *The Oxford English Dictionary*. New York: Oxford University Press, 1989.

Skorupski, John. *The Routledge Companion to Ethics*. New York: Routledge, 2010.

Sorabji, Richard. *Emotions and Peace of Mind: From Stoic Agitation to Christian Temptation*. Oxford: Oxford University Press, 2000.
Steele, Richard B. *"Gracious Affections" and "True Virtue" according to Jonathan Edwards and John Wesley*. Metuchen, N.J.: Scarecrow Press, 1994.
_____, editor. *"Heart Religion" in the Methodist Tradition and Related Movements*. London: Scarecrow Press, Inc., 2001.
Stone, Ronald. *John Wesley's Life & Ethics*. Nashville, TN: Abingdon Press, c2001.
Stout, Jeffrey. *Democracy and Tradition*. Princeton, NJ: Princeton University Press, c2004.
Swanton, Christine. *Virtue Ethics: A Pluralistic View*. Oxford: Oxford University Press, 2003.
Taube, Mortimer. *Causation, Freedom and Determinism: An Attempt to Solve the Causal Problem Through a Study of its origins in Seventeenth Century Philosophy*. George Allen & Unwin LTD, London, 1936.
Thompson, Andrew. *John Wesley and the Means of Grace: Historical and Theological Context*. Ph.D. Dissertation, Duke University, 2012.
Thorsen, Donald. "Experimental Method in the Practical Theology of John Wesley." *Wesleyan Theological Journal*, 24, (1989): 117 – 141.
Vickers, Jason. *Invocation and Assent: the Making and Remaking of Trinitarian Theology*. Grand Rapids, Michigan: William B. Eerdman's, 2008.
_____. "Albert Outler and the Future of Wesleyan Theology: Retrospect and Prospect." *Wesleyan Theological Journal*, 43, no 2, (2008): 56 – 67.
Volf, Miroslav. *Free of Charge*. Grand Rapids, Michigan: Zondervan, 2005.
_____. *Work in the Spirit*. New York: Oxford University Press, 1991.
Volf and Bass. *Practicing Theology: Beliefs and Practices in Christian Life*. Grand Rapids: Eerdman's, 2002
Wainwright, Geoffrey. "Ecumenical Dimensions of Lindbeck's Nature of Doctrine." *Modern Theology*, 4, no 2, (1988): 121 – 132.
Walls, Jerry. "'As the Waters Cover the Sea:' John Wesley on the Problem of Evil." *Faith and Philosophy*, 13, 4, (1996): 534 – 562.
_____. "The Free Will Defense, Calvinism, Wesley, and the Goodness of God." *Christian Scholars Review*, 13, no 1, (1984): 19-33.
_____. "John Wesley on Predestination and Election." *The Oxford Handbook of Methodist Studies*. Oxford: Oxford University Press, 2009.
Watson, Kevin. *Pursing Social Holiness, The Band Meeting in Wesley's Thought and Popular Methodist Practice*. Oxford: Oxford University Press, 2014.

Weber, Theodore. *Politics in the Order of Salvation, Transforming Wesleyan Political Ethics*. Nashville, TN: Kingswood Books, c2001.

Wells, Samuel. *Transforming Fate into Destiny*: The Theological Ethics of Stanley Hauerwas. Eugene, Oregon: Wipf and Stock, 2004.

——— and Ben Quash. *Introducing Christian Ethics*. Oxford: Wiley-Blackwell, 2010.

White, James F. *John Wesley's Prayer Book*. OSL Publications, 2008.

Williams, Colin. *John Wesley's Theology Today*. New York: Abingdon Press, 1960.

Wittgenstein, Ludwig. *Philosophical Investigations*. Malden, MA: Wiley-Blackwell, 2009.

Nicholas Wolterstorff. "Are Concept Users World Makers?" *Philosophical Perspectives*, 1, (1987): 233 – 267.

Wood, A. Skevington. "John Wesley on Religious Affections: His View of Experience and Emotion and their Role in the Christian Life and Theology." *Evangelical Quarterly*. 64, (1992): 83-84.

Wood, Laurence. *Pentecost and Sanctification in the Writings of John Wesley and Charles Wesley with a Proposal for Today*. The Study of World Christian Revitalization Movements in Pietist and Wesleyan Studies. Lexington, KY: Emeth, 2018.

Wright, John. *Postliberal Theology and the Church Catholic: Conversations with George Lindbeck, David Burrell, and Stanley Hauerwas*. Grand Rapids: Baker Academic, 2012.

www.ingramcontent.com/pod-product-compliance
Lightning Source LLC
Chambersburg PA
CBHW070727160426
43192CB00009B/1345